Praise for *The 32 Principles*

"I learned these 32 principles over decades of jiu-jitsu practice and I've applied them in every aspect of my life. But Rener codifies them in a simple, clear, digestible way, making them accessible to any person in any situation, regardless of whether they are a black belt in jiu-jitsu or have never learned a martial art. The complementary videos in each chapter provide a one-of-a-kind experience for every reader, adeptly bridging the gap between the combat and life applications of the 32 principles."

—Jocko Willink, retired Navy SEAL, author, podcaster, and entrepreneur

"Thirty years ago, I began learning jiu-jitsu from the Gracie family, and to this day it remains one of the best decisions of life. By presenting the 32 principles in such a clear and easy-to-learn format, Rener extends the profound benefits of his family's fighting system far beyond the world of martial arts and into the realm of how to live a meaningful life."

—Ed O'Neill, actor

"Jiu-jitsu is a super power. Whether it's used to protect yourself and your family, or in your professional pursuits, it provides an incalculable advantage. Rener is incredibly articulate in *The 32 Principles*. He brilliantly breaks down these universal problem-solving principles in real time for use in any environment."

—Tim Kennedy, former UFC fighter, US Special Forces, author, and entrepreneur

"A must-read for anyone seeking to succeed in life through a winning mindset. I love the analogies and practical advice this book has on how the principles of jiu-jitsu can be applied beyond the mat to achieve success in all aspects of life."

—Cynthia Rothrock, five-time undefeated martial arts champion, action star, and inductee in the Black Belt Hall of Fame

"I wish I had this book when I was playing professional baseball. It is filled with tons of wisdom, told in a simplistic way with engaging stories. It's a book that after you read it, you will go back to it again."

—Ila Borders, pro-baseball pitcher and coauthor of *Making My Pitch*

"Rener Gracie is, without question, one of the most talented teachers I have ever met—on any topic. And jiu-jitsu is among the most useful and personally rewarding forms of knowledge our species has produced. The importance of this coincidence should be obvious: when the student is ready, the teacher appears . . ."

—Sam Harris, neuroscientist, *New York Times* bestselling author, host of the *Making Sense* podcast, and creator of the Waking Up app

"Rener Gracie and Paul Volponi make a great team in explaining the benefits of martial arts to non-martial artists. *The 32 Principles* is an easy read and full of great information."

—Christine Bannon-Rodrigues, nine-time World Champion martial artist and Hollywood stuntwoman

"Paul Volponi and Rener Gracie do an outstanding job of making *The 32 Principles* a guide to daily living for everyone."

—Wendy Behar, author of *Disarming the Narcissist* and founding fellow of The Academy of Cognitive Therapy

"To watch a top-notch novelist like Paul Volponi weave a narrative through a nonfiction book such as *The 32 Principles* is a thing of pure beauty."

—Lenny Shulman, Emmy Award–winning writer and author of *Justify*

"It's amazing how the principles of martial arts connect so directly to life, and Paul Volponi's writing here is simply superb."

—William Moy, Ving Tsun kung fu grandmaster

The 32 Principles

Also by Paul Volponi

Novels

Black and White (2006)

Crossing Lines (2011)

The Final Four (2013)

Game Seven (2016)

The Hand You're Dealt (2010)

Homestretch (2009)

Hurricane Song (2008)

Marcus and Eddie (2021)

Response (2010)

Rikers High (2011)

Rooftop (2006)

Rucker Park Setup (2008)

Top Prospect (2016)

Non-Fiction

The Great G.O.A.T. Debate: The Best of the Best At Everything From Sports to Science (2022)

Phyllis George: Shattering The Ceiling (2022)

SpongeBob SquarePants: The Unauthorized Fun-ography (2023)

Streetball is Life: Lesson Earned on the Asphalt (2020)

Superhero Smart: Real Life Facts Behind Comic Book Characters (2023)

That's My Team: The History, Science and Fun Behind Sports Teams' Names (2019)

The 32 Principles

HARNESSING THE POWER OF JIU-JITSU TO SUCCEED IN BUSINESS, RELATIONSHIPS, AND LIFE

RENER GRACIE

Paul Volponi

BENBELLA

BenBella Books, Inc.
Dallas, TX

BENBELLA
BenBella Books, Inc.
10440 N. Central Expressway
Suite 800
Dallas, TX 75231
benbellabooks.com
Send feedback to feedback@benbellabooks.com

BenBella is a federally registered trademark.

Printed in the United States of America
10 9 8 7 6 5 4 3 2 1

Library of Congress Control Number: 2022061163
ISBN 9781637743669 (hardcover)
ISBN 9781637743676 (electronic)

Editing by Herb Schaffner and Rachel Phares
Copyediting by Scott Calamar
Proofreading by Kellie Doherty and Rebecca Maines
Text design and composition by Aaron Edmiston
Cover design by Morgan Carr
Cover photograph by Racquel Kussman
Printed by Lake Book Manufacturing

For Mom: Thank you for always inspiring me to apply jiu-jitsu when it mattered most.

—R. G.

This book is dedicated to all of my teachers—from classrooms to street corners—who proved to me that nothing comes easily unless you take self-direction and truly work for it.

—P. V.

Jiu-jitsu is like a philosophy. It helps me learn how to face life.

—Helio Gracie, founder, Brazilian jiu-jitsu

Contents

Foreword

"Jiu-jitsu is life." This statement is often made by practitioners of the art of jiu-jitsu.

Some mean it in a playful way: jiu-jitsu is so fun and engaging that it seems to permeate every aspect of life.

Others mean it in a more serious way: the power of jiu-jitsu becomes an obsession, and every waking moment is spent trying to learn, develop, and improve jiu-jitsu skills.

But for me, the statement "Jiu-jitsu is life" has always been about the actual correlation between jiu-jitsu and life. Yes, the struggles, trials, tribulations, and triumphs that are part and parcel of jiu-jitsu also reflect what we all experience in life.

I was introduced to jiu-jitsu in the early nineties by a revered Navy SEAL master chief. I was a young SEAL at the time and was overseas on my first deployment. During our morning muster, the master chief asked if any of us wanted to learn how to fight. I raised my hand—and my life changed forever.

A few hours later, this lanky master chief, who was much older and smaller than I was, was tying me in knots—placing me in positions where I had no option other than to tap out, to surrender. I was dumbfounded. It didn't make sense. No matter what I did, I could not survive for more than 30 seconds with the master chief.

I tried over and over again to do something, anything, to survive, but I could not. Neither could any of my fellow SEAL teammates who had also joined me for the lesson.

After almost an hour, the master chief looked at our exhausted faces and said: "Welcome to Gracie jiu-jitsu."

I had no idea what that meant at the time. But it seemed like I had been exposed to some kind of magic—a magic power that I did not understand. But I did understand one thing: I needed to learn this magic power—this power of jiu-jitsu.

The master chief, whose name was Steve Bailey, had trained at the legendary Gracie Garage in the late eighties and early nineties in Torrance, California. He was by no means a master of the art. By his own admission, he was just a beginner. But even with the most basic jiu-jitsu moves, he was able to completely dominate and easily make my teammates and me submit over and over again.

So began my jiu-jitsu journey. I continued to train with Master Chief Bailey on deployment. When I got back to the States, I found a jiu-jitsu instructor named Fabio Santos, whose jiu-jitsu lineage traced directly back to the Gracie family.

I trained as often as I could, sometimes speeding to the jiu-jitsu academy for lunchtime training, then returning at night for more classes. I was obsessed. I learned the basic positions of jiu-jitsu: the mount, the back, the guard, the half guard, and side control. I learned the basic submission holds of jiu-jitsu, the moves to actually make opponents tap out: the straight armlock, the kimura, the americana, collar chokes, the guillotine choke, the rear naked choke, and foot, ankle, and knee locks. Over time, I learned how to fight. But I also slowly began to recognize that jiu-jitsu was not just a catalog of individual moves. Instead, all the moves were interconnected—they worked best when combined together in sequence to support each other. That lesson soon led to the realization that jiu-jitsu was not just combinations of moves either, but that there were underlying principles of jiu-jitsu that made the entire system work.

But most importantly, over time, I realized that the principles of jiu-jitsu were not just a way of fighting—they were a way of *thinking*. I saw the correlations between the principles of jiu-jitsu, leadership, combat, and life itself. I began to apply these principles to everything I did. And the more I applied these principles in other aspects of my life, the better I was able to execute: I became a better SEAL, a better leader, and a better person.

So, when Rener Gracie, grandson of the founder of Gracie jiu-jitsu, Helio Gracie, asked me to review his book, I was thrilled when I saw the title, *The 32 Principles: Harnessing the Power of Jiu-Jitsu to Succeed in Business, Relationships, and Life*. This title made perfect sense to me considering Rener's direct personal connection to the co-founder of Gracie jiu-jitsu, his vast knowledge of the art, his unique ability to adapt jiu-jitsu so that anyone can learn it, his success in various business ventures (many unrelated to jiu-jitsu), and his honorable position as a grandson, son, husband, brother, and father. All this represented the statement "Jiu-jitsu is life." I could not wait to dig into the book. I was not disappointed.

The book spells out the underlying principles of jiu-jitsu, how they apply on the mats, and how they apply in life. These are principles that I also learned from jiu-jitsu and that I applied in every aspect of my life. But Rener codifies them in a simple, clear, digestible way, making them accessible to any person in any situation, regardless of whether they are a black belt in jiu-jitsu or if they have never learned a martial art. These principles have been tested on and off the mat and are sure to help anyone who implements them. Here are some of the principles readers will learn:

The Detachment Principle teaches us that there are certain situations where it is advantageous to break away, let go of, or make distance from an opponent. The same is true in some situations in life: There are times when the best option is to simply let go. If a person is in a bad relationships or an unfulfilling job, sometimes the best thing to do is just to detach and move on.

The Creation Principle is rooted in taking action in order to set up a reaction that is advantageous. On the mats, this means executing moves that provoke a response from the opponent. In life, it means taking action in order to create a scenario that will help move toward a desired goal—like asking your boss specific questions to help you get a raise or proactively taking on a project to show you're ready for a promotion.

The Fork Principle requires a jiu-jitsu practitioner to utilize multiple attacks simultaneously, which will all result in a predicament for the opponent—each available outcome ends with the opponent skewered on one prong of the fork or another. For instance, a skilled jiu-jitsu player will simultaneously set up a triangle choke, an armlock, and a sweep on their opponent. In order to defend the triangle, the opponent extends themself, becoming vulnerable to an armlock, so they collapse their weight, lose their balance, and get swept. The life application of this principle teaches us to pursue win-win relationships in our personal and professional lives. So, whether it's a strategic alliance between corporations or a shift in how you relate to your children, if it's win-win, then you're applying the Fork Principle.

The Depletion Principle utilizes patience, persistence, and pressure to defeat an opponent. In jiu-jitsu, this principle is self-evident: A jiu-jitsu practitioner uses certain positions to conserve energy while their opponent struggles. Over time, the opponent becomes exhausted and can easily be defeated. In life, this principle is equally effective—instead of trying to forcefully impose a new idea on someone, which may result in unnecessary friction and conflict, it is better to slowly introduce the new idea over time so that it can be fully understood and willfully accepted.

The Sacrifice Principle teaches us there must be sacrifices in order to achieve success. We all understand this idea from the game of chess: We might give up a pawn to take a rook. In jiu-jitsu, we might sacrifice the danger of a triangle choke in order to pass the guard or give up the mount to attempt an armlock. In life and business, we must also make sacrifices. Sometimes we must sacrifice short-term profit for long-term growth or perhaps resist the temptation to give our children something they *want* in order to teach them the life lesson they *need.*

The Redirection Principle can turn negative situations into positive ones. In jiu-jitsu, this often means using your opponent's energy against them. For instance, if an opponent uses excessive force to push you, you can redirect that energy and trip them with relative ease. This principle is invaluable off the mats as well. It can be used to de-escalate an angry individual by redirecting their focus, or it can be used to redirect your child's excess energy from annoying their sibling to something more productive, like exercise or exploration.

These are but a few examples of the principles outlined in this book. Some of them seem like common sense, while others are more nuanced and subtle. But all of them are effective—both in fighting and in life. Since physical jiu-jitsu principles can be difficult to explain through words alone, Rener has included a scannable QR code at the beginning of every chapter that links the reader to a video in which he and his brother Ryron visually demonstrate and teach the combat application of that chapter's featured principle (if only Sun Tzu had access to the same technology when he wrote *The Art of War*). These complementary videos provide a one-of-a-kind experience for every reader, adeptly bridging the gap between the combat and life applications of the 32 principles.

Once the reader understands these principles, they will see they can be applied everywhere and to everything.

That is the purpose of this book: to share the powerful principles of jiu-jitsu with as many people as possible so that they may be learned and utilized, allowing people to become Grandmasters of life.

But remember what the final principle in the book says about being a Grandmaster: The co-creator of Brazilian jiu-jitsu, Helio Gracie himself, never stopped seeking knowledge. He never stopped learning. He never believed he knew it all. Nor should we.

We must always be learning. And this book is a great source to learn.

Learn the philosophies. Learn the principles. Learn the lessons.

Learn, without a doubt, that "Jiu-jitsu is life."

Thank you, Rener Gracie, for distilling the art down to its 32 core principles and for making them so easy to learn and implement.

Thank you to the Gracie family for everything you have given to the world and to me through the techniques and philosophies of jiu-jitsu.

—Jocko Willink
December 2022

Introduction

Hello, my name is Rener Gracie. Brazilian jiu-jitsu (BJJ) is one of the most effective and efficient self-defense systems on the planet, and I have had the privilege of being born into the family that created it. Though I never earned a college degree, I spent the first nineteen years of my life mastering the art of BJJ by perfecting the thousands of physical techniques that have enabled me to control and defeat larger and stronger opponents. Once I had mastered the physical techniques, I dedicated the subsequent decades to distilling the art down to its core principles. I have used these principles to navigate challenges and achieve great levels of success in my personal and professional life. With this book, I hope to share these principles—the keys to my success—so you too can overcome obstacles and enjoy life with the confidence, clarity, and the conviction of a BJJ black belt—and the best part is that all your growth will be possible without ever taking a single step onto a jiu-jitsu mat.

Until the advent of Brazilian jiu-jitsu, there hadn't been a martial art that could be used by smaller, weaker individuals to defeat larger, more athletic opponents in "no-holds-barred" fights with daunting consistency. My grandfather Helio Gracie, who stopped attending school in Brazil in the third grade due to intense bouts of vertigo as a frail and sickly child, invented BJJ during the 1920s, alongside his brother, as a way to use leverage instead of strength in approaching traditional jiu-jitsu. How successful was it? Just a decade later, my 140-pound grandfather had become Brazil's first national sports hero, accepting challenges and regularly defeating all comers, no matter their weight class, martial art discipline, or nationality. Helio Gracie wasn't on a mission to prove his own self-worth but rather the worthiness of the art form he had created.

My family's pursuit of proving Brazilian jiu-jitsu's mettle didn't stop with my grandfather—he passed the tradition along to his children, whose passion for the sport matched his own. In 1993, my father, Rorion Gracie, who'd immigrated to the US in 1978 and for years had taught the art of BJJ out of his garage, co-created the Ultimate Fighting Championship (UFC). His objective was to pit accomplished fighting experts from the most prominent martial arts against one another in a no-rules, eight-man, single-elimination tournament, so that the world could see what really works in personal combat and what doesn't. There were no time limits, no weight classes, no gloves, and no rules. Chosen as the family representative to compete in the first event, my uncle, Royce Gracie, walked into the octagonal cage at McNichols Sports Arena in Denver as a biblical David facing a trio of Goliaths in one night, armed only with a slingshot called BJJ. And after Royce defeated all three in under five minutes, it became clear that the martial arts world would never be the same. A year after the first UFC event, Royce's repeated success in UFC 2 (and later in UFC 4) caused every serious martial artist to completely rethink how they approached fighting. Three decades have passed since that pair of high-profile tournament victories, and now not a single Mixed Martial Arts (MMA) fighter enters the cage without first investing heavily in their BJJ skills.

As for me, I learned to walk on a grappling mat. I don't know life without jiu-jitsu, nor do I know life without the confidence the art has instilled in me. Whenever I encounter an obstacle in life that stops my forward momentum, I don't walk away in frustration, feeling helpless and believing that the world has gotten the better of me. Instead, I discover a solution for that seemingly insurmountable problem. But before anyone, including me, can identify a potential solution, you have to believe that such a solution actually exists. That's part of what jiu-jitsu has taught me. Whether it's an individual technique or a core principle of the art, I have the ability to reach into my jiu-jitsu–honed mental and physical toolbox to address problems—whether they be personal, professional, or anything in between—and find solutions.

I've been teaching BJJ professionally for over 25 years. Between live instruction and video courses, I've taught millions of people from every age and demographic. From bullied children and Navy SEALs to entrepreneurs and sexual-assault survivors, they all come to me to learn how to use leverage-based techniques to prevail in the chaotic circumstances of a violent physical altercation. After just a few months of practice, my students arrive at the conclusion that with the correct technique at the right time, they are far more capable than they ever imagined. Once they experience this inevitable breakthrough, they begin to look at life through an entirely new lens, and that's where the real growth begins.

In 2020, when the COVID-19 pandemic struck, my older brother Ryron and I were forced to close the doors to in-person classes at Gracie University, our jiu-jitsu school in Southern California. It was a total gut punch to our passion and livelihood. But rather than sitting on our hands and waiting for permission to get back to doing what we love, we started seeking answers from jiu-jitsu in a way we never had before. We began asking questions and conducting jiu-jitsu experiments to see if there was a finite number of clearly definable, easy-to-understand principles on which *every* technique relied. While the apex principle of jiu-jitsu has always been *efficiency*, and the macro principles of *timing* and *control* are generally well known, we had a strong inclination that there was something deeper we could extrapolate from the art that could provide great value to practitioners everywhere. After several months of study and countless hours on the mat, we identified what we called the "32 micro principles of jiu-jitsu." We concluded that every technique in jiu-jitsu was made possible by one or more of these core concepts, and that realization gave us a new perspective on the art. Excited to share our findings, we produced an instructional video series called *The 32 Principles of Jiu-Jitsu*, and the response from the BJJ community exceeded our wildest expectations. In the first 72 hours after it was released, the course generated monumental sales, making it the fastest-selling martial arts instructional video course of all time.

The "Alphabet" of Jiu-Jitsu

In our pursuit for sincere feedback on how the 32 principles were impacting BJJ students around the world, this analogy surfaced several times: *Imagine struggling to learn a new language by ear. Then you discover that there's a 32-letter alphabet, one that allows you to visualize and understand the formation of words right before your eyes.* With these 32 principles, my brother and I had seemingly discovered the "alphabet" of Brazilian jiu-jitsu, and based on feedback from both longtime practitioners and relative novices, it served as a crucial component to their overall fluency in the art.

Life Through a New Lens

After spending much time reflecting on how the 32 principles had shaped my own development in jiu-jitsu, I couldn't help but wonder if the same principles were subconsciously being used to shape my life off the mat as well. As it turns out, the answer was a resounding "Yes!" Having started working for the family business at 13 years old, jiu-jitsu shaped how I interacted with the world, so it came as no surprise that I had been relying on these same 32 principles to overcome obstacles and achieve success in my personal and professional life for as long as I could remember. To illustrate, here is a brief summary of how just the first six jiu-jitsu principles had guided my thoughts and my actions in the face of adversity over the years, and how they changed the course of my life in the process:

- The Connection Principle enabled me to turn a catastrophic back injury into a global online enterprise that would exponentially increase the impact of the Gracie family.
- The Detachment Principle helped me navigate the challenges and complexities surrounding the untimely and very tragic passing of my mother.
- The Distance Principle taught me how to manage the difficulties of personal relationships with two people I trusted that ended in betrayal.
- The Pyramid Principle inspired me to create a solid foundation of proprietary products that launched our organization to the front of a saturated industry.
- The Creation Principle enabled my family to transform countless traditional martial artists into Brazilian jiu-jitsu fanatics using methods they never expected.

- The Acceptance Principle saved my marriage before it even started by allowing me to see that just because my wife didn't fit the mold I thought I wanted, that didn't mean she wasn't exactly who I needed in my life.

. . . and the list goes on.

As I reflect on my life, there isn't a single obstacle that I successfully overcame without attribution to one or more of the 32 principles. Even though I didn't have labels for them at the time, after going through the process of identifying, naming, and defining each principle, it became crystal clear that they were there guiding my sails all along.

Eradicating BJJ's One Limitation

Having dedicated nearly forty years to the practice of the art, I concluded that the *only* limitation I had identified in BJJ was that in order to benefit from the life-altering impact of the art, you first have to suit up and step on the mat to learn the physical techniques. But with this book, I intend to overcome that limitation.

Along with multi-award-winning author and journalist Paul Volponi, I have created a comprehensive problem-solving curriculum based on the 32 principles of jiu-jitsu that anyone can use to navigate personal and professional challenges with the same confidence, conviction, and clarity that practitioners of this art have demonstrated in combat for almost a century.

This book features 32 chapters, one for each principle. While the chapters are meant to be experienced in the order presented, if you decide to explore the chapters out of order, you'll still find stand-alone value in every one. Each chapter is comprised of sections that outline how the principles can be used in every aspect of your life, including, but not limited to: combat application, life application, personal application, and societal application.

Combat Application

I speak to executives and entrepreneurs at leadership conferences all over the country about the impact and application of the 32 principles in life and business. It is by no means a traditional keynote as I normally begin by demonstrating several BJJ techniques on stage, which not only excites the audience but also visually contextualizes each principle in its combat application before I proceed to explain its life and business applications. As I contemplated writing this book, one of my biggest concerns was that readers would not get the same visual experience as would the attendees in an audience. In my search for a solution, I leveraged the Tagalong Principle (chapter twenty-three), and decided to add a QR code at the beginning of each chapter.

When scanned with a smartphone, these QR codes will launch short videos in which my brother and I demonstrate the principle of interest in the context of a physical altercation. By the time you're done watching a video, not only will you be better prepared to defend yourself in a physical altercation, but you will be fully primed and eager to dive into the chapter itself, where you will learn the life applications of the very same principle.

Even though QR codes were invented in 1994, it wasn't until the COVID-19 pandemic of 2020 that their use became ubiquitous. While I could have done without the pandemic, I am happy that the resulting technological improvements have allowed me to give you a front-row seat to one of my Fortune 500 presentations.

Personal Application

In every chapter, I will also share a personal anecdote to illustrate how profoundly the 32 principles have influenced my life at every turn. I recount the time I used the Buoyancy Principle to catch a thief, the time I used the Posture Principle to convince my high school teacher to change my report card grade, the time I used the River Principle to "accidentally" create an apparel company that landed on ABC's *Shark Tank*, and the time I used the Clock Principle to rescue a teenage boy suffering from an extreme case of social anxiety. We'll also be joined by well-respected contributors in different fields—from elite athletes, coaches, performing artists, and entrepreneurs to everyday people focused on forging a better place for themselves in the world—who'll provide us with perspective from their own experiences with our core principles.

Once you grasp how each of the 32 principles have shaped my outcomes, you'll be ready to begin adopting and applying them as your own. To help guide you on the journey, we'll provide a range of hypothetical situations and historical anecdotes to illustrate some of the most common and powerful applications of each principle.

Principles in Practice

Sometimes the biggest challenge is knowing *which* of the principles to use in a given situation. On the mat, when thrust into a challenging position or situation, my mind subconsciously conducts a "32 Principles Diagnostic," and in a matter of seconds, my body adopts the most applicable principles and then uses them to produce a customized technique to overcome the obstacle presented by my opponent. Even though the position I'm in may be unfamiliar, and the technique I come up with may be one I've never used before, my mastery of the 32 principles allows me to be comfortable where others are not and to improvise in a way that is quasi magical.

To end each chapter, I've included simple everyday examples of how you can apply the featured principle in your own life to maximize leverage and increase efficiency at every turn. So that you truly grasp the limitless problem-solving potential of the 32 principles, the examples will touch on everything from business challenges to parenting problems to relationship difficulties and everything in between. In the end, my goal is to develop your knowledge of and your confidence in these principles to such an extent that you too can conduct a "32 Principles Diagnostic" anytime you face hardship in your life.

Simply put, all our problems are just techniques waiting to be discovered, and when the 32 principles become part of your DNA like they are part of mine, the right techniques will reveal themselves at the right time. By the time you finish this book, you will have the 32 principles of jiu-jitsu in your personal problem-solving arsenal, and you will be enjoying life through the lens of a Brazilian jiu-jitsu black belt, even if you never step foot on the mat.

—Rener Gracie

Psst . . .

Here are some brief definitions to assist those of you who are new to jiu-jitsu. You'll encounter several of these terms in the text's description of jiu-jitsu's 32 core principles and hear them mentioned in the demonstrative videos at the start of each chapter.

A "gi" *(gee)* is a loose-fitting jiu-jitsu garment (uniform), which is normally secured by a belt that displays the practitioner's ranking. Though a gi is also worn in other martial arts such as karate and tae kwon do, the jiu-jitsu gi is usually made of a thicker material to prevent potential rips from grappling sessions.

Most of us are familiar with the phrase "Keep your guard up." We hear it in boxing and other striking arts as a fundamental technique of using your hands to protect your head. However, in jiu-jitsu, the term "guard" is most often used to describe when a practitioner is on their back and has the opponent on top, positioned between their legs. You'll also hear the phrase "passing the guard." That's when the opponent on top escapes the legs of the practitioner who is on their back and gets to either their left or right side, gaining "side control."

The "sweep" was made famous in the film *The Karate Kid*. But in jiu-jitsu, it means more than just sweeping your leg and bringing an opponent to the ground. For us, a sweep also means using leverage and any number of limbs to escape an inferior position in a ground fight, where we are underneath our opponent, to a dominant position, where we are on top of our opponent.

We'll end this linguistic journey the way most jiu-jitsu practitioners hope their grappling sessions end: with a "submission." That's when we put the opponent in an inescapable position, via a choke or a joint lock, and the opponent signals their surrender by "tapping out," usually a repetitive tap of their hand upon the mat or their rival.

That's enough for now; you'll learn a lot more throughout this book. Just think of me as Merriam-Webster in a gi.

Scan here to learn the combat application of

The Connection Principle

Chapter One

The Connection Principle

Optimizing your success by constantly evolving the tools and tactics you use to connect with others in the world around you.

Our lives are connected by a thousand invisible threads. And all along these sympathetic fibers, our actions run as causes and return to us as results.
—Herman Melville, author

The Connection Principle is where our jiu-jitsu journey begins. We all yearn to be connected—to our family, friends, the world, and especially to ourselves. If jiu-jitsu is the language we will speak throughout the pages of this text, then the Connection Principle will serve as our first exposure to its alphabet. We will learn to string its connective resources together, not to make literal words, but rather to create positive actions and potential solutions to the problems and situations we encounter.

On the jiu-jitsu mat, there are dozens of body parts that practitioners of the art can use to make a physical connection with their opponents. They include our hands, feet, arms, legs, thighs, hips, wrists, shoulders, fists, elbows, and even armpits. These are the connective tools with which most of us are born, and which we learn to use to our advantage from an early age. But jiu-jitsu opens the door for us to use our natural ability to connect in ways we never imagined. As a practitioner of the art, I can use these connective tools to grab, control, hook, push away, or pull in an opponent—all aimed at either keeping myself at a safe distance from an attack or totally stifling one.

Of course, jiu-jitsu has ramifications in life well beyond the borders of a mat. The art, once internalized, becomes woven into your thinking process and instinctual reactions. The more you practice it, the more you find its core principles taking root in your daily life. How has that worked for me with the Connection Principle? I've learned that the connective tools of my body have their mental and personality-driven counterparts—what I use to relate to the people with whom I come in contact. It's not the heel, chest, glutes, triceps, or biceps creating a physical connection to them. Instead, it's my ability to communicate, listen, negotiate, observe, problem solve, escalate, de-escalate, empathize, pacify, praise, embrace, or perhaps totally avoid that helps me to maintain control in everyday social situations.

Taking the Reins

I was only 19 years old when my brother Ryron and I began running the family business. We had just assumed the roles of co–head instructors at Gracie Jiu-Jitsu Academy (later to become the Gracie University of Jiu-Jitsu), and one day, at the conclusion of a training session, I felt a strange numbness in my right leg, which later developed into a sharp pain. It was like nothing I'd ever felt before. I thought to myself, *Did I tear a muscle?* But ignoring the discomfort, I continued to train on it. After several more weeks, the pain got so bad that I couldn't stand up for more than a minute at a time. That's when I understood that I needed help. I went to the doctor, accompanied by my mom.

The scans were conclusive; I had a herniated disc in my lower back. The surgeons would have to operate and clean it out. As a young man believing that my body would never fail me, it was a substantial blow to my psyche. Thankfully, the operation was a complete success. The doctors, however, said that I couldn't participate in jiu-jitsu for ten months, which meant nearly a year on the sidelines.

Growing up in the Gracie family, I had been taught that your body was the only tool you needed to make an impact on the world. I had witnessed everyone important in my life use their bodies to teach, express their creativity, and earn a living, including my grandfather Helio, who had been active well into his nineties. For the first time, this injury forced me to question my life's path. *What if this happened to me again? What if I had to retire from physically teaching jiu-jitsu by the time I was in my forties?*

That's when I turned to the Connection Principle. I realized that I needed to connect to my students on more than just a physical plane. So I started to focus on my communication skills and use of language. I also began concentrating on connecting with my students on a deeper emotional level, becoming even more attuned to their hopes, fears, and personal goals. But above all, I became consumed by a new approach to teaching jiu-jitsu, something that would initially be viewed as radical and almost heresy in the martial arts world. During the time that I was prohibited from practicing jiu-jitsu, I created the road map that would allow us to connect to a global community of students through a computer monitor, teaching the art of jiu-jitsu on the internet.

Creating a comprehensive curriculum on video, one that mirrored the way my brother and I were taught, would be an extremely difficult task. But the potential reward of bringing jiu-jitsu to people beyond our physical reach, as if they were our own personal students participating on the mat at Gracie University in Torrance, California, was exciting and revolutionary. The completion of such a video curriculum would also afford us the opportunity to document everything we had ever learned from our teachers, so those incredibly valuable lessons could never vanish from the face of the earth. But back in 2008, our idea was met with stinging condemnation from the established jiu-jitsu community. *No one can properly teach this art over the internet! It will be a joke!* Internally, it was even called a "disgrace" by several members of the Gracie family.

Undeterred by our critics, Ryron and I plowed forward and painstakingly dedicated half a decade to developing the Gracie University Interactive Online Curriculum. The connections that have been enabled by these efforts are beautifully encompassing. Not only does it connect us to our global student base through a comprehensive linear video curriculum, it also allows the students to connect to us by permitting them to upload videos of their developing skill sets for evaluation and personalized feedback by our team of certified instructors. Furthermore, in cases where an online student doesn't live near a Certified Gracie Jiu-Jitsu Training Center but is looking for a training partner to practice with, the online platform connects them to other students in the area who are also seeking a training partner. Over just a few years, these community connections grew so strong that we added a new location classification called "Gracie Garages" to identify unofficial at-home training groups of dedicated students who didn't have access to an accredited school but were using our interactive online curriculum as their sole source of instruction. Not only had we pioneered new ways for people to connect to jiu-jitsu, we pioneered new ways for people to connect *through* jiu-jitsu.

Today, we reach over 350,000 students in nearly 200 countries. And in the wake of both our success and the COVID-19 pandemic, ironically, many of our initial critics have tried in some way or another to duplicate our model.

On more than one occasion, I have been asked if, in retrospect, I view my back injury as a type of blessing in disguise. My answer to that question has always been consistent. I believe that life doesn't happen *to* you. Life happens *for* you. So whether that injury was a cosmic gift or not, I made it into a gift for myself. That's the beauty of approaching life with the 32 principles of jiu-jitsu in your arsenal. For every worst-case scenario, there's a technique just waiting to be tapped into to solve it.

Connecting the Dots

Scott Butler lives in Shepparton, Australia, roughly 100 miles north of Melbourne, with a population of approximately 50,000. In 2009, when Scott decided to learn Brazilian jiu-jitsu via Gracie University's distance-learning program, it was clear to him that his success, in part, would rest on finding training partners.

"I own a real estate company. That meant I knew a lot of people, so it became all about prospecting to find training partners who would want to do jiu-jitsu," said Scott. "I would talk to all of my clients, friends, family, and neighbors just to try to get people involved and come over to my garage and train. Early on, that wasn't so easy to do. It was difficult to find interested people, and I needed to be really persistent."

Scott's persistence and desire to learn eventually paid off. "At one point in the garage, I regularly had 12 to 14 adults and about 25 kids. The kids being there was important to me because at that stage of my life my wife and I were having children of our own. I wanted to learn how to teach kids so I could eventually teach mine and have grappling partners for them in the future," said Scott, who is now the father of three.

In 2013, Scott went to Sydney to participate in a seminar I was teaching. A year later, he started making regular trips to Gracie University in Torrance to continue his progression in the art. Scott now operates a burgeoning Certified Gracie Jiu-Jitsu Training Center in Shepparton where he trains more than 150 students. What does Scott consider to be the key to his successful journey? "I knew that this was the right path. That all I needed to do was commit to a daily training routine and the skills would come. For me, success is a multi-tiered process: Your career needs to be in check. Your family has to be happy, which gives you support. Then your interests can be enhanced and achieved."[1]

For Scott, the Connection Principle reinforced multiple contact points in his life, creating a stable bridge that he traversed to his desired destination.

From the Mat to the Supermarket

In jiu-jitsu, our connectedness to an opponent is used to supply us with a trio of important outcomes: to prevent motion, to promote motion, or to predict motion. For example, we can thrust both palms forward, connecting them to our opponent's upper arms, preventing an incoming strike upon us. That very action will undoubtedly prompt the opponent to execute an offensive move. One of the most likely moves the attacker will make is to retract an arm in an effort to punch. Our connectedness allows us to feel that motion and predict the still-evolving punch well before it ever happens.

1 Scott Butler interview with Paul Volponi (February 19, 2022).

Our reaction? It may well be to rush further in, closing the gap between us and denying that punch the space and extension it would need to gather any significant power.

Now imagine you're in a local supermarket. You've just advanced the cart you're pushing toward the checkout line. Somebody behind you believes that you've cut the line. They're also screaming that you have twelve items in your cart instead of ten (the allowable limit), and you don't belong at the express register. They become overly angry at you and are on the verge of losing control. The person takes a step forward toward you. You quickly spin your grocery cart around, using it as a buffer, a safe space, between you and this irate customer. You begin to use your words as a secondary buffer, assuring the person that you respect them and had no intention of cutting in front of them. Despite your efforts to quell the conflict, this person shoves their cart into yours. Yes, it's way over the edge on their part. But thinking as a jiu-jitsu practitioner, you realize that you now have a physical connection to something. You can feel the tension of their cart pushing up against yours. As the angered customer rears their cart back to ram yours again, you feel the release of tension. Your connectedness has allowed you to predict the next move in real time. So you advance your cart forward in the direction of theirs, reestablishing the connection and not allowing their cart the kinetic energy to rush forward with any real momentum. All the while, you're continuing to use your language and communication skills in an effort to connect to their better judgment, in hopes of defusing the situation. It's an example of how the Connection Principle can provide you with information during a tense encounter without ever having to put your hands on someone.

Nothing exists in isolation. We have to stop pretending
we are individuals that can go it alone.
—Margaret J. Wheatley, author, teacher

Sightless Connections

Over the years, I've taught jiu-jitsu to many students who are blind. The idea of being connected to their opponent is something that usually strikes a very personal chord with them, and they typically master the Connection Principle quicker than most sighted students. Though no sighted person can ever truly know what it's like to be blind, there is an exercise that I use with my students that gives them a glimpse at it, while also perfectly illustrating the Connection Principle. After removing the belt from around my jiu-jitsu gi, I hand one end of it to a student. I hold the other end, with approximately four feet of slack belt hanging loosely between us. Then I ask the student to close their eyes and predict when I will rush forward to throw a strike at them. Because the belt is slack, with no tension in our connectedness, the student is indeed defending blindly, guessing at when the attack will come. However, when the belt is pulled taut between us so there is tension in our connectedness, as I move forward to strike, the student feels the tension in our connection release and perfectly predicts my attack. We call connections with tension "reliable connections," while connections with a lack of tension are termed "unreliable connections."

Profile: Maria Liana Mutia

Maria Liana Mutia has represented the US in judo at the Paralympics. Governed by the International Blind Sports Federation (IBSA), men's judo debuted in 1988 during the Seoul Games and women's judo was added at the Athens Games in 2004.

"Judo has influenced how I conduct my everyday life largely in terms of confidence," says Maria Liana Mutia. "I became visually impaired and began judo in my teens. Had I not done so, I am certain that I would have much less spatial awareness, as well as less confidence in my physical movement.

"As a blind woman, judo has taught me to be unafraid. Many times, I was followed while taking the train when I lived in the city—whether it was because of my gender, appearance, or obvious disability, I cannot be certain," said Maria. "While the experience of judo may be different for sighted or able-bodied individuals, judo training has taught me to be confident, aware of my surroundings, and surer of my ability to defend myself. Judo training allowed me to address potential situations by giving me the spatial awareness to prevent the situation from escalating further."[2]

Rely on the Connection Principle when . . .

- **Owning Your Identity:** You've become so consumed with being who others want you to be that you've lost connection with who you are, so you begin to spend more time on self-discovery.
- **Empathy:** If you suspect someone you care about is struggling with depression, communicate and connect with them so that when they are ready to open up, they know you're there for them.
- **Marketing:** Your goal is to acquire new customers, but the marketing methods your company is using are old and outdated, so you consult with experts about new ways to connect to your target demographics.
- **Parenting:** You feel that your relationship with your teenage child is suffering, so you explore different ways of connecting that are meaningful for them.

2 Maria Liana Mutia interview with Paul Volponi (January 5, 2022).

Belts

The modern belt system in martial arts had its beginnings in Japanese judo during the late nineteenth century. It was devised by a man named Kano Jigoro (1860–1938), who is widely recognized as the founder of modern judo. The belt system began as a way to visually identify a student's proficiency, while also clearly designating the student's ability level within a larger group.

Most students studying martial arts today receive a new belt whenever they rise to the next level of their training. Originally, students kept the same belt throughout their entire course of study and would simply dye it another color upon being moved up. That's why the belts normally progress in colors from light to dark, making the dying process easier. There is an interesting superstition among some jiu-jitsu practitioners of not washing their belts, believing all of their hard-earned knowledge could possibly be washed away. Added to that is the belief that an unwashed belt will literally turn from white to black, mirroring the practitioner's increasing knowledge over many years of usage and study.

Scan here to learn the combat application of

The Detachment Principle

Chapter Two

The Detachment Principle

Recognizing when holding on does more harm than good, and when letting go does more good than imagined.

Detachment doesn't mean you don't let the experience penetrate you. On the contrary, you let it penetrate you fully. That's how you are able to leave it.
—Mitch Albom, author

You've undoubtedly heard of the Chinese philosophy of yin and yang, which puts forth the idea that opposite and contradictory forces can be complementary to one another. Many martial arts borrow from this concept, and jiu-jitsu is one of them. The Connection Principle explains how keeping ourselves connected to our opponent can prevent, promote, and predict movement. If that is our yin, then the Detachment Principle is certainly its yang. The Detachment Principle grants us optimal efficiency through the deliberate *disconnection* from our opponent. For it is equally as important to know how to disconnect, even if only momentarily, to maintain an advantage and good position. Whether it's a physical encounter, an argument, or the internal struggle of reaching a future goal, mastering the Detachment

Principle of knowing when it is advantageous to release our hold on something will improve both your jiu-jitsu and your life.

Peace for Mom

The Detachment Principle is extremely personal to me. In the spring of 2021, my mother's husband, Mark (my parents Suzanne and Rorion Gracie divorced when I was twelve), was diagnosed with stage 4 prostate cancer. It was shocking news for our family, and my mother instantly went into caretaker mode, helping to plan all of his possible treatment options. Several months later, my mother was scheduled to watch my two boys while my wife, Eve, and I went out to dinner. But those plans changed. Less than an hour before we had planned to leave the house that evening, my mother called and said, "I'm not feeling well. I have this pain in my abdomen." She had suffered from gallstones in the past, so we all figured that was most likely the cause. She went to the doctor the next day for some tests, and within weeks my mother was diagnosed with a rare form of bile duct cancer, one of the most aggressive forms of the disease. I was devastated. As the mother of five children, she had always been a rock to lean on for me and my four siblings, being especially helpful with her many beloved grandbabies. In her younger days, she earned the reputation as "the Mother of Jiu-Jitsu in America," because she single-handedly ran the household and looked after us kids while my father taught long hours in our garage turned into a makeshift school.

We all became intensely focused on finding the right doctors and clinic that could somehow deliver our mom a miracle cure. My mother, who'd been living an active lifestyle just several weeks earlier, was growing considerably weaker every day and had become bedridden. That's when she summoned me to her side and in a pained voice said, "Honey, I've lived such a good life, longer than I ever imagined. I've been fulfilled on so many levels and I'm very content with where I am." Even though it tore me apart to hear her say this, her words were clear and the underlying message was unmistakable. We'd been doggedly fighting a battle for my mother of which she wanted no part. She was clinging to life, in pain, just to satisfy us. It was the hardest decision of my life, but the Detachment Principle was speaking to me. It was saying: *Sometimes the people closest to us don't need the type of help we want to give. They need a different type of help from us. They need for us to realize it's all right to let go.*

I finally accepted that detaching from my mother was the most powerful way to love, and the most powerful way to give her what she ultimately needed. Peace. Convincing her husband, Mark, of this was no easy task. But the two of us had a long and emotional talk. My mother, a caretaker by nature, couldn't move on unless she knew that her husband could find his own way. I stressed to Mark how important it was for both of them that he learn to detach, releasing my mother from her perceived obligations. Ultimately, he agreed. Within a week after Mark left for a clinic to receive his own much-needed treatment, my mother finally found peace, surrounded at her bedside by her loving children.

> *Detachment is not about refusing to feel or not caring or turning away from those you love. Detachment is profoundly honest, grounded firmly in the truth of what is.*
> —Sharon Salzberg, writer and meditation teacher

Better to Be Next?

Imagine you are waiting to be served at a bakery on a busy Sunday morning. Just as someone behind the counter begins to take your order, another customer aggressively says to you, "I was here when you walked through the door. Don't jump me in line." Both you and the counter person explain that you were indeed there first. Only, the other customer is becoming more roiled with every word. You sense that the other customer is about to completely lose control. This is obviously not about who gets the last rye bread in the bakery. It's more likely that the other customer has had a bad morning, week, or month, and that this moment has become their tipping point. You decide that a further tug-of-war over this issue wouldn't serve anyone's best interests, especially the other customer's emotional state. That's when you politely step aside and let the issue go.

On the jiu-jitsu mat, we often discuss the concept of detachment for survival. You might be on your back, tightly grasping your standing opponent. If your opponent tries to lift you up with the idea of slamming you down, you'll need to use the Detachment Principle and counter by detaching your grip. Never let your back come off the ground, allowing your opponent to use gravity against you.

Always remaining grounded, in jiu-jitsu and in life, will serve you extremely well. It mirrors the scenario at the bakery. Don't let your opponent bring you to a place where you don't want to be, physically or emotionally. Remember, the Detachment Principle works in two ways: Sometimes we dictate when to detach, other times our opponent dictates that moment for us. Either way, the student who masters the Detachment Principle reaps the benefits.

Detachment is not that you should own nothing.
But that nothing should own you.
—Ali, philosopher/prophet

Consider the Detachment Principle when . . .

- **Preserving Dignity:** After several years of marriage you realize that irreconcilable differences are leading you toward hatred, so you commit to a healthy divorce process to preserve the dignity and respect of the relationship.
- **Meditating:** Work and family challenges have caused your stress levels to reach all-time highs, so you adopt the habit of meditating for 10 minutes at the beginning of each day.
- **Starting Anew:** You hate your job, so you decide to turn your passion into your profession in spite of the fact that the decision will bring a degree of uncertainty.
- **Letting Go:** You worked hard on a project at work, but management decided to go "in a different direction," so you detach from your ego and support their decision.

The Dualism of Yin and Yang

To help you understand the concept of yin and yang, consider this: As the sun rises and then slowly moves across the sky, a mountain and the valley below it become a visual theater of an interconnected relationship. Throughout the early hours, the north face is the darkened area, or yin, shaded by the mountain's immense presence. The south face, which for the moment is bathed in light, plays the temporary role of yang. But as the sun makes its journey across the sky, the pair begins to slowly trade places. Yin becomes yang, as what was visible becomes obscured, and what was obscured becomes visible.

The dualistic idea of yin and yang finds its roots in ancient Chinese cosmology, which believes that the universe, including humans, was created out of such a duality. The philosopher Confucius, born in the sixth century BC, said, "Yin and yang, male and female, strong and weak, rigid and tender, heaven and earth, light and darkness, thunder and lightning, cold and warmth, good and evil . . . the interplay of opposite principles constitutes the universe." In ancient Chinese medicine, good health was also thought to be the by-product of a proper balance between yin and yang. Science, philosophy, martial arts, and various forms of exercise all have foundational elements of the pair in Chinese culture. The circular design representing yin and yang is a Taoist symbol, which is divided into twin teardrop shapes, one black and one white. A smaller circle of the opposite color is often contained in each opposing half. The symbol's construct is meant to represent the undifferentiated unity that supposedly gave birth to the universe and still persists to this day.

Scan here to learn the combat application for

The Distance Principle

Chapter Three

The Distance Principle

Understanding the impact that distance has on your effectiveness.

We can only see a short distance ahead, but we can see plenty there that needs to be done.
—Alan Turing, mathematician and philosopher

One of the simplest principles of jiu-jitsu, as well as one of its most universal, is the Distance Principle. Most of us are familiar with the concept of someone trying to strike us, be it with a punch or kick. If not, we're certainly familiar with someone reaching out to either hug us or shake hands. Managing the distance between ourselves and others to correctly perform predictable movements is a concept to which we've been exposed and practiced since we were very young. Even a toddler quickly learns not to reach out for the cookie jar until they are at a proper distance to do so.

In all forms of fighting, whoever manages the distance manages the damage that can be done. Why? Opponents who wish to strike you need to establish the proper distance to deliver any type of blow with substantial power. And if we view distance as maintaining proper position, including the positions we grant to others in our daily orbits of work, school, and personal relationships, then the Distance Principle perfectly equates to our own internal human resources department.

Keeping Closer Tabs

This story about the Distance Principle is one of which I truly regret being a part. My brother Ryron and I meet a lot of people through our position as jiu-jitsu instructors and running the worldwide interests of Gracie University. We partake in a myriad of relationships, and positioning ourselves with others in a way that is both authentic and safe is an ever-evolving challenge.

Several years ago, a person who had been allowed inside our circle of trust for more than a decade hit rock bottom both morally and ethically. Although he lived beyond our spectrum of daily sight, many miles away in a different part of the country, we considered him a close friend. To our shock and dismay, my brother and I were made aware of multiple substantiated allegations of sexual assault against this person.

We were left to wonder: How could he have hidden his true nature from us for so long? He posed as someone with high levels of integrity, which made the disappointment hit deeply. But what made matters even worse was that his public and private relationships with Gracie University we believed had, in part, made it easier for him to take advantage of innocent people.

After some rather intense soul-searching, my brother and I came to the conclusion that we had mismanaged the Distance Principle in this relationship. How so? Because of the extended distance between us, we were never physically close enough to him on a regular basis to witness how he treated others in his own orbit. Instead, we were perpetually caught in the relationship "red zone" with him, that inherently dangerous space where his unforeseen actions could deliver a power-packed blow to our feelings and reputation (we'll see how this plays out on the jiu-jitsu mat in the very next section). We had let him into our circle, and we felt close. But unfortunately, not close enough to see who he truly was and to mitigate the damage-causing potential of his true character.

While there were no criminal charges filed against him, the volume and severity of the allegations were substantial enough for us to make the decision to cut all ties and fully distance ourselves from him.

Sadly, within months, a series of similar allegations arose surrounding yet another person who existed in our relationship "red zone." He, also, lived hundreds of miles away in a different state and was trusted implicitly.

While we've always recognized that the Gracie name carries clout, it took these back-to-back incidents to drive home that there are always going to be those who try to forge a relationship with us to enhance their own reputations, for good or for evil. Through our failed application of the Distance Principle, we've learned that we must remain ever vigilant about the trusting bonds we build with others.

I'm not suggesting that managing the distance in something as free flowing and fragile as a friendship is either easy or can be quantified through a concrete formula. It can't. Obviously, I'm looking back at the situation with 20/20 hindsight, and it's always possible to be blindsided by disappointment, even from people who are very close to us. But the Distance Principle, applied to relationships in general, can be both viable and valuable. If you're close with someone, be close enough to assess their true nature. Or remain positioned just far enough back that you can sidestep and react to unexpected circumstances. Otherwise, what happens in the red zone may cause irreparable damage when it hits you in a way you never expected.

Punch Protection

We refer to managing the distance during a street fight as "punch protection." It's even color coded, much like a traffic signal. You occupy the green zone when you're standing outside of the distance to receive a blow, where the opponent can't reach you. If the opponent moves forward, you can simply move back an equal amount, continuing at a safe distance. Jiu-jitsu, though, has an opposite green zone that exists when you are so close to the opponent that their blows can't gather enough momentum to deliver optimal force. That's a distance where your jiu-jitsu techniques can begin to be applied.

In between those green zones is our red zone, with red representing danger. It's where the opponent can manufacture enough power to hurt you. And yes, we have to learn to move through the red zone in order to reach our jiu-jitsu–applicable green zone. We learn to pass through the red zone quickly, considering our own timing along with that of our opponent's. Once you are engaged, however, a pair of pertinent questions should immediately come to mind: Which jiu-jitsu techniques can I use against my opponent, and which might be used against me?

The overall number of possible techniques in the art is staggering. So how do we reduce the idea of preparing for that massive number? The answer is by fully understanding distance. The relative space and distance between you and your opponent will begin to dictate which techniques can successfully be executed by either party, and which, at the moment, cannot.

Distance has the same effect on the mind as on the eye.
—Samuel Johnson, author

Personal Space

Recognizing and computing distances between ourselves and others is a function that we perform constantly. And whenever we fail at that function, or more likely, have a difference of opinion, we may hear the phrase: *Please, you need to respect my boundaries. My personal space.* Personal space is commonly defined as the physical space immediately surrounding someone into which any encroachment feels either threatening or uncomfortable for them. How does it work? Researchers in the fields of neuroscience, psychology, sociology, and zoology maintain that the brain, in a mostly unconscious manner, computes a "safe zone" around the body. It's a purely defensive mechanism. In the animal kingdom it's referred to as the "flight zone," where animals will either choose to make a stand and fight or take flight from predators.

In human society, our accepted personal boundaries are always being recomputed depending upon the situation. It has long been observed that a quartet of strangers in an elevator are very likely to occupy the four corners of the elevator car, giving each other plenty of personal space. However, when the elevator takes on more passengers, usually an arm's length of distance (the very edge of the red zone for a jiu-jitsu practitioner) leaves most people feeling comfortable about their boundaries. But if the elevator adds several additional riders on the next floor, we further adjust our accepted personal space. Those who cannot accept the change in their personal boundary may even choose to get out of the car and wait for the next elevator.

Remember the Distance Principle when . . .

- **Managing Tasks:** You are overwhelmed with tasks hitting you from every angle and recognize the need to close in on one mission at a time to make measurable progress each day.
- **Relating at Work:** You are beginning to form a negative opinion about a work colleague, so you purposely create distance and limit interactions in hopes that your perspective will shift.
- **Reacting Emotionally:** You get an email from your boss that is upsetting, and you furiously type a response, but before hitting send you go for a walk, and when you return to your desk you re-write the email with a measured tone.
- **Overseeing Emotions:** You are emotionally drained by a friend with whom you've existed in the emotional "red zone" for too long, so you get closer to them to try and resolve the issues, but when that fails, you distance yourself fully.

How Does a Punch Generate Power?

The power behind a punch comes from technique. All the natural strength in the world won't deliver a truly powerful punch without the proper execution. Momentum (the mass of an object multiplied by its velocity) is a big part of delivering a powerful blow. So the greater the force and speed, the more potential for overall power and even a knockout.

In the case of a boxer, force is generated from the floor to the fist via a kinetic chain. That chain has a multitude of moving parts, which are dependent upon one another for maximum efficiency. Force from the floor is transferred to the feet, then to the legs, up through the hips and midsection, to the shoulders, and finally to the fist. Any disruption along the kinetic chain can severely minimize a potential punch.

That's why when boxers are in close quarters, they often try to tie each other up in a "clinch," disrupting the kinetic chain. In that case, a referee will separate them, allowing each to reestablish their proper distance to generate power. The jiu-jitsu practitioner wants to minimize a striker's space, controlling the distance and giving the striker's blows less of an opportunity to gather momentum, thus inhibiting the kinetic chain.

Scan here to learn the combat application of

The Pyramid Principle

Chapter Four

The Pyramid Principle

Investing in a strong foundation.

Next to love, the most important thing is balance.
—John Wooden, champion basketball coach

In jiu-jitsu, the Pyramid Principle is vitally important. It is what allows us to stay in control of ourselves and our opponents. Our structural foundation rests upon it, providing the practitioner with a solid base that gives us balance and stability. It applies to both the horizontal plane, when we might be on top of an opponent, and the vertical plane, when an opponent might attempt to bring us to the ground from a standing position. In both scenarios, the Pyramid Principle gives us a solid connection to incoming force. Reflected in its name, the Pyramid Principle finds its roots in mathematics.

Consider this: A triangle has three connection points and an incredibly stable base. If you stood straight up and down with your feet together, you'd essentially have a single connection point to the ground. Yes, it's strong, bearing the weight of gravity, but fairly easy to unbalance by physical forces from the front, back, and sides. If you spread your feet shoulder-width apart, you'd have a pair of connection points to the ground, stronger but still susceptible to having your balance disturbed, especially from the front or back. But add a third connection point by crouching down and placing one hand on the ground (like an offensive lineman in football), forming a triangle between the base points, and your stability increases dramatically in all directions. Adding a third connection point also typically lowers your center of gravity, another plus.

Suppose you're riding the city bus on your way to work. An elderly person walks onto that bus, but all of the seats are already taken. Instantly, you rise up and offer that elderly person your seat. Now the bus is suddenly moving. You have a computer case slung over one shoulder and a cup of coffee in the opposite hand. You're standing upright with your feet slightly apart, swaying a bit to the movement of the vehicle and the various forces of motion. As the bus picks up speed and begins to make a turn, you start to waver like an unbalanced Jenga tower. Any major bump in the road or quick stop could seriously topple you. So what do you instinctively do? You reach an arm out and connect yourself to either a handrail or the back of the nearest seat. That action provides you with a third connection point and instantly improves your balance. On the jiu-jitsu mat, we might use a hand, a leg, our head, or even our opponent to create a third balance point, forming our triangle.

Jiu-jitsu is dynamic, resulting in constant motion. It is also performed in a three-dimensional world. So let's exchange our triangle for its three-dimensional equivalent, a pyramid. Flip a pyramid on its side, mimicking the free-flowing and transitory movements of a jiu-jitsu practitioner, and it still has a trio of connection points and a strongly balanced foundation. Why? A pyramid design has most of its weight closer to the ground with less force pushing down on it. This makes the design incredibly stable, and for our purposes, mobile, as our posture/structure shifts with each succeeding jiu-jitsu position. Hence, the Pyramid Principle. Of course, the ancient Greeks and Egyptians, who used the pyramid design in architecture so their monuments would stand the test of time, were a model of this type of thinking. In our own lives, we should always invest in building a strong foundation.

There were times when I didn't leave the factory for three or four days—days when I didn't go outside. This has really come at the expense of seeing my kids. And seeing friends.
—Industrialist Elon Musk on a period of imbalance in his life when he put in 120-hour work weeks[3]

Balance in Business

For all practical discussions, my grandfather Helio, alongside his brother, Carlos, invented Brazilian jiu-jitsu. My father, Rorion, immigrated to the States with his primary passion being to disseminate the art, which was basically his only means of financial support, on these shores. Then, as co-creator of the Ultimate Fighting Championship (UFC), my father was responsible for choosing his brother Royce to be the new standard-bearer of the art by fighting in that competition.

As I mention in the introduction, standing six feet tall and weighing 176 pounds, my uncle Royce very much resembled David going up against Goliaths when viewed side by side against his massive opponents in both UFC 1 and UFC 2. His high-profile championship victories in those no-hold-barred tournaments truly opened people's eyes and created an incredible demand for Brazilian jiu-jitsu. But with hundreds of thousands of people seemingly knocking down the doors of martial arts schools everywhere to learn the art, the Gracie clan didn't own a patent on it. And rightly so. The art, despite my family's invaluable propagation of it, belonged to the world. It was purely public domain.

Anyone could hang a shingle outside their door that read: *Bob's Brazilian Jiu-Jitsu*. That also meant lots of people would be learning *generic jiu-jitsu* from non-Gracies, often taught by instructors without a substantial passion for the art or the required knowledge to teach it correctly. The logo for our brand of jiu-jitsu is a triangle, which is a revered shape in the jiu-jitsu community because it provides three points of balance for a strong foundation, fully representing the Pyramid Principle.

3 David Gelles et al., "Elon Musk Details 'Excruciating' Personal Toll of Tesla Turmoil," *New York Times*, nytimes.com, August 16, 2018 (accessed on January 17, 2022).

As Ryron and I assumed the co-leadership roles at Gracie University in 2002, we realized that the proliferation of schools offering Brazilian jiu-jitsu around the country would greatly affect our organization's position in the martial arts industry. No longer would our family name, alone, be a strong enough pillar on which to build a lasting jiu-jitsu empire. If we were going to create something that would impact the world for generations to come, we would need to strengthen our foundation, but where would we find these additional balance points? It began with the recognition that although we couldn't claim ownership to the art of Brazilian jiu-jitsu as a whole, we could stake a claim to our family's unique curriculum and teaching methodology.

That realization was the spark that gave birth to a series of proprietary beginner jiu-jitsu programs. Our flagship program, Gracie Combatives, is based on the fundamental techniques of jiu-jitsu that every practitioner should learn at the beginning of their journey. Gracie Bullyproof is aimed at children ages three and up. It gives kids the courage and confidence to overcome bullies without the use of violence. Women Empowered is a self-defense program based on Gracie jiu-jitsu techniques and the art's core principles to confront twenty of the most common types of physical attacks perpetrated against women. Because we recognize that successful deployment of the Pyramid Principle requires constant reevaluation and reconfiguring of your base points to support future growth, the Women Empowered program (originally written by me and Ryron in 2011) was rewritten several years later by my wife, Eve, a purple belt in BJJ. She specifically brought a point of view and inherent balance to the program that two men simply couldn't.

In stark contrast to the one-size-fits-all approach used by the vast majority of BJJ schools around the world, Ryron and I took tremendous pride in creating these proprietary programs to provide a custom-tailored beginner jiu-jitsu opportunity for students of all ages and athletic abilities. Not only did the success of these programs give our business greater stability in the crowded marketplace, but they served as the foundation for Gracie University to scale globally in a way that exceeded even our most ambitious expectations.

Profile: Kayla's Story

Kayla Harrison is a two-time Olympic gold medalist, and the first American—man or woman—to ever win gold in judo. She is also an MMA champion. Kayla has been kind enough to speak to us about her life in judo. She shares several of her anecdotes relating to our 32 principles throughout this text. But Kayla is also a survivor of teenage sexual abuse. Her moving account of that experience is detailed in her book, Fighting Back: What an Olympic Champion's Story Can Teach Us about Recognizing and Preventing Child Sexual Abuse—and Helping Kids Recover. *She is also the founder of the Fearless Foundation, an organization aimed at shining a light on child sexual abuse.*

"I truly believe that we all have a purpose in life. And although something terrible happened to me, I feel like everything happens for a reason. Winning two Olympic gold medals is great, and being an MMA champion is great. All this stuff is fantastic but it's very selfish and doesn't do anything to give back to the world," said Kayla Harrison. "My goal is to leave the world a better place than I found it. So I decided to use my story to shine a light on sexual abuse and educate people. The Fearless Foundation is like my third child. It's the thing I feel most strongly and passionate about. It's the reason I want to have a big platform, the reason I want to continue to fight and have people pay attention to me. My hope is that we can have this conversation about sexual abuse, have the numbers go down, and help survivors to not just survive, but to thrive."[4]

Courage and Fear

As with every other principle, the Pyramid Principle is relevant to our lives off the mat. We should aim to develop the foundational emotional and

4 Kayla Harrison interview with Paul Volponi (January 18, 2022).

communicative tools that help us to navigate a myriad of potential social obstacles while remaining balanced. Among these tools and traits are a healthy self-esteem, humility, personal reliability, confidence, respect for others, the ability to deal with pressure, a strong will, and the possession of a moral compass. If you can bring any three of these tools to a given situation, the chances of you controlling that situation, rather than the reverse, will increase substantially.

A healthy measure of self-esteem will insulate you from falling into many of the intentional and unintentional traps that people set for you. When you believe in yourself, the words and actions of others, especially those who would disparage your character, are far less likely to either harm you emotionally or goad you into responding in a manner that you normally wouldn't.

> *Once you give [others] the power to tell you you're great, you've also given them the power to tell you you're unworthy. Once you start caring about people's opinions of you, you give up control.*
> —Ronda Rousey, MMA champion

Fear of failure is something that unbalances plenty of people, including students, athletes, salespeople, artists, teachers, entrepreneurs, medical personnel, and many others. The phobia is so common that it actually has a scientific name: atychiphobia. The condition can cause paralyzing anxiety. And when it does, that frozen posture tends to neutralize a person's many other positive traits because the progression of moving from one point of experience to another becomes derailed.

The most difficult part of being a white belt in jiu-jitsu is dealing with the frustration of continually being dominated on the mat. There are students who never make it past the earliest stages of their training because they believe the journey will be too difficult, and they equate the learning curve of being dominated with a type of failure. I believe the students who persevere past that point have a number of the positive traits we've discussed here, enabling them to find a balance between early failure and eventual success.

I've missed more than 9,000 shots in my career. I've lost almost 300 games. Twenty-six times, I've been trusted to take the game-winning shot and missed. I've failed over and over and over again in my life. And that is why I succeed.
—Michael Jordan, NBA Hall of Famer

Turn to the Pyramid Principle when . . .

- **Pursuing Growth:** You're seeking a promotion at work, but you haven't mastered the skills in your current role that would give you the leverage to make the request.
- **Empowering Your Child:** You've insisted that your child take a stand against a bully, but you haven't given them the self-confidence and the physical self-defense skills to make it possible.
- **Diversifying:** Your business leans too heavily on a single product or service and competitors are catching up.
- **Setting Your Routine:** Life is hard, so you create a morning routine that gives you the energy, optimism, and mental clarity to make the most of each day.

Helio's Phenomenal Focus

A submission is usually signaled by the opponent "tapping out," a literal phrase in which the defeated practitioner taps his hand on the mat, the opponent, or himself, signaling to the referee that they are submitting. One of jiu-jitsu's most well-known submission holds is called a "Kimura," which hyper-rotates the shoulder. It is named after Japanese champion Masahiko Kimura, who used the hold to defeat Brazilian jiu-jitsu founder Helio Gracie in a 1951 challenge match in Sao Paulo, Brazil, in front of 20,000 fans at Maracanã Stadium. It should be noted, though, that Gracie, who had his arm broken twice during the intensely painful hold, never submitted himself. Instead, Gracie's corner, concerned about his safety, finally threw in the towel signaling the end of the contest. Helio Gracie's tenacious performance was a testament to his phenomenal focus, as well as his intense pride in himself, his art, and his country. In the history of athletic competition, it is truly one of the handful of times when a participant's reputation grew even larger in defeat.

Scan here to learn the combat application of
The Creation Principle

Chapter Five

The Creation Principle

Beginning with the end goal in mind and then using targeted actions to make your vision a reality.

Thus, what is of supreme importance in war
is to attack the enemy's strategy.
—Sun Tzu, military strategist, writer, and philosopher

When people hear the word "creation," their mind can conjure many different images. Perhaps they're fans of various artists—or creators—in fields ranging from fashion to music to architecture. They may be responsible themselves for the creation of a recipe, invention, painting, poem, story, or a new system of completing a task more efficiently at their job. Their minds may also focus on much broader ideas, such as the creation of time, space, and all that encompasses our universe. In jiu-jitsu, the Creation Principle is not quite so abstract. This principle teaches us to use a deliberate action to force a specific reaction from the opponent. That reaction, which we're trying to promote, is something that can be used to our advantage.

My grandfather once noted, "Jiu-jitsu is a mousetrap. The trap does not chase the mouse. But when the mouse grabs the cheese, the trap plays its role." Correspondingly, jiu-jitsu is an art that makes full use of counterattacks. The opponent moves or attacks and we respond accordingly, so the action, by nature, is very free flowing. The Creation Principle is designed to put the jiu-jitsu practitioner in charge of that timing and flow. We don't have to wait around for things to happen by chance. Instead, we can force our opponent's hand through the Creation Principle and dictate the flow of events to follow.

On the jiu-jitsu mat, you often know what's coming through experience. Practitioners with higher ranked belts usually make their subordinates feel as if their minds and movements are being read in advance, as if their superiors are several steps ahead of them. That's because those with experience are asking themselves: *What do I want my opponent to do?* Then they apply the stimulus to make that happen, creating a submission, an escape, or a reversal.

We like to say: Be first and third. What that literally means is that those in control of a situation make the first move, knowing what the opponent's response (the second move) will be. Then we capitalize on that opening through the third move, the move we set up for ourselves. As you begin to apply the Creation Principle to your everyday life, start with a specific goal in mind. Then focus your subsequent actions on being stepping-stones to make that goal a reality.

Creating a Buzz

Before my father engineered a global buzz over Brazilian jiu-jitsu through his co-creation of the UFC, he had begun the same task on a much smaller level in Southern California, influencing people, one by one, with the ultimate goal of creating a domino-type effect and disseminating the art of BJJ to as many people as possible. While teaching out of his garage, he offered every person he met a free lesson. And if any of those people brought in a friend to train, my father would give them each a free lesson, offering a sort of finder's fee. That was considered stage one of his plan. Stage two? Well, that basically took care of itself.

Beyond just being fun, some consider jiu-jitsu training to be addictive. It wasn't long until that garage was packed with people, many of whom had been training in other disciplines of the martial arts. They'd go back to their former schools and tell the instructors there: "Have you heard of Brazilian jiu-jitsu? This stuff really works!" Of course, those instructors, worried about losing business, would tell their students: "Brazilian jiu-jitsu is a load of crap." After hearing about these retorts, my father would invite those instructors to the garage for a *friendly* challenge match. I emphasize the word "friendly" because my father never wanted to hurt these opponents. He wanted to defeat them in the most humane way possible. For my father, it wasn't about personal ego or accomplishment. It was solely about proving that our family's martial art was more effective than others.

As a youngster, I witnessed dozens of these challenge matches. The garage would be filled with my father's students, eager to view the outcome. What struck me the most about these matches was how fast my father would win. They lasted 16 seconds, 24 seconds, 30 seconds. A minute or two at most. The opponent would attempt to set up one devastating strike, punch, or kick. Often before that ever occurred, my father would quickly rush in, and in anaconda-like style, wrap himself around the opponent and bring him to the ground where he would succinctly tap out. That created an incredible buzz about our art in the California martial arts community. From there, the carefully seeded reputation of Brazilian jiu-jitsu and the legendary Gracie challenge matches would only grow, eventually bringing to fruition an influx of students from all corners of the globe. Generating maximum awareness and adoption of our jiu-jitsu was always the goal, and in the garage days, engaging in these frequent challenge matches against all comers served as the perfect application of the Creation Principle.

Profile: Richard Bresler

Professor Richard Bresler was the first official Gracie jiu-jitsu student in the US.

Richard Bresler met Rorion Gracie during the late 1970s, becoming his first student in the United States. Bresler was introduced to the art during a very rough stretch in his life. He had just started therapy to address his recreational drug use, something that had been steadily escalating. "I was at a place where I was extremely unhappy in my life. I thought drugs were my problem. But they were just a symptom of my problem, not the whole problem," said Bresler. "I wanted to change. I didn't like who I was becoming, so I found a therapist. I was searching for something better when jiu-jitsu came into my life, and it helped me in keeping my focus."

Bresler continued with both therapy and jiu-jitsu, eventually kicking his drug habit. As one of Rorion Gracie's most trusted students, Bresler arranged a good number of the challenge matches that took place at the Gracie Garage and elsewhere. Bresler recalled a conversation between Gracie and an instructor of a different martial art prior to one such match. "I don't think it's the jiu-jitsu. I think it's you, Rorion. You're just that good," said the opposing instructor. To which Rorion promptly replied, "No, it's the jiu-jitsu."[5]

Counterattacks in Games and Sports

Most people already have a vast amount of experience with the Creation Principle without even realizing it. Anyone who has ever sat at one end of a chessboard pondering their next move and then their opponent's succeeding move has experienced the principle in action. And if chess doesn't interest you, how about poker? A player with a good hand early in the proceedings might make a strong bet in order force opposing players to fold their potentially promising hands that still need to be filled out. The flip side of that would be a player with an outstanding hand betting as if they had an average hand, therefore encouraging their opponents to raise the stakes.

Football coaches often put their best receiver alone on one side of the field. This forces the opposing defense to either double-team the receiver, leaving the other side of the field short one defender, or to play that talented receiver one-on-one. Either defensive option can create incredible scoring opportunities for the creation-minded offense. Scoring opportunities via the

5 Richard Bresler interview with Paul Volponi (January 14, 2022).

counterattack are also prevalent in both soccer and ice hockey whenever the opposing offense is encouraged to commit too many players to an offensive wave, conceding their defensive positions.

The word "counterattack" was first coined in 1800 by military strategists and used in war games. The tactic of a military counterattack comes into play when one side successfully defends the opposition's initial attack and then starts to put the enemy on its heels through an attack (counterattack) of its own.

Take time to deliberate. But when the time for action comes, stop thinking and go in.
—Napoleon Bonaparte, general and French emperor

The Car Dealership

Suppose you're sitting in a car dealership. You have your eye on leasing the previous year's model, and the salesperson is willing to make a deal with you because the brand-new models are already on the showroom floor. The financing options are fine, and the dealership even has a car in stock in your favorite color, vermillion red. The only negotiating point left is the mileage over the course of the lease. You have a child attending college several states away, and you plan on making a number of road trips to visit. The mileage they're offering is standard. But you want something better, and you're willing to invest your time haggling at the dealership to get it—you've made this your end goal. They're not going anywhere until closing time, so you've adopted the same stance to put yourself on equal ground with the salesperson.

The paperwork is all drawn up, awaiting your signature. The only blank that remains in the lease agreement is the space for mileage. The manager has already come out and talked to the salesperson for you to hear. "We don't go over that standard mileage on leases for any reason," stated the manager, almost two hours ago. But you're still sitting there, tying up the salesperson from dealing with other potential customers.

You can read the frustration on the manager's face in having to make a reappearance at the salesperson's desk. That's when you decide to make your move and put the Creation Principle to work. You take out your phone and call a second dealership, one representing a different car company. "Hello, what time do you close the showroom tonight?" you ask, in a voice just loud enough for your pair of opponents to hear. "There's no need to go anywhere else," says the manager, waving for you to put the phone away. "We want you to be a customer of ours. Today and for the future. You can have the mileage you're asking for." Waiting for the most opportune time, you made a probing move and received the reaction you wanted. It was the Creation Principle in full bloom.

Call on the Creation Principle when . . .

- **Garnering Support:** You've identified the best way forward for your company, but you still need to gather consensus from your colleagues to get everyone on board.
- **Asking for More:** You desire increased compensation at work, so you meet with your supervisors to ask them exactly what they need to see from you to make it happen.
- **Negotiating:** You want to buy a car for $20,000, but it's listed at $30,000, so you offer $10,000 and hope to split the difference.
- **Managing Tantrums:** You sense a tantrum from your child is inevitable, so you begin planning your deescalation strategy in advance in hopes of reaching an amicable outcome.

Scan here to learn the combat application of

The Acceptance Principle

Chapter Six

The Acceptance Principle

Recognizing when it's better to yield than to resist.

A bend in the road is not the end of the road
. . . Unless you fail to make the turn.
—Helen Keller, author, disability rights advocate

A fight is a fight. An obstacle is an obstacle. We resist and battle against them. We invest our time, strength, and emotions in confrontations both large and small nearly every day of our lives. But not every outcome, whether it's momentary or long-term, plays out in our favor. That realization is especially useful on the jiu-jitsu mat. If our opponent applies a successful technique against us, there will be a time during its application when it becomes abundantly clear to us that the opponent will prevail in gaining a desired position. In fact, that truthful view can present us with a very useful and important opportunity to improve our own future position. It's called the Acceptance Principle. Consider this: If you are the first to accept the inevitability of an action performed against you, then you also have the opportunity to be the first one prepared for the outcome of that action. And that acceptance can be extremely valuable in determining what happens next.

Widening My Point of View

My sister-in-law, Victoria, had set me up on a blind "introduction" with her friend, Eve Torres, whom she described as incredibly intelligent, athletic, and per her initial assessment, "probably too good" for me. Our introduction? Naturally, I gave her a first jiu-jitsu lesson on the mat at Gracie University. Fast-forward eighteen months later, Eve and I are in a serious dating relationship. One evening, in a totally unplanned way, the subject of marriage and children came up. Having never broached those topics before, we were suddenly in an intensely focused conversation on the roles of a husband and wife in raising kids.

My family hails from Brazil, a Latin American country where gender roles have been clearly defined for centuries. Growing up as a Gracie, it had been ingrained in me as much as the art of jiu-jitsu that the ideal family model was that of the woman staying home to care for a couple's children. But when I introduced that idea into the conversation, Eve essentially straightened me out, shaking my cage with a different point of view. "I totally disagree," she said. "I think a woman can be a great mother and still have a career." It was a discussion that, at the time, bordered on an argument, one that lasted almost five hours (in the middle of the night), with us each passionate about our opinions.

Finally, Eve said, "Rener, there was never a time in my life when my mother (a federal attorney) wasn't working. I never had a mom who didn't have a career. She'd wake up every morning and go to work, and I never once felt like she didn't love or care for me. I don't just love her as my mother, I admire her." That's when it hit me. She was absolutely right. Someone I thought was so amazing, whom I wanted to marry, came from a household where both parents worked. Not only are Eve and her siblings educated and successful, they are three of the most socially and emotionally healthy people in my life. I also had to face the fact that her parents were still married after thirty years, while my parents divorced when I was twelve, and my father was working on his third marriage.

I was being presented in real time with the Acceptance Principle. At that moment, though it partially felt like a defeat, I knew I needed to make a leap of faith and let go of that outdated machismo-inspired approach. And

I certainly didn't need to force my past onto our future together. How did this approach go over with my family? After Eve and I got married and she became a working mother of two amazing boys, Raeven and Renson, my father never commented on it. My mom, however, totally embraced Eve's pursuit of a career. In fact, we purchased a home right next door to hers, and my mom was always there to lend a hand with our kids when needed. During her marriage to my father, my mom assumed the role to which she was assigned—that of a full-time stay-at-home mom. I know that, in a very real sense, my mother felt like she was walking in Eve's shoes beside her through the support she gave us.

Today, Eve is chief of staff at Gracie University and is instrumental to the organization's success at every level. After she completely reinvented our Women Empowered program, she went on to evaluate each department within our growing business to determine where systematic improvements might lead to increased efficiency for personnel and processes (a role that came quite naturally to her considering her achievement of a bachelor's degree in industrial engineering from USC).

Eve has exceeded all of my expectations of what a mother could be, and it pains me to think of what might have come of us if I didn't have the Acceptance Principle to save me so many years ago.

You may encounter many defeats, but you must not be defeated. In fact, it may be necessary to encounter the defeats, so you can know who you are, what you can rise from, how you can still come out of it.

—Maya Angelou, poet and author

Combat/Company Picnic

At what point should you begin to put the Acceptance Principle to use? Ideally, just after the inevitable outcome of an action against you becomes clear to you, but just before the outcome of the same action becomes clear to your opponent. A good guideline is when an action is approximately 60 percent completed against you. When the action is past the halfway point and no longer worth your effort to resist, yielding will grant you a space of time (the remaining 40 percent) for positive actions, such as conserving energy, getting a slightly better position than your opponent had planned, or preparing yourself physically and mentally for the succeeding move. Of course, no one enters a fray with a stopwatch in their hand to time these events, so it's hard to calculate exactly.

Knowing when to shift gears from resistance to acceptance is a matter of timing that can only be sharpened with experience on the mat. It's the same way in life: The more experience you have, the easier it is to recognize when to let go of something that is not to your benefit. After successfully applying the Acceptance Principle, you should welcome your new position with full awareness. Ask yourself: What are the forthcoming possibilities? Which technique do I flow into next, and which principle or combination of principles are most applicable from where I am?

Changing your stance from resisting to yielding can also throw your opponent off-balance. How so? Imagine that you're at a company picnic. There are two rival departments at your workplace, shipping and receiving. And the members of each department are always bragging that theirs is more important to the company's success than the other department. At the picnic, the two departments decide to have a friendly tug-of-war, a contest staged with a deep mud puddle between the rival squads. Though there are seven participants on each side of the rope, the department against which you are competing outweighs yours by approximately 150 pounds. To make matters worse, you're at the front of the line with that mud puddle practically staring you in the face. You're also wearing a brand-new pair of white sneakers.

Thirty seconds into the competition, you can feel the inevitable coming. Your side's strength is slowly but surely beginning to wither, with you inching closer to that impending mud-soaked fate. "Heave, ho!" the other squad hollers in an attempt to end it. Just as they put all of their effort into one ferocious tug, you scream out, "Now!" to your teammates, who all release their grip on the rope. Your already forward momentum helps you to leap the mud puddle as the rival squad tumbles to their now grass-stained backsides. "Congratulations, you were truly the stronger team," you acknowledge with all sincerity, in a much cleaner position than you'd be if you hadn't employed the Acceptance Principle.

Profile: Anthony Pepe

In his second career Professional Bowlers Association tournament, Anthony Pepe found himself in the finals of a 2014 event being televised on ESPN. The left-handed Pepe was already being recognized by longtime professionals and commentators for his remarkable balance during his approach and delivery of a 15-pound bowling ball to a waiting tensome of pins 60 feet away. "Balance and tempo. That's the key to ability and repeatability," said Pepe who, in a three-way match to determine which opponent would face the tournament leader, bowled a 295, just one strike short of a perfect game, reaching the final. "I only got five pins with my last ball. I was all nerves and a little too quick to the line. Let's just say after eleven straight strikes, it wasn't my best attempt." But Pepe, quickly accepting the results of his poorest attempt of the day, brushed aside any disappointment before decidedly dispatching the tournament leader to secure the tournament victory. "It's about visualization and imagery. Before you can achieve it in reality, you need to see yourself doing it in your mind."

The Acceptance Principle didn't just prove effective for Anthony Pepe in his professional pursuits. He wanted to be the truest reflection of himself possible. "When I made the announcement about my sexuality, at the time, I became just the second openly gay bowler," said Pepe. "I mainly made the announcement for myself. I felt like I needed to have closure with my own feelings. I honestly didn't know what to expect from the sport. I did experience some worries and stress about making the announcement. But that didn't stop me. In the end, I received an incredible amount of support from the bowling community. And it's certainly been a positive in my life to have their acceptance of who I truly am."[6]

6 Anthony Pepe interview with Paul Volponi (March 14, 2022).

My happiness grows in direct proportion to my acceptance,
and in inverse proportion to my expectations.
—Michael J. Fox, actor and activist

Lean upon the Acceptance Principle when . . .

- **Surviving:** You're driving on ice and you've lost control of your car so you wisely begin bracing for impact, and you survive with only a few bumps and bruises as a result.
- **Arguing:** You're in a heated argument with a friend when you realize that winning the argument may cause you to lose the relationship.
- **Moving On:** The news breaks that everyone in your department will be laid off so you're on the phone before the end of the day searching for a new position.
- **Keeping Motivated:** You haven't reached your personal fitness goals, but rather than fixating on where you fell short, you let the little progress you did make motivate you to keep going.
- **Adapting:** You realize that your child isn't growing up to be exactly who you wanted them to be, and rather than trying to change your child, you accept who they become and make the necessary changes to serve as the parent they need you to be.

The Public Eye

Change is something everyone has to deal with. But *how* we choose to deal with that change, and whether or not we accept it into our lives to find the best possible position forward, isn't always easy, especially for talented artists. Actor Michael J. Fox was in the midst of a high-profile film and television career when, as early as 1991, he started showing symptoms of Parkinson's disease, a degenerative disorder of the central nervous system that can severely affect motor skills. In 1998, Fox announced his condition to the world, becoming a public advocate to raise awareness and research funding for the disease. More than a decade later, prior to his retirement from acting, Fox appeared on an episode of *Curb Your Enthusiasm* in which he shakes a bottle of soda before handing it to the show's protagonist, Larry David. When David opens the bottle and gets showered in soda, he asks, "Did you do that on purpose?" Fox coyly responds, "Parkinson's." What a remarkable gift to be able to make others laugh through the acceptance of your own health issues.

French artist Henri Matisse (1869–1954) was an incredible painter and sculptor known for his marvelous images filled with light and bright colors. During his later years, however, Matisse became stricken with cancer. The resulting surgery made it exceedingly hard for him to get out of bed. Standing at a painter's easel was out of the question. That's when Matisse began a new phase of his career. Using scissors, he cut small bits of colored paper, arranging them in a collage-like fashion to depict striking images. Matisse's commitment to adapt to the changes in his life continued to bring him personal joy, while giving the world great beauty and art.

Scan here to learn the combat application of

The Velocity Principle

Chapter Seven

The Velocity Principle

Adapting your speed to maintain balance and optimize outcomes.

There is more to life than simply increasing its speed.
—Mahatma Gandhi

I'm always preaching to my students that they need to be less predictable and more in control of their surroundings. Reflecting that premise, the Velocity Principle can make a big difference in your ratio of positive outcomes. On the jiu-jitsu mat, we want to regularly change the speeds at which we grapple, from slow to fast and fast to slow. Why? It keeps our opponents constantly guessing what approach we'll take next. And that can create incredible opportunities, both in jiu-jitsu and in life.

When you're in charge of going from slow to fast or fast to slow, others are following your lead, and not the other way around. Imagine you're staging a sprint race between you and several of your friends. Everyone is standing at the starting line. Now, wouldn't you want to be the one to say "Go"? Wouldn't you have more overall success if you knew exactly when that signal to sprint was coming? Consider this: There is always going to be someone who is naturally faster than you, someone whose reactions are simply quicker.

So how are you ever going to beat that person to the punch, to a particular spot, or to a desired action? The answer is by being in control of the timing. As a grappler, if you're always fast, you're predictable. If you're always slow, you're predictable as well. Switching between the two extremes is far more effective. It makes you much more difficult to read and keeps your opponent off-balance, especially when you change speeds continually.

Suppose one of the friends you're racing against is the US's two-time gold-medal–winning Olympic sprinter Sydney McLaughlin. She is as fast as any woman in the world. You're simply not going to defeat the native of New Jersey in a full 100-yard sprint. But you might beat Sydney in a series of 10-yard sprints if you were continually distracting her and also in charge of the start. It could happen something like this: "Hey, Sydney, those are some sharp track shoes you're wearing. And I also like your . . . Go!"

That's exactly what we're trying to achieve on the jiu-jitsu mat against our opponents as we grapple. Which speed is best, fast or slow? The speed that will make your next move the hardest to predict. Remember, giving energy to an opponent or partner at any speed is a form of communication. Your counterpart will most likely fall into the rhythm you establish. The larger the gap between your changing speeds, the bigger the shock and surprise. In life, always act quickly and decisively to seize opportunities when they present themselves.

Alternating Speeds

Several years ago, my wife, Eve, and I were at the very height of our combined travel schedules, constantly on the road due to our busy professions. We were taking numerous commercial flights per month, with Eve wrestling in the WWE and me giving jiu-jitsu seminars around the country. And though we mostly traveled separately, Eve and I had the same shared complaint about air travel—getting a truly restful night's sleep was nearly impossible.

It seemed that none of the travel pillows on the market, and we had tried them all, addressed the dreaded "bobble-head" syndrome. That's when you finally fall asleep and your head naturally rocks forward with gravity, instantly waking you back up with a jolt. It's something that can happen multiple times in a matter of minutes. After one particular cross-country flight, I was so frustrated by the bobble-head syndrome that I immediately went on the internet and purchased a pair of standard airline seats. I had those seats delivered to my home, and we went to work in our garage trying to solve the problem once and for all.

It quickly became obvious to me that the solution could be found through *alavanca* (the Portuguese word for "leverage"), using the most advantageous angle to secure the head in an upright position with the least amount of force. Over the course of just a few days, we had developed a working prototype with which we were extremely satisfied, so we applied for a patent. With the attachment of a simple strap to the seat's headrest or seatback, and then anchoring a padded eye mask onto the secured strap, the device provides the user with a one-of-a-kind zero-gravity seated sleeping experience. Unlike other sleep pillows, our design keeps pressure off the neck and the carotid arteries, which carry blood to the brain and can cause headaches when impeded.

What did we call this new travel pillow? The "Sleeper Hold," of course (pun intended).

How did the Velocity Principle come into play? Well, after an intense blitz of progress at the onset, we had to slow down and put the Sleeper Hold on the back burner for a few years. In chapter nine, you'll learn about my foray on *Shark Tank* with another invention I opted to focus on first. That choice was undoubtedly the correct decision since air travel ground to a halt in 2020 with the COVID-19 pandemic.

As COVID began to fade and our nation finally got back to flying, I started using the Sleeper Hold myself on flights, inciting curiosity in many of the other passengers. On a flight to Cincinnati where I would give a "Leadership–Jiu-Jitsu" keynote presentation to the executives at Procter & Gamble, a fellow passenger named Patty was intent on getting a Sleeper Hold for herself. She made such a strong case that I agreed to start a crowdfunding campaign and finally bring the Sleeper Hold to market. To say that we kicked back into gear was an understatement. In just a few weeks, Eve and I designed a company logo, built a website, filed for additional patents, and produced over a dozen marketing videos to ensure the most successful launch. But just as we were all set to launch, I had a call with my digital marketing guru, Kenny, who said, "Rener, I absolutely love the product and all the promotional materials you put together for the launch, but I have to strongly advise against launching right now."

I was gutted, and in my mind there was nothing that was going to stop me from launching. It was already October, I had waited over five years, and *finally* all the pieces were in place. So when I pushed back and told Kenny that I wanted to launch before the end of the year, he pulled no punches and said, "I got your back, and I'll support you no matter what, but based on all the available crowdfunding data, and the feedback from my colleagues who specialize in this area, the fourth quarter (October, November, December) is the absolute worst time of year to launch a crowdfunding campaign."

When I asked why the fourth quarter was such a bad time to launch, Kenny explained that the social media ad costs skyrocket in this time of year, so we could end up spending 500 percent more to reach the same number of customers compared to any other time of the year. To put it simply, he said, "If you wait until the first quarter of next year, your crowdfunding campaign could perform 500 percent better than if you were to launch right now. Are you willing to take that risk?"

Although my pride didn't want to listen to Kenny, my heart knew he was right. So as I'm writing this, we are, once again, patiently waiting for the right time to launch the Sleeper Hold. The changing of speeds surrounding this project is unmatched in my professional life: We came out fast, then we slowed down, then we rushed to launch, then we stalled for the fourth quarter, and if all goes well, we'll explode onto the scene early next year. Although this book will go to press before then, only time will tell if the perfectly timed release will make the Sleeper Hold the most successful travel pillow of all time, or if it flops. Either way, the five-year Sleeper Hold saga will live on as a powerful lesson in the Velocity Principle.

And as to being quick . . . That is only a matter of habit. If you get into the habit of being quick, it is just as easy as being slow, easier.

—Anna Sewell, author, *Black Beauty*

Velocity in Business, Sound, and Signage

In business, velocity is equated with the amount of time it takes a company to reach certain milestones in production, sales, and revenues. It is a valuable measurement of both direction and the rate of movement. For example, Buffalo Trace, one of Kentucky's most recognized distilleries, recently produced its seven millionth barrel of product since Prohibition. It took the company a decade to go from the six million–barrel mark to seven million. But the boom in the bourbon business, with strong demand from customers in the US and abroad, means the company will probably reach their next million-barrel milestone in less than half that time, creating a need for improved production facilities and a bigger workforce.

That means the rapidly growing company will also need to ensure a consistent performance in maintaining production schedules and high-quality standards in order not to fall behind the ample competition, including Jim Beam and Woodford Reserve, in either category. So high-velocity success translates into even more hard work for a company to maintain its trajectory.

Another example of the Velocity Principle in action involves the art of communication. The act of varying the velocity of your speech pattern, be it fast to slow, loud to soft, or high to low, can make a profound impression on your audience. Teachers, sales reps, broadcast journalists, tour guides, trial attorneys, public relations people, and actors are among the many professions that must keep a listener's attention for prolonged periods of time. Audiences can easily start to tune out a speaker whose voice is monotone. And whenever a particular emphasis needs to be placed on vital information inside of a longer presentation, the speaker should certainly consider changing the tone and cadence of their voice. Sometimes, even dropping your voice down to a whisper can move the listener to tune in intently. In a summation to a jury, a trial lawyer might emphasize their most important point by delivering that grouping of words in a staccato fashion, almost individually, perhaps punctuating each word with a thrust of a finger.

The Velocity Principle in music? The average pop song is three to five minutes long. Why that length? It's about keeping the audience's attention. But what about several much longer songs that have been at the top of listeners' playlists for multiple decades? Well, let's look at Led Zeppelin's "Stairway to Heaven," a multigenerational megahit. That beloved song is a shade more than eight minutes long. Does it have any help in breaking the standard mold? Yes, the Velocity Principle. The song starts out soft, slow, and low. Then just past the halfway point, it starts an increase in tempo. By the end of the song, it transforms into a full-out rock and roll anthem with fast-tempo guitar and lyrical shrieks. Of course, it makes one more musical change, ending the way it began, slower and softer. It's simply a Velocity Principle masterpiece. Want to research the Velocity Principle in other famous lengthy songs? Take a look for yourself at Queen's "Bohemian Rhapsody," Don McLean's "American Pie," and the Beatles' "A Day in the Life."

Finally, think about the signage we see every day, from most words to least. Or in terms of the Velocity Principle, from long to short, with the shortest needing our immediate attention.

Not Responsible for Lost Items

Guard Dog on Duty

No Passing Zone

Speed Limit

Stop

If the one-word stop sign doesn't get your attention, signaling a necessary action, then hopefully its red coloring and distinctive octagonal shape will.

> *People in the NBA are just as athletic as you. That's the game. You have to have the change of pace. You have to change speeds to get around people.*
>
> —Kawhi Leonard, two-time NBA champion and two-time Finals MVP

Visualize the Velocity Principle when . . .

- **Speaking:** You're giving a business presentation when you suddenly vary your cadence and the audience becomes more engaged.

- **Managing Emotions:** A child gets hurt and is in a panic, so you give them time to breathe and then speak to them in a slow, soothing voice.
- **Launching:** You've been working patiently on a project for years when market conditions change, and you seize the opportunity to launch before competitors get traction.
- **Balancing Workloads:** Shifting demand at work requires you to speed up production at certain times but allows you to slow down to avoid burnout at others.

Changing It Up

In game two of the 2021 World Series, Atlanta Braves pitcher Charlie Morton toed the rubber, staring down batter José Altuve of the Houston Astros in the bottom of the third inning. During the previous inning, Morton had taken a ground ball from the bat of an opponent to his right leg. Morton shrugged off the pain and continued to pitch. He didn't know it at the time but his leg was broken, a fracture of the right fibula. He delivered his second strike to Altuve, a 96-mile-per-hour fastball.

There is no doubt that Morton was beginning to feel the pain. Could he even deliver another pitch with that type of velocity? The question became moot when Morton decided it was time to change speeds. His next and final pitch, thrown before having to be removed from the game due to his injury, was an 80-mile-per-hour curveball. It was as slow as a major league pitcher could make a delivery to the dish. The 16-mile-per-hour difference in those consecutive pitches caught the Astros hitter completely off-balance—so much so, Altuve couldn't even get the bat off his shoulder to swing. The umpire rang him up with a called third strike. Charlie Morton's team eventually became world champions, despite losing their ace pitcher for the rest of the World Series.

Scan here to learn the combat application of
The Clock Principle

Chapter Eight

The Clock Principle

Recognizing that the right move at the wrong time is the wrong move.

The two most powerful warriors are patience and time.
—Leo Tolstoy, author, *War and Peace*

Synergy is a dominant theme within the 32 principles of jiu-jitsu, and the Clock Principle is a prime example of that synergy, operating hand in hand with several of the principles to which we have already been introduced. How does the Clock Principle apply on the jiu-jitsu mat? By disrupting the anticipated timing of the opponent's techniques or objectives, you can take better control of the eventual outcome.

Every practitioner of the art has a theoretical clock inside their head at any given time on the mat. They also have an anticipated plan as they begin an action. They know how long it will take to start and accomplish a particular technique, so they give themselves a certain amount of time to reach that desired position. But whenever you disrupt that timing, it both frustrates the opponent and burns their energy. It also provides you with the inviting opportunity to control the remaining time that your adversary was relying on for the completion of their technique.

To illustrate the Clock Principle's synergistic relationship with its 31 other counterparts, let's look at two related principles: Distance and Velocity. What the Distance Principle is to controlling the flow of action through distance or spacing between opponents, the Clock Principle is to controlling the timing of a grapple. The Velocity Principle is predicated on the practitioner using a change in timing to gain an advantage, while the Clock Principle can totally disrupt the opponent's attempt at changing speeds and velocity plays designed to be used against us. Hence, there is a superb synergy between these three closely related yet independent principles.

Fighting for Shane

A student of ours at Gracie University is a psychologist, and she believed that a teenage patient of hers would benefit greatly from studying jiu-jitsu. "Rener, this young man named Shane suffers from extreme anxiety. Whenever he's in an unfamiliar social situation or feels unsafe, he vomits uncontrollably," she told me. It was important enough for my student to suggest jiu-jitsu as something that could help, so I decided to take up the challenge of teaching Shane. For our first meeting, I chose midafternoon on a weekday when there were fewer people in our building. I was at the school awaiting the arrival of Shane and his mom, when his mom called my cell. "I'm so sorry, Rener. It doesn't look like it's going to happen. We're parked outside but my son won't come in," she said. I felt like I'd be giving up on Shane before ever meeting him if I didn't go the extra mile. "Well, can I at least come out and see him? Say hello?" I asked. "Sure," his mom responded.

I walked outside in my gi and spotted Shane's mom standing beside their car. Shane was alone in the back seat on the passenger's side. As I got closer to the car, I could hear Shane crying loudly between taking huge gasps of air, as he sat there doubled over. His mom was looking at me, and I could see the look of helplessness in her eyes. I silently mouthed the words, *Can I go in and see him?* She nodded her head. I walked around to the driver's-side back seat and got into the car beside Shane. He wailed nonstop for another twenty minutes without ever raising his head to look at me. In all that time, I didn't say a word. Finally, Shane ran out of steam (an example of my using the Depletion Principle; more on this in chapter eighteen), and except for his labored breathing, there was silence for a moment. That's when I asked, "Hey, Shane, what do you like to do for fun?" After several seconds, he answered, "Video games." We probably spent fifteen minutes discussing video games before I said, "Shane, I'm Rener and I'm really happy that you're here. If it's okay, I'd like to take you inside our school and give you a guided tour of the facility." He nodded *yes*.

Inside the school, I spent an abundance of time showing Shane our locker rooms and the Gracie Family Museum. When I felt comfortable that he trusted me, I walked Shane and his mom toward one of our private training rooms and said, "You won't believe how soft the mats are in here. Take off your shoes and come feel for yourself!" He complied, and in one swift move, I finally had him exactly where I wanted him. His mom sat in the far corner, leaving Shane and me in the center of the mats. Then I asked Shane if I could show him a jiu-jitsu technique. He agreed and actually lay down so I could assume our mount position atop of him. Once there, I said, "Okay, now try to push me off." He tried his best but he couldn't. Then we switched roles.

"All right, hold me down and don't let me up." Shane focused all of his strength on keeping me there, but I escaped in two seconds using a simple trap-and-roll technique. He was elated at my maneuver. "Let me teach you how it's done," I said. The next time I climbed on top of Shane, he escaped using that same technique. That left him with a wide smile. We practiced the maneuver several more times together, cleaning up the little details. Over the succeeding hour, I was able to teach Shane six more beginning techniques. Then I glanced over at Shane's mom and saw that her eyes were filled with tears of joy. But Shane's anxieties didn't totally disappear that day.

On his next trip to our school, it took him fifteen minutes to walk through the door. The lesson after that, it took just seven minutes. Then, for his fourth lesson, Shane actually met me inside the building. He studied jiu-jitsu with us for several years, and he even moved from private classes into a group setting. Shane eventually received his blue belt at a ceremony attended by close to 300 people, a huge step forward for the young man, who would ultimately go on to attend college.

How did the Clock Principle play into my interaction with Shane on that first day? Well, making the right move at the wrong time is still the wrong move. Timing is everything. If I had attempted to either get Shane out of the car or onto the mat too soon, before I had his trust and he was emotionally ready to do so, my best intentions would have proved totally ineffective. In fact, there were a pair of critical points in which I deliberately chose inaction over action (waiting him out in the car and allowing him to slowly become familiar with the school building), and those decisions helped make the difference. It was the ultimate test of the Clock Principle.

The experience left me with dual feelings. I was intensely satisfied that Shane had gained something valuable that day, and that I could be a part of it. But I also felt wiped, as if I had been in combat for two hours. It felt like I had just exited a tooth-and-nail battle. Only I wasn't fighting *against* someone, I was fighting *for* someone, Shane. It took literally everything I had—every tool, every technique, everything that I'd learned in my life and through my jiu-jitsu training. And it was absolutely worth every ounce of energy to help Shane take control of his life.

Time, Time, Time

Consciously, you may not be aware of it, but you know the Clock Principle well from your own life. Many times, you've felt it building momentum against your carefully timed objectives. The disruptions don't even need to be orchestrated by an actual opponent, just by the effects of Murphy's Law: Anything that can go wrong will go wrong.

Let's say you're preparing dinner for your spouse and in-laws. It's a recipe you've never attempted before. The cookbook states that between prep and cooking time, the whole meal from cutting board to dinner table will take approximately one hour. Just to play it safe, you've given yourself an extra ten minutes to spare. As you begin to chop the vegetables, the phone rings. You see from the caller ID that it's the dermatologist. You've been waiting for days for the doctor to call and let you know about that rash on the back of your son's neck. It's a call you can't ignore, so you answer it.

Five minutes later, there's a knock at your front door. It's a FedEx from your job that will require your signature, so you shut off the burner on the stove for a moment. Aren't you glad that you factored in that extra ten minutes? But the distractions don't end there. Next, your dog scratches to be let out the back door. You know what type of accident might happen if you don't let the pooch out fast enough, and company is coming. Your daughter is crying because the monster in the clothes dryer ate one of her favorite purple polka-dot socks. Distracted by all these interruptions, you use the air fryer and the microwave at the same time. Seconds later, the kitchen fuse blows. You're frustrated, mentally exhausted, and standing in the dark. And there wasn't even an opponent pulling the strings. That's the innate power of the Clock Principle.

Now, imagine there's a clock in your house that's running ten minutes slow. You would be late for everything in your life: school, work, dates, public events. And what if you had a clock that was set ten minutes ahead? Conversely, you would be early for all of the things we've mentioned. Either way, your life is thrown off-balance because your timing has been disrupted. The only thing worse than living your life by either of these two clocks is if the single clock in your actual life was even less reliable. How so? Perhaps the single clock in your life is *sometimes* ten minutes fast and *sometimes* ten minutes slow. Just when you think that you've figured it out and adjusted for the discrepancy, you haven't, resulting in total confusion. So now there's no predictability. In jiu-jitsu, that's the kind of effect you want to have on your opponent: unpredictable and a disruption in their timing, whether you're forcing a slow clock or a fast clock.

> *I need to know how the clock is made after you tell me what time it is. I want to know all the details so I can understand how it works.*
>
> —Sandra Bullock, actress

Profile: Mari*time* Clock Principle

The tradition of staging organized rowing races began with eighteenth-century water taxis along England's Thames River. By 1852, the US saw its first intercollegiate athletic contest in the form of a boat race, called a "regatta," between Yale and Harvard. Today, Coach Bill Porter has been at the helm of the women's rowing team at Yale for more than two decades and has brought the Bulldogs several national titles. How does the Clock Principle reflect on rowing? Well, it's actually the Clock Principle played out in reverse. Timing and being in sync with your teammates is important in most arenas of sport, but it is absolutely vital in rowing, especially for a team of eight.

A lot of that team timing falls on the shoulders of a model rower referred to as "the stroke," whose job it is to establish a rhythm for the other rowers to emulate, placing their oar blades in and out of the water simultaneously. "Finding someone to occupy the stroke is the first piece. It requires someone with rhythm and a movement that's easy to follow, someone that the other rowers can fall in behind and then start to work combinations [changes of speed]. Remember, though the entire team is seated, everyone is of a different height and has different leg and arm length. It's great when the bodies are all in sync, but even more significant are the angles of the oars entering and leaving the water, as well as the load on the oar beneath the water," noted Coach Porter, who despite the advent of tech equipment to measure these various angles still prefers to coach by eye.

Even though rowing isn't a contact sport, it's possible to disrupt the timing of another boat. "If the other crew has a lead and you start to close the gap, because rowers face backward and might be caught looking at an oncoming boat, you can throw off their timing and fluster them while emboldening your own crew." Races are typically 2,000 meters, or 1.2 miles in length, and call for a crew that can operate under a relaxed type of tension. "You need to relax and have a relative level of elasticity. But it's certainly one of the most agonizing, physically grueling, and painful sports, which is counterintuitive because from the shore it all looks beautiful . . . The movement in rowing a big boat is very rhythmic. The boat actually ebbs and flows beneath you, and you can feel the hull moving once you get the boat up to speed. For the rowers, it's about finding each other's rhythm and breath. So it's similar, in a sense, to music and dance. A good, fast boat is very well choreographed with everyone dialed in," Coach Porter explained.[7]

On the Playing Field

In baseball, the Clock Principle is constantly at work. And that's really a statement considering baseball is the only major team sport without a game clock—a new pitch clock, however, will be instituted for the 2023 season. Whenever the pitcher is in a good rhythm and wants to work quickly on the mound, you'll see the hitter step out of the batter's box or go to the on-deck circle for a rag of pine tar (now a hitter can only call time out once per plate appearance), any excuse to slow the pitcher down. In retaliation, a frustrated pitcher might even throw high and tight on a batter (utilizing the Distance Principle), resulting in a *friendly* warning called "chin music."

The pitcher can also use the Clock Principle to frustrate a runner on first base who might be intent on stealing second. A pitcher can make numerous throws over to first base, on pickoff moves, both fast and slow, to break the base runner's rhythm in getting a quick start (a demonstration of the Velocity Principle). In a nifty double-edged sword scenario, the runner at first base can combine the Distance Principle and Clock Principle to throw off the timing of the pitcher. How? By taking a long enough lead, the base runner can almost force the pitcher to throw over to first base instead of home, interrupting his good rhythm to the plate. If the pitcher doesn't comply, the runner receives the distinct advantage of a longer lead. So the pitcher is forced to choose between the conflicts presented by the pair of principles.

That synergy of principles can also clearly be observed in the relationship between defensive backs and receivers in football. Defenders might sacrifice the idea of keeping a safe distance between themselves and a receiver (so a fleet receiver doesn't run right past them) in order to get up into the receiver's face mask at the line of scrimmage. The instant the football is snapped, the defensive back will jam or block the receiver in order to diminish his ability

7 Bill Porter interview with Paul Volponi (March 15, 2022).

to run a clean pass route. That also hurts the timing between the quarterback and the receiver. However, if the receiver can sidestep that jam with a velocity-driven move, he now has the distinct advantage of the defender without a cushion or margin of error in trying to deny him the ball. Through the lens of the Clock Principle, it's clear that timing truly is everything.

The only reason for time is so everything doesn't happen at once.
—Albert Einstein

Consider the Clock Principle when . . .

- **Prioritizing Family:** You're spending much-needed time with your family when you get a call from the office and you choose not to answer.
- **Connecting:** You get home from work, and before you start talking about your day, you ask your spouse how their day went.
- **Timing Communications:** You want to talk to your boss about getting a raise, but you realize she is stressed out about a new product launch, so you decide to wait for a better time.
- **Parenting:** Your child behaves poorly, but they're not emotionally ready to hear your input, so you put it off for another day.

Scan here to learn the combat application of

The River Principle

Chapter Nine

The River Principle

Overcoming obstacles by flowing around them.

Intelligence is like a river: the deeper it is, the less noise it makes.
—Unknown

Jiu-jitsu mirrors a number of processes in the natural world, so it's appropriate that several of its core principles, like the River Principle, are inspired by events found in nature. Imagine water swiftly flowing along in a river current. Suddenly, a huge rock appears, reaching above the surface. That onrushing water smartly wastes no time on the rock. The water doesn't butt heads with its opposition, trying to prove which is more powerful. It's not about power. It's about persistence. You only need to look at the immensity of the Grand Canyon, produced by five to six million years of continual water erosion, to know that water can eventually carve a path of its own choosing through solid rock. This loss of efficient focus applies only to humans who become distracted by a challenge on their journey forward. The water has naturally devised a better way, a more efficient way. Water doesn't focus on where the rock is. Instead, water focuses on where the rock is not. It takes the path of least resistance, never losing sight of its primary goal of reaching the sea.

Don't misunderstand the River Principle—it is not an exercise in passivity. Consider the concept of a dam. When confronted with a dam, there will be times when a river's progress and seizing upon the path of least resistance isn't immediately possible. But the idea isn't to flow forward at all costs. Don't be afraid to err on the side of patience. When stopped by a dam, the water behind it begins to rise. It continues to amass potential energy, waiting for an exploitable weakness. During that time, we are recouping previously spent energy and planning our next move. When an exploitable weakness appears, perhaps a slight crack in the dam, we seize upon it instantly. Whether on the mat or in life, the River Principle is comprised of a very persistent mindset.

Swimming with Sharks

Two days after Christmas 2016, I was enjoying an early-morning walk at the park with my young son Raeven. I'd worn a hooded sweatshirt because it had rained the night before, and there was still some dampness in the air. But as the California sun came out in full force, I took off my hoodie. My first thought was to tie it around my waist. Only I never liked that look, and I wanted to be the *cool dad* at the park. So I casually slung the hoodie over my shoulder. But when I bent down to pick up my son, the jacket fell onto the damp, muddy grass. Instantly, my jiu-jitsu problem-solving mind kicked in. I thought, *there has to be a better way.*

The moment I arrived home, I locked myself inside my office with the hoodie, some paper clips, shoestring, duct tape, and a pair of scissors. Thirty minutes later, I had fashioned my first working prototype of a hooded sweatshirt that could transform into a backpack when it wasn't being worn. That's how my apparel company Quikflip was born. Fast-forward six months later and several improvements to the product, I took the first public samples to Venice Beach, approaching people carrying jackets and sweatshirts. I recorded their amazed reactions to how comfortable my hoodies were and how easily they could be turned into a backpack. Well, that video went viral and, within thirty days, I sold the first batch of 5,000 Quikflips I'd produced. Then something even more amazing happened. Producers from the hit ABC TV show *Shark Tank* called me. It was like a fantasy come true. I had long dreamed of being on that show and negotiating against the sharks, but I had no intention of selling our jiu-jitsu school. This opportunity, though, would give me the prospect of pairing Quikflip with an all-star, black-belt-level business partner, from whom I could undoubtedly learn some things.

On the day of the taping, standing on that famed entrepreneurial carpet beneath the hot studio lights, I found myself face-to-face with a quintet of heavyweight obstacles in the form of sharks Mark Cuban, Daymond John, Kevin O'Leary (a.k.a. Mr. Wonderful), Lori Greiner, and Robert Herjavec. But I had come focused on both my presentation and on using the River Principle to keep flowing forward to my destination of showcasing Quikflip to an audience of well over a half-million viewers. After my initial pitch, which included me thwarting a pair of attacks from my brother Ryron (because we weren't going to miss the opportunity to share some jiu-jitsu magic on primetime television), the sharks began bombarding me with questions.

"Rener, I want to hear about sales," said Mr. Wonderful. But I wasn't done pitching yet. He wasn't going to be an obstacle that interrupted my progress. So I reached for the River Principle and continued an alternate path forward. "Just real quick," I said, acknowledging him but not relinquishing control. I made the point that we'd added to the catalog, going beyond only hoodies. "This is not a product, guys. It's a company," I affirmed. Then, without permission, I grabbed Mr. Wonderful's glass of drinking water from the table in front of him. After donning a second convertible garment, I poured the water over my head to demonstrate that it was waterproof, and in one bold move, the Dryflip Rain Jacket was introduced to the world. It was a more than fitting move on my part, considering I was in the midst of using the River Principle. I just kept talking, kept pitching, and kept pushing because I knew there would be no second chance. "Rener, will we be able to talk at all during the pitch?" asked Daymond John, in a semi-frustrated tone, "I'm just trying to get there." But I was trying to *get there* too. To my own destination, not his.

"You're a force of nature," Mr. Wonderful conceded, eventually making an offer. Then Lori began to get serious about arriving at a deal with me, though Kevin's voice remained persistent. "Kevin is talking to me. But I'm not talking to Kevin," I assured Lori, keeping eye contact with her. "I'm talking to you." Ultimately, I chose to close a deal with Lori, presenting her with an honorary business black belt (the only way to earn a real belt is on the mats, no matter how famous you may be). In the end, I flowed past every obstacle and spent considerably more time pitching my product than negotiating, which was exactly my goal. Lots of *Shark Tank* deals made on air never get consummated in the weeks and months afterward, and that's exactly what happened to my proposed deal with Lori. For Quikflip, though, the high-profile exposure was a huge win.

The river is everywhere.
—Hermann Hesse, Nobel Prize–winning author

Test Taking and Evolving Work Responsibilities

Of course, you don't have to be competing on a jiu-jitsu mat to encounter major obstacles. They can crop up in any facet of your life, from work to school to our daily relationships. Importantly, these impediments appear even bigger than their reality when we become fixated upon them, stopping our own progress with an inefficient mindset.

Perhaps you're a student taking an important exam. Maybe it's a mathematics final or midterm, with just fifty minutes to answer forty questions. The teacher places the exam facedown on your desk. Looking at the multiple pages stapled together, you take a deep breath. You're concerned about not having enough time to finish, because that's been a problem for you in the past. "Students, you may begin," says the teacher. You turn the exam over and hurriedly write your name at the top of the page. The first several questions offer you little to no resistance. Confident in your answers, you develop a rhythm. A flow. Everything is moving smoothly. Then comes the question that stops your natural momentum forward.

To make matters worse, there's a specific equation involved in solving that question. It's an equation that you had committed to memory five minutes before the exam started, but now you're drawing a blank. You become frustrated. Suddenly, you're at a standstill. You can hear the other students turning the pages on their exams. They're moving forward while you remain immobilized. The River Principle teaches you to move on to a better position, to understand that you've hit an obstacle that shouldn't consume all of your energies. You need to sacrifice that smaller struggle with an individual question in favor of the larger battle with the many questions that still lie ahead—and the ultimate goal of passing the test. Test-taking experts will tell you exactly the same thing, not to mismanage the allotted time over a single problem.

Work environments are often evolving. The duties of almost anyone's job description can undergo challenging changes. Perhaps this has happened to you. Many of the things you did so well, that had earned you accolades, are no longer among your work-related responsibilities. You are frustrated by the complexity of your new duties, convinced that even if you eventually master these tasks, all of your hard work will go unnoticed. In essence, your workflow has hit the proverbial rock. You've become unhappy, fixated, and stagnant, dwelling on the things that have upset your previously established rhythm. However, what you need to remember is that the world is not static and that change is a continual part of life. The River Principle teaches us to be better attuned to a dynamic environment, flowing around all kinds of obstacles, especially the ones that are self-imposed. It takes a strong belief in yourself to make such changes in midstream or midcareer. But that's exactly what the River Principle inspires in its practitioners.

Profile: No Soup for You!

Actor Larry Thomas stormed onto TV sets in 1995 in an episode of Seinfeld *entitled "The Soup Nazi." Thomas played Yev Kassem, a proprietor of a New York City soup stand, and was nicknamed "Soup Nazi" by the cast of characters. His curt, no-nonsense tagline "No soup for you!" resonated with audiences worldwide. Thomas is a trained martial artist in Shotokan karate, which is typically considered a "hard" martial art reflecting more yin (harder side) than yang (softer side).*

As a beginning actor, Thomas initially considered running over the obstacles placed in his path. "Karate, of course, made an insecure kid confident as a man, and resulted in helping me protect myself on the street. Acting, on the other hand, could not be muscled. I needed to develop a different confidence **. . .** I had to surrender. Get hit and not hit back. Yes, the Soup Nazi was impatient and stood up for his own rules. But in the end, he was defeated for his actions," noted Thomas, who prior to acting held jobs as a bail bondsman, bartender, and janitor. How can acting draw a parallel to the River Principle? "When starting out as an actor I had to lose a lot of the standing ground and concentration that was prevalent in Shotokan for the more floating feeling you get when you give yourself over to a character. In acting, you must surrender to the moment and bend to the script."[8]

Remember the River Principle when . . .

- **Building Habits:** Your goal is to get your child to consume more fruits and vegetables, but they hate eating them, so you introduce tasty smoothies as a first step in the right direction.
- **Finding Solutions:** You're working on a project to increase efficiency in your organization, but the budget gets cut, and instead of tapping out, you pull together available tools to create an alternate solution that achieves the same outcome.
- **Forgiving:** Your girlfriend cancels your scheduled lunch date on short notice, but rather than dwell on disappointment, you decide to sit at the bar where you enjoy a meal and great conversation with an absolute stranger.
- **Aging Wisely:** You reach the point in your life when your aging body can no longer perform the sportive activities you once loved, so you begin learning the gentle art of jiu-jitsu, and your only regret is that you didn't start sooner.

8 Larry Thomas interview with Paul Volponi (April 2, 2022).

The Impactful Bruce Lee

Bruce Lee's most iconic quote echoes the power of the River Principle. "Empty your mind. Be formless. Shapeless. Like water. You put water into a cup, it becomes the cup. You put water into a bottle, it becomes the bottle. You put it into a teapot, it becomes the teapot. Now, water can flow or it can crash. Be like water, my friend," emphasized Lee, who eventually constructed his own martial art called Jeet Kune Do, or the Way of the Intercepting Fist, which stressed personal efficiency. His words on the strength of water are a cry against rigidity, of being fixated by a particular form or single-mindedness instead of reveling in flexibility and freedom.

Lee, whose given name was Lee Jun-fan, was born in the Chinatown neighborhood of San Francisco. However, he was raised in Hong Kong where his father was a Cantonese opera star (the equivalent of a US pop star today). That connection to the world of performance gave Lee the opportunity to be cast in several films as a child actor. As an adult, Lee is often credited with changing the way Asians are perceived in film, TV, and, ultimately, Western society.

Prior to the early 1970s, Asians working in Hollywood were primarily cast in subservient roles such as waiters and household servants. Lee began on American TV in *The Green Hornet* (1966–1967) as a sidekick/manservant named Kato. But Lee's staggering success abroad as a lead actor in a pair of martial arts–based films, *The Big Boss* (1971) and *Fists of Fury* (1972), brought him the bargaining power to write and produce his own material for a Western audience. Warner Bros. Studios backed Lee's *Enter the Dragon* (1973) with an immense $850,000 budget, which would probably translate to more than $500 million today. "The true [Asian] should be shown . . . I think [what we've seen in film] is very out of date. I want to think of myself as a human being," said Lee, who sadly died of a cerebral edema at the age of 32 in 1973.

Many martial arts–inspired cinematic stars such as Jackie Chan, Donnie Yen, and Rina Takeda owe Lee a debt of gratitude for the doors he opened.

Scan here to learn the combat application of

The Frame Principle

Chapter Ten

The Frame Principle

Increasing effectiveness by enhancing systematic efficiency.

Every idea that is a true idea has a form, and is capable of many forms. The variety of forms of which it is capable determines the value of the idea.
—Frank Lloyd Wright, architect

Jiu-jitsu practitioners can be viewed as architects, constantly constructing new body positions throughout a free-flowing grapple. These positions must be structurally sound enough to withstand the forces applied by our opponents, as well as supporting our own attacks. This can best be witnessed in the Frame Principle. Because we always assume that our opponents are going to be bigger, stronger, and more athletic than us, whenever possible, we try to use our skeletal structure to take the place of physical strength and sheer muscle mass. This technique is referred to as "framing."

The framework of a house usually consists of studs (vertical members of a wall), plates (horizontal members of a wall), joists (beams arranged parallel from wall to wall to support flooring or a roof), rafters, girders, and flooring. The human body's framework is our skeletal system of bones, which serves as the attachment point for muscles, ligaments, tendons, and joints. In jiu-jitsu, we use the skeletal framework to optimize our leverage in many situations including blocking, shielding, breaking a hold, or keeping an opponent at a safe distance. It also enables us to buy space to create an opportunity for ourselves while stopping our opponent's progress. The Frame Principle was tremendously important to my grandfather Helio's creation of Brazilian jiu-jitsu because he was not a large man who possessed great strength. He stood five foot nine and weighed a mere 143 pounds.

What are the advantages of relying on framing over muscular strength? Get into a push-up position, lower yourself until your elbows are bent at 90 degrees, and stay there. Your only opponent at the moment is gravity. Even without the additional pressures that a human opponent might bring to bear, fairly soon you'll begin to feel a burning sensation in your triceps, biceps, pectorals, and deltoids. That feeling is due to a buildup of lactic acid, which comes with prolonged muscle exertion. Conversely, if you straighten your arms to the top of the push-up position, you will not incur the same fatigue factors since the bones of your arms are aligned and presented at a perpendicular angle to the ground. In a physical altercation, bones such as the cervical spine, humerus, ulna, radius, femur, tibia, and hips can unite in different sequences to create frames that can outlast and overcome muscular force. And for the opponent, the experience of pitting their muscular strength against a well-conceived frame can be both exhausting and demoralizing.

Finding the Proper Structure

Most people know that I hail from a family of fighters. But I was also born into a family of teachers. And I'm equally as proud of that. If you would have asked my grandfather, "Helio, why did you step into the ring as an undersized opponent against those heavier championship-caliber fighters?" he would have absolutely answered: *to prove to my students that everything I taught them is the truth. That they can put their trust in me as teacher and in Brazilian jiu-jitsu as the art of efficiency.*

I taught my first class in jiu-jitsu at the age of 13 and currently have over a quarter-century of experience in how to impart that knowledge. A little more than a decade ago, as Gracie University began to expand in step with the seemingly insatiable global desire for Brazilian jiu-jitsu, I came to realize that the Frame Principle was going to be vitally important in effectively disseminating the seeds my family had cultivated. On the mats, the Frame Principle concerns itself with properly aligning the skeletal system to create maximum leverage. That principle is mirrored in the marketplace as well, where the major components of any business, including our jiu-jitsu school, also need to be in proper alignment to produce at a high level. How does that concept directly relate to Gracie University? Besides teaching students, which provides Ryron and me amazing gratification in opening new eyes to our beautiful art, we also certify instructors in the proprietary Gracie programs we created, and then we subsequently license them to teach these programs at their schools.

Potential Gracie-approved instructors participate in a twelve-month intensive study of our materials, methodology, and techniques, submitting videos of their progress along the way. When that phase of the process is complete, they spend a week at Gracie University in Torrance, California, attending our Instructor Certification Program and must grade out high enough to ultimately be approved. For all of their hard work and commitment, our instructors are guaranteed that we will not certify another Gracie instructor to operate within a five-mile radius of their school. Eventually, though, we discovered a serious flaw in our business model. A potential instructor, say located in the Dallas/Fort Worth area, might not know that someone else within their radius was applying to the Instructor Certification Program too. What would happen if after ten months or so of rigorous study, that *other* person became certified first? It seemed terribly unfair. So we used the Frame Principle to reorder our model's components, making them stronger and more efficient.

Now, anyone interested in being our representative pays the full cost of the Instructor Certification Program up front, and by doing so, we allow them to reserve their territory for a term of one year. This new frame brought about two additional benefits: Because of their financial stake, it made our potential instructors more committed to successfully completing the process in the allotted time. In turn, that meant Ryron and I received a better return on the time we invested in training them, since fewer potential instructors dropped out. Why is it so important for us to have these representatives? Yes, it creates extra revenue for our business. But more importantly, it supports our family's century-old mission of developing a far-reaching network of Gracie team members to pass along the art of Brazilian jiu-jitsu. Remember, we can teach only so many classes per day and can only fit so many students on the mats. Through our global network of certified instructors, that number has grown exponentially.

Of course, none of this global expansion would be possible without our prior use of the Pyramid Principle, which had given Gracie University better balance and more stability in the martial arts marketplace. Since the Gracie family doesn't own Brazilian jiu-jitsu (no one can patent or copyright an art form), Ryron and I developed proprietary programs such as Gracie Combatives, Gracie Bullyproof, and Women Empowered. Witnessing the Frame Principle and Pyramid Principle complementing each other in business as powerfully as they do on the mats continues to prove the strong synergy between our 32 core principles.

Profile: Ballet's Fighting Spirit

George Birkadze is the artistic director of the Dallas Conservatory, a private performing arts school. His personal and professional life has been dedicated to blending a pair of intense passions: ballet and martial arts.

George Birkadze grew up on the streets of Soviet Georgia where being a male adolescent dancer meant he would also need to learn how to fight. "My initial connection to the martial arts was to defend myself. To fight off the bullies on the streets who knew I was a dancer and associated that with some type of weakness," said Birkadze, who studied at the famed Bolshoi Theatre in Moscow. "But as I began to mature, reached the age of maybe sixteen, I developed a deeper understanding of how [dance and martial arts] fit together. After all, they are both arts with organized movements and patterns. I heard Muhammad Ali say, 'Float like a butterfly and sting like a bee.' Also, I recognized that many of the martial arts had animal totems they tried to emulate such as tigers and cranes, just like several ballets. Both require dedication and training to perform their movements and techniques at a level of mastery."

How do the Frame Principle and Pyramid Principle blend into ballet? "Framing and balance are very important in dance. An airplane can't fly properly, overcome the natural forces it needs to, unless it is properly balanced. In martial arts, I try to unbalance my opponent [an illustration of the Kuzushi Principle, which we'll discuss in chapter eleven]. But in dance, the opposite is true. I use my framing abilities to keep my partner in perfect balance. These principles also reflect on the audience, which I believe feels more tranquil and secure when the positions of the dancers on stage are correct." Though the legendary Russian ballet dancer Mikhail Baryshnikov had defected from Soviet oppression for the artistic freedom of the West nearly a decade before George Birkadze was born, the aspiring artist stumbled upon his work and instantly adopted Baryshnikov as one of his early heroes. "The government tries to suppress the legacy of people like that. But I came upon a pirated video of Baryshnikov dancing. I was blown away by the movements he could do in midair. I remember thinking to myself, *How does this dude do it?*"

When the Soviet Union fell apart, Birkadze left Georgia to embark on an odyssey of teaching dance and choreography in countries including Portugal, Spain, and France, before eventually settling in the US. "It's important for people to realize that dance and martial arts have a shared history. There's Brazilian capoeira. The katas in karate resemble a dance. African war drums and dances were performed before battles. And in Renaissance France, a true gentleman knew how to both dance and duel with a sword."[9]

Framing in the World

Off the jiu-jitsu mat, we frame ourselves at many different times during an average day. Whether we're opening the refrigerator door, sitting behind the steering wheel of a car, raking leaves in the yard, vacuuming a rug, or pulling open a pop-top on a carbonated beverage, we properly align our skeletal

9 George Birkadze interview with Paul Volponi (March 28, 2022).

system to perform the task efficiently. Those are things at which we have a vast amount of practice. We do them almost automatically and with little forethought. But there are an equal number of times in life when we more carefully plan our posture and create frames to take on bigger forces.

Peak performance is meditation in motion.
—Greg Louganis, Olympic diving champion

Consider the simple act of diving into the deep end of a swimming pool. The goal is to align and streamline your body upon entry so the impact of hitting the water is minimized. That's a type of framing. We all know what happens when your framing is poor and the result of the dive is a belly flop. And depending on the height of the dive, that faulty framing can seriously sting or even knock the wind out of you. The proper framing? In a flat palm-up position, the diver's hands are normally clasped together, cutting through the water first with a frame designed to create a type of window through which the rest of the body passes. The framing of professional or Olympic divers is so well constructed that they can often achieve an entry with no splash whatsoever, called a "rip" because it sounds like the ripping of paper. The secret to such an entry is to be perfectly perpendicular to the water. That's also what we try to achieve in jiu-jitsu. The Frame Principle is at its most efficient when our deployed skeletal structure is perfectly perpendicular to the opponent's force.

Frank Lloyd Wright (1867–1959) is perhaps the most revered architect to ever live. He was known for a philosophy of design termed "organic architecture," which combines human and natural elements into its structures. That philosophy is a wonderful reflection of the Frame Principle's ability to align the skeletal structure to bear loads. Wright's crowning achievement was the construction of a house called Fallingwater, built over a 30-foot waterfall in Pennsylvania. It has been said that the house appears to defy the laws of physics, floating on air over the falls. Obviously, from what we know of architecture and the Frame Principle, this cannot be true. Like a jiu-jitsu practitioner searching for the correct technique to fit a given situation, Wright used a series of cantilevers, which are long beams fixed only at one end, to support the house while the unfixed ends hover almost magically in the air.

The Frame Principle can also be interpreted socially. After all, aren't we all architects of our own lives? No one wants their life to resemble a house built out of playing cards. Why? There isn't much internal support to such a structure. Because it lacks the proper framing, a house of cards can easily be brought down by stray vibrations or even a sudden sneeze. In building a better life structure, we can envision our friends and family as the supporting members, acting as the vertical studs and horizontal plates in the walls around us. The rafters and roof over our heads, as well as the flooring beneath us, can be bolstered by our health, hobbies, work life, and emotional well-being. It's another example of one of jiu-jitsu's principles extending beyond the mat to influence our daily life.

It had long since come to my attention that people of accomplishment rarely sat back and let things happen to them. They went out and happened to things.
—Leonardo da Vinci

Rely on the Frame Principle when . . .

- **Planning Ahead:** Your company is overly reliant on a small number of key employees, so you take steps to minimize risk by documenting all the responsibilities and procedures that govern their roles.
- **Prioritizing Love:** You're so consumed with work and parenting obligations that you forget to prioritize time with your significant other, so you commit to weekly date nights.
- **Setting Deadlines:** You insist on not falling victim to Parkinson's Law, which states that "work expands so as to fill the time available for its completion," so you develop the habit of setting deadlines for important tasks in your life.
- **Setting Parameters:** Your child's performance at school is suffering due to their addiction to video games, so you start requiring that they finish their homework each day before they're allowed any tech time.

Scan here to learn the combat application of
The Kuzushi Principle

Chapter Eleven

The Kuzushi Principle

Seeking first to understand, then to be understood.

Balance isn't something you achieve "someday."
—Nick Vujicic, author and motivational speaker

Whenever a jiu-jitsu student witnesses someone taking a fall, be it physical or figurative, the two questions they should immediately ask themselves are: *How did that happen?* and *At which point did their balance begin to become compromised?* We were introduced to the importance of these questions in discussing the Pyramid Principle. If there is a direct inverse to the Pyramid Principle, a mathematically driven concept that allows us to stay in control of ourselves and our opponents by building a solid foundation to provide balance and stability, it would certainly be the Kuzushi Principle. Kuzushi comes from the Japanese verb *kuzusu*, meaning to pull down, level, destroy, or demolish. In jiu-jitsu, we are focused on breaking the balance of our opponent. That means we need to compromise the stable pyramid or base on which our opponent's weight rests.

The Kuzushi Principle, through the dynamics of math and gravity, enables us to unbalance opponents who are heavier and stronger. One common way to put the Kuzushi Principle into practice is to sweep, or completely remove from contact with the ground, one of our opponent's standing legs. And if the opponent's center of gravity stays the same, unable to use the Pyramid Principle to reconfigure their balance points, they will be taken to the ground.

A second way to use the Kuzushi Principle in jiu-jitsu is not to attack the opponent's appendages, but rather to directly attack their center of gravity by lifting, pushing, or pulling them past their point of balance. This is most often used from the bottom position of a grapple, either to escape, roll to a better position, or even completely reverse the position, switching the bottom for the top.

You've undoubtedly seen the classic jiu-jitsu hip throw, where an opponent is hoisted onto the practitioner's hip and then thrown to the ground. It's an absolutely beautiful technique, resembling a ballet of body mechanics in motion. However, not every opponent comes ready-made to succumb to the hip throw. Even if the practitioner gets excellent position, thrusting his hip directly into the opponent, if the opponent's balance remains centered, the throw will be nearly impossible. Imagine trying to toss a 180-pound bag of wet cement over your shoulder. It just doesn't want to move. But if the practitioner first makes a move, such as hooking the opponent's leg to upset their balance, and then attempts the hip throw, that heavy sack of wet cement can suddenly transform into a feather. The use of that additional move reflects the Creation Principle, which uses a specific action to force a deliberate reaction from our opponent that we can use to our advantage. It's another prime example of synergy between the principles, how they are all interconnected.

The Yelp Review

In order to break my opponent's balance in a fight, I must first understand where their balance is rooted. Similarly, in life, if I am looking to influence someone's way of thinking, I must first understand *exactly* where they are. For instance, several years ago, an elementary school–aged student named Miranda attended one of our Gracie Bullyproof classes for the first time. Though I wasn't teaching that class, I came to know Miranda and her mother, Myra, quite quickly after Myra posted a one-star review of our school on

Yelp. Even though I've become immune to the occasional hateful comments directed at me by anonymous and often misinformed keyboard warriors, if an actual student at Gracie University has a bad experience, I'm willing to go to any length to make it right. I was so concerned by what this mom had to say about the experience that I really wanted to speak with her, but since her review was anonymous, I had my staff dig through our attendance records, and through the process of elimination we identified the student and found the mom's phone number.

I brought a pair of our managers into an office with me, closed the door behind us, phoned the mom, and put the call on speaker. "Myra, this is Rener Gracie. I understand that you were dissatisfied with the experience at our school. Would you please tell me what happened?" For the next twenty minutes, Myra went on to recount how her daughter Miranda, once she walked through our doors, completely slipped through the cracks. That none of the instructors on the mats seemingly understood that she was a new student amid a large class. To make matters worse, Miranda was paired to do techniques with a student that both she and her mom viewed as too aggressive. Then Myra went on to describe the feeling of utter helplessness watching Miranda on the mats. She detailed the uneasiness in her stomach, the growing pounding in her chest, and then the intense burning in her throat until she finally called for an instructor to step in between Miranda and her partner.

I could hear in Myra's voice how difficult the story was for her to retell. But it was also difficult for me to hear, to understand that this parent and child put their trust in Gracie University, and we had completely let them down. I vowed that it would never happen again, that Miranda would be the last child to ever have a negative first experience on our mats.

As a school, we immediately put new protocols into place, readjusting the ratio of instructors to students, and ensuring that an instructor always recognizes a new student, partnering with that child for techniques themselves. But that wasn't enough for me. I needed to set things right with Myra and Miranda. "Myra, I feel badly that your daughter's introduction to jiu-jitsu went so poorly. I want to offer Miranda free private classes here for a month, and I'll personally teach the first one." Earlier during our call, Myra had mentioned that she had always wanted to study jiu-jitsu herself but never had the chance. That was one of the reasons she'd brought Miranda to our school, to make sure her daughter had more opportunities than she had. "And Myra, I'd be pleased for you to take these classes with Miranda," I added. They were both thrilled to accept my offer, and I was grateful for the chance to set things right.

When we eventually got together on the mats, I brought along one of my top female instructors, Bobbie, who would be training them for the succeeding private sessions. Miranda and her mom had a great time. A few weeks later, Myra deleted her review, replacing it with one that assigned us five stars.

The key to my success was in listening without judgment, so I could fully understand why Myra was so upset. With that information, I was able to craft a plan that not only gave Miranda the amazing introductory jiu-jitsu experience she deserved, but one that recruited her mom onto the mat as well. Thanks to the Kuzushi Principle, we flipped a one-star Yelp review into two long-term students.

Profile: Kayla's Kuzushi

"One of the most beautiful things about being a martial artist is that you develop this inner peace, this inner sanctuary where your mind is at one with your body. You're capable of controlling yourself in almost any situation. Because of the rigorous training and all the work I do, it's really hard to off-balance me in life," said Olympic champion Kayla Harrison. "The crazy thing is that you spend hours and hours going through the repetition of Kuzushi, of off-balancing your opponent. There are three parts to every throw: the off-balance, the entry, and the finish. The beautiful thing about the sequence is that you can't get to step two without step one, and you can't get to step three without step two. You get your opponent up on their toes, using their momentum against them. There's really no feeling like it. You've mastered your mind and body and found a way to put it all together. There's no greater high than when you execute a perfect throw."[10]

10 Kayla Harrison interview with Paul Volponi (January 18, 2022).

Balancing Act

How can we view the Kuzushi Principle in our daily lives? Well, we clearly don't want to be that opponent whose balance becomes so compromised that we're either swept or thrown to the hard ground by the reality of life's challenges. For example, it's all too easy to become unbalanced financially. Do we spend more money per week than we earn in our paychecks? Rent or mortgage, food, tuition, car, gas, phone, internet, and insurance are most people's primary expenditures. Our checkbook can easily fall on the wrong side of the plus/minus ledger through no fault of our own due to sudden unanticipated expenses such as medical bills, or home, vehicle, and computer repairs. How long could you remain financially balanced if you lost your job?

Balancing our time between work, school, and family is something that could easily send us sprawling emotionally, trying desperately to remain upright. What happens when your boss needs you to work through the weekend, but your spouse or children were counting on spending time with you? Lots of people take work home with them every night, especially educators, just to be prepared for the next day's assignment. How do you properly balance that work/home equation in your life when work is work and home is partly work too? The inverse of that problem is also possible. With many people performing their professional duties from home since the COVID-19 pandemic, there are those who find it exceedingly difficult to concentrate on work amid all of the possible household distractions including children, spouses, pets, neighbors, TV, and noise. Finding the proper balance for yourself, and learning how to maintain it, is key to establishing control over such situations.

> *You're juggling these four balls that you've named work, family, friends, [and] spirit. Now, work is a rubber ball. If you drop it, it bounces back. The other balls, they're made of glass.*
>
> —James Patterson, author, *Roses Are Red*

Suppose you've been carefully balancing your diet. You're down almost sixteen pounds, and everyone from your immediate family to your doctor is proud of you and being supportive. But tonight is your cousin's birthday party, and your aunt, whom you love dearly, has just one motto in her home: My joy in life comes from cooking for my family and watching everyone eat. You're smart enough not to mention your new diet to your aunt. She'll just tell you that you're already too skinny, and you'll become the topic of conversation around the dinner table. Not something in which you're terribly interested. So far, you've stayed away from the homemade bread and heavily buttered mashed potatoes. Filling your plate with a double serving of vegetables beside your main protein has seemingly satisfied your aunt's desire to lavish food on her guests. But now it's time for dessert, a huge birthday cake for your cousin. After everyone sings and the candles get blown out, your cousin gets the first slice of cake. To your surprise, the aunt places the second slice in front of you, a huge mound of chocolate fudge cake with strawberry icing. Your aunt smiles widely at you and says, "It's your favorite from when you were a child. I baked it especially for you." Deep down, you've been fighting the urge for a few weeks now to ditch your diet. Sticking to it has been anything but easy. You know that you need to taste at least a few forkfuls for your aunt. But you wonder to yourself: *Will this start me on a downward spiral of eating out of control?*

There are no easy answers to any of the above quandaries. Life can seem like walking a tightrope with the wind blowing in every direction, intent on unbalancing us. The Kuzushi Principle we use on the jiu-jitsu mat can certainly serve as a model, though, to understand how our stability can become compromised, and whether or not we've contributed to that process ourselves. Can we readjust our center of gravity as in the Pyramid Principle before we topple over? That's a matter of how well we know ourselves, and what we do emotionally to readjust as we sense the first degrees of slippage. That valuable readjustment can even take place outside of ourselves by asking friends, family, and neighbors for help. If we communicate with others about our potential unbalancing and the intense feelings that normally accompany it, their responses could play an essential role in keeping us upright. Yes, jiu-jitsu gives us the basic tools for life. But we still need to become skilled artisans at living in order to get the best use out of them.

We need to do a better job of putting ourselves higher on our own "to do" list.
—Michelle Obama

Consider the Kuzushi Principle when . . .

- **Influencing Others:** Your company needs to implement new software that doesn't have employee buy-in, so you communicate with employees to understand their concerns that will, in turn, enable you to highlight the features of the software that will help get the support you're looking for.
- **Overcoming Fears:** Your child is scared of the dark, so you take small steps to create positive associations with varying levels of darkness.
- **Communicating:** You call your ex-husband and ask him to pick up your child from school, but he immediately reacts aggressively until you inform him that you got a flat tire, which causes him to soften his stance and comply.
- **Healing from Trauma:** You realize that you have an aversion to long-term relationships, so you seek therapy that will help you identify and heal the trauma that is holding you back.

Martial Arts Etymology

We have Mars, the Roman god of war, to thank for the phrase "martial arts." It comes from Latin and means the "arts of Mars." The phrase first appeared in sixteenth-century Europe and was originally used to describe the skills and knowledge of professional warriors. Nowadays, however, people study and train in martial arts for a variety of reasons such as health, exercise, self-discipline, improved focus, and fun.

The term "jiu-jitsu" comes from the Japanese language, and it literally translates as a gentle, soft, or yielding art. It's a spot-on description considering that jiu-jitsu manipulates the opponent's own force against them. It was first developed to combat feudal Japan's fierce samurai warriors, with the art's written history dating back to the beginning of the eighth century.

"Karate" has a pair of translations. It originally meant "Chinese hand" or "a martial art for China." Then a homophone was introduced into its character spelling and karate became more commonly interpreted as "empty hand." It was a martial system embraced by several provinces of Japan after starting to trade with China's Ming dynasty in the fourteenth century. Its forms, comprised of sequenced moves, are called "katas," meaning "shapes" or "models."

The Chinese art of kung fu translates as "time plus effort equals a skill." Of course, in Chinese culture, the term "good kung fu" doesn't exclusively refer to being adept at fighting and self-defense. It also means being a good-hearted or skilled person. It's not uncommon to see Chinese shops with names such as Kung Fu Tea or Kung Fu Bread, suggesting that, over time, their proprietors have developed great skill at their particular craft.

The art of sumo hails from Japan and literally translates as "striking one another." It is a form of full-contact wrestling where the combatants attempt to force each other out of a circular ring (*dohyo*), or have any part of the opponent's body, except the soles of their feet, touch the ground. Even in modern Japanese culture, women are barred from participating in professional sumo under the archaic tradition that their menstrual blood makes them not pure enough to enter the sacred ring.

Tupi is a language spoken by the aboriginal people inhabiting the southern coast of Brazil. It is responsible for the etymology of the martial art capoeira, which translates as "forest round," referring to the areas of low-lying vegetation or underbrush where runaway slaves might hide. To disguise the fact that they were practicing fighting, practitioners incorporated the element of dance and music into the art, which for more than a half century was banned by Brazilian authorities nearing the conclusion of the nineteenth century. Capoeira is recognized for its acrobatic elements, including hands on the ground for balance and thrust while executing inverted kicks.

Scan here to learn the combat application of

The Reconnaissance Principle

Chapter Twelve

The Reconnaissance Principle

Believing that the answers you seek do exist, and never underestimating the power of new information.

How you gather, manage, and use information will determine whether you win or lose.
—Bill Gates, businessman and philanthropist

I learn something from every person with whom I grapple. What becomes most ingrained in me via that process? Their strengths, weaknesses, and ultimately, what I need to do to be successful in my encounter with them. On the jiu-jitsu mat and in life, you've already learned half of what you need to know to succeed. The other half? You'll discover that during your impending personal interaction, be it a business meeting, a first date, introducing yourself to the new neighbors, or a sparring session. That's called the Reconnaissance Principle, which centers on your keen observations of the opponent. In total, it's the culmination of the information gathered both before and during the encounter, whether you've gleaned that knowledge from watching the opponent interact with others or from what you've accessed firsthand through a process of touch and feel.

In jiu-jitsu, I use a technique referred to as "drummer," especially when sparring with someone with whom I've never grappled before. From either the top or bottom position, I'll use my hands much like a drummer would, slapping and touching, often in rapid-fire fashion. With every touch, I'm gaining information on what the opponent will do in certain situations and how they react to different stimuli. It's a matter of taking a personal survey, like an auto mechanic running a diagnostic on a car. Throughout the process, I'm being extremely observant and proactive in acquiring knowledge to use later on. Usually, I'll do something very deliberate to evoke a response. But other times, the reconnaissance is incidental. The more relaxed you are as a practitioner, the more information you can gather. Once you know what your opponent's predictable response will be, you can more easily create counters using the Creation Principle. And the better you understand which boulders the opponent will use in an attempt to stop your flow, the more prepared you'll be to use the River Principle to find an alternate path.

Consider trying to discover the exact location in which air is leaking from a car or bicycle tire. You absolutely know there's a leak because every few days your tire pressure is low and you need to pump additional air. So how can you pinpoint the leak? Submerging the tire in water will do it instantly. Just follow the escaping air bubbles coming to the surface. It's the same on the jiu-jitsu mat. Put the opponent under pressure, and he or she will display to you their weaknesses. That's the theory behind the Reconnaissance Principle.

Teaching "For" Instead of Teaching "To"

Never underestimate the power of new information. That's one of the staples of the Reconnaissance Principle. And that is clearly evident in how we currently present Gracie Survival Tactics (GST), a jiu-jitsu-based program that teaches defensive tactics to police officers around the country. The Gracie Family has long believed that law enforcement learning jiu-jitsu would equate to safer physical encounters for both officers and the citizens with whom they come into contact. But approximately two decades ago, the program ran into some stiff resistance. At our weeklong seminars, which normally hosted officers from several different neighboring departments, my father sensed the resentment of some officers who were not eager to learn, either being too prideful to accept new ideas or too close-minded to accept advice from civilians.

As a 19-year-old, I was scheduled to travel to Texas and run a GST seminar with my father. Only, he had a family emergency he needed to deal with. So he sent me to the Lone Star State alone to face a gymnasium full of officers. It was very intimidating. I could tell what they were thinking by their faces. *You don't know anything about the job we do, kid. And now you're going to tell us how to do it better?* They had a valid point. I was an expert in jiu-jitsu, but I'd never arrested nor handcuffed anyone in my life. So I turned to everyone in the crowd and said, "I'm not a police officer and I'm not going to pretend that I am one. I'm here to share with you my knowledge of jiu-jitsu. But I'd also love to hear your feedback on how to make every technique more applicable for law enforcement use. My father's not here and I know you're disappointed in that. So I'll make everyone this promise. At the end of the week, if you're not 100 percent satisfied with what you've learned, simply ask for a refund and you'll get it."

That week, after demonstrating every technique, I opened the floor up to questions. I turned no one's inquiry away. We examined every suggestion made, trying it their way to see if it fit their unique circumstances any better. And in several instances, it did. Eventually, I wrote modifications of those Texas-based scenarios, and many others, into the actual GST curriculum. At the end of the course, I restated my refund offer to everyone on the mat. Not a single department took me up on it. (It *may* have helped that prior to offering the refunds, I sparred with all fifty-plus cops in the room and made them all tap out, one after another, without any rest or water breaks.) My father missing the seminar was fortuitous in a way. He came from an era in which the instructor absolutely knew best, and he rarely asked for input or improvements from the students. But I had forever changed that in the way we would run GST in the future.

My Texas debut was so successful that my father no longer needed to travel to teach GST courses around the country. From that point on, my brother and I became the head instructors for all law enforcement courses. I'm partial to saying, "The Gracies used to teach jiu-jitsu *to* police officers. Now we teach jiu-jitsu *for* police officers. I'm just the messenger." That's the type of improved vision the Reconnaissance Principle can produce when you're receptive to the power of new information.

> *When in doubt, observe and ask questions. When certain, observe at length and ask many more questions.*
> —George S. Patton, general, United States Army

Advanced Scouting/Sports and Games

The word "reconnaissance" comes from the military and its need to gain advance information about both opposing forces and the terrain over which a potential battle might take place. Its usage can be traced back to the Napoleonic Wars of the early nineteenth century.

Today, lots of people who participate in a wide range of activities use the Reconnaissance Principle to further their cause. For example, both marathon runners and cyclists are always eager to scout the course in advance, wanting to know the location of the hills and their steepness. The Tour de France, the world's most important bicycle race, even has an official doing reconnaissance years in advance to select the French towns through which the cyclists will compete.

Poker players often employ the Reconnaissance Principle to feel out new competitors at their table. They want to gather information on potential "tells" or signals as to when others might be holding a strong hand or bluffing. Football is a sport in which the coaches and players watch hours of video detailing the opposing team in order to discern their tendencies. Whenever a baseball player is mired in a deep batting slump, you can often find that player in counsel with the hitting coach, comparing video of the hitter's recent at bats to when the hitter was doing much better, searching out positive and negative tendencies. In fact, iPads are now a staple for reconnaissance in baseball dugouts and football benches during games for use in real-time scouting.

Assigning the Right Jobs

In our everyday lives, the Reconnaissance Principle doesn't exclusively need to be used in gaining an edge to defeat an opponent. The idea behind it is so versatile that we can flip it completely around and use the Reconnaissance Principle to help us work *in concert* with others, with everyone coming out a winner and better for the experience.

Imagine it's your job to hand out assignments to a trio of brand-new interns, college students looking for work experience and possibly future employment at your company. The three assignments are vastly different in nature. The first requires someone to "cold call" potential clients on the phone. It will require a discernible speaking voice and the ability to read a prepared script with feeling, speed, and accuracy. The second assignment needs someone who can build spreadsheets and record information. The third has an element of creativity to it: Your company needs a dozen different signs to be put up around the office complex. Though the text has already been written, your boss wants different fonts and colors used to make each sign stand out from the others.

So how can the Reconnaissance Principle be applied here? Before you hand out the assignments, you invite the three interns to have lunch with you in the break room. It's really your first chance to speak with them since their arrival. You ask about their prior work experience, what they're studying in school, their hobbies, and goals for the future. Soon, you discover that one of the interns, though interested in business, is actually minoring in art at school. There's your poster person. Of the two remaining interns, one is definitely more outgoing than the other, with a far more pleasant, upbeat voice. But that intern also has experience with spreadsheets, while the last does not. Ultimately, you decide that it would be best to teach the third intern how to make a spreadsheet than lose all of the positives the second intern would bring to sales calls.

How about a neighborly example? You saw the new neighbors move in this morning. An hour or two after the moving vans leave, you decide to knock on their door carrying a vase of flowers from your garden as a housewarming gift. You're excited to meet them. The neighbors who previously lived there were standoffish and rarely spoke to you, despite your best efforts to have a relationship. The door opens and the house inside is in total disarray. There are tall stacks of boxes waiting to be unpacked, a dog barking loudly in the background, and a frustrated voice hollering from the kitchen, "Where did we pack the dishes?" The new neighbor is smiling at you, but clearly flustered by the surrounding circumstances. So you hand your new neighbor the flowers and say, "I can see this isn't a good time for you. I just wanted to welcome your family to the neighborhood. Feel free to ring my bell if you need anything."

As you walk away with a friendly wave, you can take pride in knowing you've used the Reconnaissance Principle to learn that your neighbors were too haggard for company, the Acceptance Principle to realize you had chosen the wrong time for a conversation, and the River Principle to smoothly transition into leaving your neighbors an open invitation to call on you. Maybe the name on your mailbox reads Jiu-Jitsu Master.

Profile: Sweet Smell of Success

Howie Freilich began in business as a teen, selling flowers and plants on the streets of New York City. The invaluable lessons he learned from that experience helped catapult this self-made entrepreneur to the founding of Blondie's Treehouse, an interior and exterior landscape company that brings in over $40 million a year in revenue while supporting more than 200 employees. Below, Freilich shares his business acumen as it relates to the Clock Principle, Velocity Principle, and Reconnaissance Principle.

"What I learned about respecting the clock in business is that nothing literally takes five minutes," said Freilich, whose workplace is no longer a street corner in Queens, but rather suites of offices in Manhattan and Denver. "A client calls and says, 'I need you to water some plants on my terrace. It'll only take five minutes.' Well, what the client didn't consider is that it takes more time than that to reach their floor on a slow-moving elevator. Then there's the protective paper they'd like for us to put down before walking across their carpet. And what if they forget to turn the water on from its source? Sure, it's five minutes to water the plants but probably forty-five minutes to get ready to do it. If you give them a price for a five-minute job, monetarily, you'll be on the losing end."

Freilich, who built his company on customer relations, is finely attuned to the emotional needs of his clients. "Velocity is important, whether it's time to move fast or slow. The time to move quickly is when a client is either waiting on a written proposal or for service, maybe to check on a plant that might not be looking well at the moment. Every client wants to feel important. Your speed of service will ensure that feeling. When they begin to feel unimportant, you just might lose them. But if you respond to their needs immediately, even if all aspects of their concerns aren't completely addressed, they'll feel good about your response. On the opposite end, I've learned to move slowly and take a full step back whenever I'm personally dissatisfied with a client's actions or behavior. I usually take twenty-four hours to give a thoughtful response that's less driven by emotions to such instances."

How important is reconnaissance in business? "I go into every meeting having done my homework. Everyone on both sides of a business negotiation has a goal. I need to understand what the client wants to achieve. Is it speed of service or the lowest price? If a client's goal is for me to service plants and flowers as quickly as tomorrow, then I can charge a premium for that. Also, that higher price point will be established for future jobs down the line. But if I don't do the proper reconnaissance and lead with the lowest possible price to that same client, I may have to meet their time demands anyway, leaving profits on the table. That will ultimately hurt my business and my employees."[11]

It is a capital mistake to theorize before one has data. Insensibly one begins to twist facts to suit theories, instead of theories to suit facts.

—Sir Arthur Conan Doyle, author/creator, Sherlock Holmes

11 Howard Freilich interview with Paul Volponi (April 17, 2022).

Acknowledge the Reconnaissance Principle when . . .

- **Empowering Children:** Your child has been experiencing separation anxiety, so you get into the habit of communicating the day's activities in advance, which helps increase their sense of control.
- **Understanding Others:** You're considering a long-term relationship with a significant other, but before you commit, you ask you partner several questions to understand their beliefs on important issues that may come up down the line.
- **Marketing:** You invent a new product, but before you spend the time and money to bring it to market, you conduct the research needed to determine if there is sufficient demand to make it worth your while.
- **Managing Health:** You've been experiencing persistent discomfort in your abdominal region, and rather than ignore it, you decide to have a doctor conduct the tests to identify the source of the problem.

Scan here to learn the combat application of

The Prevention Principle

Chapter Thirteen

The Prevention Principle

Accepting that sometimes the only way to win is to avoid losing.

If you don't lose, you will eventually win.
—Helio Gracie

In a fight or in life, it's natural to prioritize our own needs, wants, and overall successes before anyone else's in pursuit of our goals. The Prevention Principle, however, teaches us to consider an alternate path to success. Whenever you're up against a much bigger, stronger adversary, instead of focusing solely on what you want to do to them, your main goal should be to stop the opponent from achieving their objectives against you. After all, self-defense is one of the art's primary goals. Accepting the Prevention Principle, and therefore changing your definition of success, allows you to take control from every position in a grapple. That's because the basic mindset of an opponent is to keep advancing forward. So, no matter which position you occupy at any given moment, be it superior, neutral, or inferior, stopping your opponent's progress puts you in control. And that is a victory. Consider this: How do you get the tug-of-war toy out of a dog's clenched jaws? Simply stop pulling.

If you can stop your opponent's progress for any length of time, say for thirty or forty seconds, it may very well result in you achieving victory in a different form such as a submission or an escape from any inferior position. How so? Your opponent will certainly get tired and discouraged. Your patience will perhaps open the door to securing your own progress by provoking in your opponent an overreaction. Remember, during the process of stopping an opponent's progress, we experience much of what they have to offer. The Prevention Principle and the Reconnaissance Principle are extremely similar in that respect, and they often work together. We want to know what's on an opponent's mind, what his reactions will be. Your success in this, though, rests upon your knowledge of the techniques, because you can't stop what you don't understand. This process of gathering information might even make it seem as if we have no place better to be than to block, hold, and posture. But once we know that we can neutralize an opponent, we can move more efficiently toward another victory, however it may be defined.

The Triangle Choke

Perhaps the most high-profile use of the Prevention Principle occurred on the night it was unveiled to the world. It was put into play out of absolute necessity by my uncle Royce in UFC 4 (1994) as he squared off in the final match against Dan "The Beast" Severn, a two-time Division I NCAA wrestling champion. Severn outweighed Royce by approximately 75 pounds, an advantage that wouldn't be allowed in any sanctioned MMA bout today. It was the third match of the night for my uncle, who quickly found himself on his back after Severn executed a double leg takedown. The spectators and announcers feared that this was the end of the David-like Royce's chances against this Goliath of an opponent. But Royce had The Beast secured with both legs wrapped around his torso—a technique called "the guard." At the time, the idea of the guard was a novel concept, with martial artists outside of jiu-jitsu having little exposure to its effectiveness. Not only was the guard used to redirect much of Severn's crushing weight, it allowed Royce to neutralize punches, elbows, and head-butts by disrupting The Beast's balance and distance. Royce was, in effect, in a position of relative safety during the midst of the raging storm above him.

The two combatants remained entrenched in their positions for fifteen grueling minutes. My uncle smartly realized that utilizing the Prevention Principle was the only way for him to ultimately succeed against a highly skilled fighter who possessed a colossal weight advantage. The Prevention Principle allowed Royce to accept the bottom position and employ an opening strategy of finding a way not to lose, because winning was most likely not among his early options. There was beautiful synergy here as well with the Depletion Principle (upcoming in chapter eighteen) as The Beast slowly burned through his energy supply. Eventually, Royce recognized an opening. He slid one of his legs over Severn's shoulder, and then locked onto his other leg in a figure-four configuration. With his two femurs restricting the blood flow in Severn's neck and his tibia placed directly behind the neck to prevent escape, Royce introduced the world to the now-famous technique that epitomizes Brazilian jiu-jitsu, the triangle choke.

Seemingly out of nowhere, Severn, who appeared to be in complete control and on the verge of victory, tapped his hand on the mat signaling his acceptance of defeat. The announcers and the crowd were in total shock as Royce, through the highest level of patience and jiu-jitsu efficiency, triumphed on the shoulders of the Prevention Principle.

"Patience" is an incredible understatement. No one expected a UFC match to last fifteen minutes, including those responsible for the pay-per-view broadcast. In fact, many viewers around the world who purchased the event didn't witness its stunning conclusion as the broadcast timed out in multiple areas, resulting in massive refunds.

Profile: The Open Car Door

Professor George Kirby is a retired California schoolteacher. He's also an internationally recognized teacher of Japanese jiu-jitsu. Despite excelling on the mats for more than half a century, his advice for both his students and himself is one of prevention first. "Do anything you can to avoid a physical confrontation." Kirby recently put this creed into practice while on a picnic at a park with his wife. He went back to their car alone to retrieve something when two men approached him and requested a small amount of money. "I already had the car door open so I got on one side of it and kept them on the other side. This is something I teach black belts, using objects in the environment to prevent people from getting to you. Once I had the door between us and kept eye contact, they decided to back away," said Kirby. "Maintaining eye contact and responding in a calm, assertive voice can be [disarming]."

Kirby got into martial arts while in college to relieve the stress of studying for his MA in social science. Upon graduation, he began teaching at a junior high where he promptly formed an after-school jiu-jitsu club to try and stem the school's increasing dropout rate. The club's attendance grew so large that the school's administrators decided to make it a regular class during the day. "It actually kept kids in school," said Kirby, who often used admission to his jiu-jitsu class as a motivation for students to buckle down in other subject areas. "If they put out the effort, they got there."

Over the course of his career, Kirby's reputation as an educator became so sterling that after the 1994 Rodney King incident (in which King was the victim of police brutality), the Los Angeles Police Department brought him in as part of a team of consultants to help teach officers less violent arrest and control tactics. "It was personally rewarding and I do believe [the LAPD] listened to us regarding their use of force levels," said Kirby. "Most people who are being apprehended aren't trying to fight with officers. They're trying to run away."[12]

Theater Etiquette/Not-So-Hard Scrabble

Suppose you're sitting in a movie theater with your popcorn and soft drink. It's the most exciting part of the film, a car chase through crowded city streets. Your mind is in motion with those fleet vehicles. You're leaning left and then

12 George Kirby interview with Paul Volponi (February 12, 2022).

right in your chair with every turn of the steering wheel. Suddenly, you feel a hard kick at the back of your seat. The person behind you is totally revved up and involved in the movie too. So you think nothing of it. A moment later, your seat gets kicked again. It's both annoying and hurts. This time you turn completely around, get the attention of the person behind you, and ask them to stop. There isn't much of a reaction on their part, just an expressionless face. A few seconds after the car chase ends, you feel a third kick and hear a hint of laughter.

There are many things that could happen next, including you completely losing your temper. But let's not go there. Let's remain calm and think. Exactly how would you put the Prevention Principle to use here? I suppose you could give this person a speech on movie etiquette or briefly leave and return with the theater management in tow. But neither of those options feels completely correct. Just like on the jiu-jitsu mat, you would need to ask yourself, "What does this person want to achieve and what can I do to stop their progress?"

The person apparently wants to control you. He or she is making the silent statement that their actions can create a reaction in you that they will somehow find pleasing. But remember, their control of you requires opposition on your part. Perhaps the perfect Prevention Principle reaction would be to get up without a word and move several rows behind this person to a new seat. That would instantly take away whatever position they believed was theirs. Why move to a seat behind and not farther in front of them? Now you can utilize the Reconnaissance Principle as well. You can watch this person's movements without having to turn around. You could see what they might be preparing to do and not do. And if they approach you to carry on this annoyance, you'll have time to prepare.

Naturally, as we go about our daily lives, we can invert the Prevention Principle to bond with people instead of vying against them. Imagine you're teaching someone to play a game for the first time—say, Scrabble. Yes, you'll explain the rules. You'll show them how to make words, link them together on the board, and which types of words, such as proper nouns, are unacceptable. But when the game begins will you go on an immediate scoring rampage? Will you call them on every mistake they might make and penalize them with losing a turn?

Perhaps the best way to start would be to show them your rack of seven tiles with the letters exposed. Then build a word in front of them, place it on the board, and explain to them why you are saving your *s* for later on in the game when it could prove more valuable. Now you'll have them expose their rack of letters. They happen to have one of the blank tiles in their hand. Instead of encouraging them to use it in building a simple low-scoring word such as "hotel," with the blank becoming a *t*, which they currently do not hold, you explain to them how a blank might help them in building a prized seven-letter word, or to reach a triple-word score on the board.

As based on the Prevention Principle, you are changing your definition of success. Instead of crushing someone with little to no experience at Scrabble, you're giving them the tools to eventually provide you with a competitive game. That's the same basic scenario when almost anyone takes their first lesson in a martial art. Your older brother or sister at the school can probably defeat you quite easily. But at some point, the more experienced practitioner will have to hold back and allow the novice to explore how to apply a successful technique.

An ounce of prevention is worth a pound of cure.
—Benjamin Franklin

Paul's POV: The Preventative Power of Names

Coauthor and journalist Paul Volponi, an ardent street basketball player, also spent sixteen years with the New York City Department of Education. Six of those years were spent teaching adolescents awaiting trial on Rikers Island, which at the time was the world's largest, most overcrowded and dangerous jail.

I played an incredibly aggressive, defensive style of basketball. I spent thousands of hours on a court learning how to stick to someone like flypaper. My constant goal was to physically smother my offensive opponent at every opportunity. I wanted to turn the 94-foot length and 50-foot width of a basketball court into an inch-by-inch war. I would go from ballyard to ballyard in NYC searching for dominant scorers, and then I would focus on locking them down. But when you bring that type of attitude into a street game, and you do it in yards where you're a stranger, intense altercations are naturally going to come with the territory.

How did I use the Prevention Principle to try and insulate myself from these impending scuffles? I would approach my opponent before the game, introduce myself, and shake their hand. I would usually say something like, "I watched you playing from the sideline. I have a lot of respect for your game, and I'm going to give you everything I've got on defense. So be prepared. It's nothing personal. I just really like to play hard." Of course, their teammates would also be upset with me for hounding their scorer all over the court, and they would consider trying to put a stop to it by being overly physical with me. In anticipation of this, I would go out of my way to learn everybody's name. When you can talk to people using their names, I've found that it reduces the chance of serious conflict.

Years later, when I was teaching high school students on Rikers Island, the world's biggest jail, I would stand at the door of the school trailer and attempt to call each adolescent by their name as they entered. Rikers is an inherently dangerous place, in part because it's normally so overcrowded. When you can call someone by their name, there's less anonymity. Hence, people are less likely to do the wrong thing in front of you. That can insulate you and those in your immediate area from problems. Learning people's names, especially those with whom you may be in conflict, can be a powerful tool in implementing the Prevention Principle.

Rely on the Prevention Principle when . . .

- **Managing Disasters:** Your company suffers from the effects of a global health pandemic, so you decide to lay off half of your workforce to avoid bankruptcy.
- **De-escalating:** Your children are fighting over a toy and it's getting heated, so you take the toy away to prevent further escalation until the emotions cool down and an amicable toy-sharing plan is agreed upon.

- **Surviving:** You're out jogging when a man grabs you and tries to drag you into a van against your will, so you drop to the ground and start yelling to prevent the attacker's progress while increasing the chances of bystander intervention.
- **Intervening Medically:** You're first on scene at a car accident site, and a person is bleeding profusely due a compound fracture of their arm, so you quickly remove your belt and use it as a tourniquet until medical services arrive.

Scan here to learn the combat application of

The Tension Principle

Chapter Fourteen

The Tension Principle

Recognizing when tension is an asset and when it is a liability.

To be a human being is to be in a state of tension between your appetites and your dreams.
—John Updike, author, poet

Normally, tension isn't something that you want in your life. It can seriously affect your health, relationships, and work. But in jiu-jitsu, there is bound to be physical tension between practitioners during a grapple. It's only natural. There will be grips, grabs, and the stretching of muscles and joints, pushing the limits of their elasticity to execute techniques and gain superior position. Physical tension, though, can be an incredible form of communication, particularly in how it reveals your opponent's intentions. As a jiu-jitsu player, you'll want to become keenly aware of how to interpret tension, using its revealing information to your advantage. That's where the Tension Principle comes into play. In addition to providing us with important information about our adversaries' objectives, this principle affords us many physical opportunities, including but not limited to: the slingshot technique, the grip break, and the advancement nullification of a grip.

The Slingshot. If you pull someone toward you, it's only natural that they will pull back in the opposite direction. In fact, the harder you pull, the more likely they are to resist. As you feel the tension building and the absolute committal of force against yours (remember, force has only one direction), simply release. By doing so, you will slingshot your opponent in the direction of their own pull, breaking their balance to set them up for a possible sweep, takedown, or submission. We witness this in real life all the time. Perhaps two children are having a tug-of-war over a toy. Then one child unexpectedly decides to let go, sending the other sprawling backward to the floor via their own force. "But I didn't do anything," states the still-standing child to a scolding parent. Their statement is technically correct. The other child actually did it to himself. At this point you may be thinking, *Hey, I also see the Kuzushi Principle of unbalancing the opponent in the slingshot technique.* If so, you are becoming acutely attuned to the synergy between jiu-jitsu's core principles.

The Grip Break. It's difficult to break a rubber band or string that's hanging loosely between two people. However, if those people begin to apply force in opposite directions, and that rubber band or string starts to pull taut, it becomes much easier to break with the added tension and shearing forces at work. It's the same in trying to break a grip or hold in jiu-jitsu. The more tension applied in a grip or hold, the more rigid it becomes, and ultimately, more susceptible to being broken.

Advancement Nullification. Here's the thing about tension in a grip: The harder you grasp something, the more stationary that grip becomes. Why? The muscles, which are already tense, must loosen before that grip can advance or retreat to another position. So an opposing practitioner with a tension-filled grip on your wrist will have to release that tension in order to advance their grip to your forearm. And that is a form of communication that is very readable. As you feel that tension ease, it is an ideal time for you to either apply a capitalizing technique yourself or frustrate your opponent with a defensive maneuver. That moment, signaled by the release of tension, takes in the attributes of several interconnected principles, including

Connection, Detachment, Distance, Creation, Velocity, Clock, Reconnaissance, and Prevention. Imagine all of that transpiring from what the opponent believed was their tight grasp on the situation.

Tension Revealing Truth

In a fight and in life, tension is a uniquely reliable way to reveal truth. By putting a skill or system to the most extreme test and under daunting pressure (as in the Tension Principle), its mettle can be proven and recognized beyond a shadow of a doubt. That's exactly what my father, Rorion, envisioned it doing in 1993 when he co-founded the Ultimate Fighting Championship (UFC). The challenge matches that my dad had conducted in our garage gained Brazilian jiu-jitsu a local following in Southern California. But he truly believed that the art deserved a bigger stage and, if it succeeded, wider recognition.

All through the 1980s and '90s, the public devoured Hollywood's depiction of martial arts. Directors demanded flashy hand movements and spinning kicks that looked good on camera. Even icons like Bruce Lee and Jackie Chan traded a tangible degree of their martial sensibilities to perform less efficient moves that shined on the big screen. Brazilian jiu-jitsu was absolutely the antithesis of that, more beautiful in its efficacy than its anaconda-like appearance. My father focused on having his eight-fighter tournament between different martial disciplines mirror the uncertainty of a street fight. He ratcheted up the tension by foregoing multiple rounds with rest periods. Instead of ropes, he had a chain-link fence surrounding the ring. That way no one could purposefully fall through the ropes and cause a stoppage, stealing a breather. His initial notion was to have a crocodile-filled moat in wait beneath the fighting surface. Only that never came to pass.

Colorado was chosen as the site of the first event because it was one of the few states where combat between consenting parties in unsanctioned fights was legally allowed. The night of UFC 1, my uncle Royce, the Gracie family's representative, was a decided underdog. Some in the media even referred to him as *the little guy in the pajamas* (gi). But when Royce used his mastery of jiu-jitsu to defeat a trio of giants that night, many in the martial arts world cried *the fight was fixed!*

Above all else, the tension surrounding UFC 1, both inside and outside the octagon, revealed one unequivocal truth: when it comes to a no-rules fight between two people, Brazilian jiu-jitsu is the superior art form.

Of course, Royce had a seemingly unfair advantage. Both he and my dad had done their reconnaissance and put it to work against the other competitors. After all of those challenge matches in our garage taking on all comers, the Gracie family knew what to expect, that the fight would end up on the ground, leaving the opponents absolutely lost in Royce's domain.

Incidentally, for several days leading up to the event, there was some real tension at home as well. You see, I was ten years old at the time and not allowed to make the trip to McNichols Arena in Denver to witness the event live. Meanwhile, my brother Ryron, age twelve, got the opportunity to go. I put up a real fuss about it, trying to reverse that decision.

In the end, I watched UFC 1 on pay-per-view, along with approximately 86,000 other households. My only solace came after Royce, who'd lived with us when he first came to the US from Brazil and was more like my older brother, was crowned champion. That next Monday at school, most of my teachers and classmates were talking about it. At some point, I looked in the mirror and asked myself, *Does this mean I'm famous too?*

For centuries, martial artists have debated over which fighting discipline is superior when it comes to real combat. It wasn't until the arrival of the UFC—when the masters of all the most prominent arts were pitted against one another for the world to watch—that this age-old question was answered, once and for all, and we have the Tension Principle to thank for that.

Don't let what you don't know scare you because
it can become your greatest asset.
—Sara Blakely, entrepreneur

Positives vs. Negatives

Off the jiu-jitsu mat, relationships can also suffer and become broken through the tensions caused by overly tight holds. Giving someone edicts—telling them what they can and cannot do—makes it extremely difficult to maintain an enduring relationship. In life, two people are best connected through a less-than-taut hold. Think of relationships as music. Musicians who play stringed instruments know that if they tune their strings too tightly, those strings will break. If they string them too loosely, the sound will not resonate properly. So somewhere in between is probably just right.

The Tension Principle applies to business as well. In fact, businesses often refer to their competing needs as "tensions." For example, there may be internal tensions (opposing forces) between the needs of satisfying customers versus profits, potential growth versus liability, increased advertising versus short-term debt, and introducing new products versus warehousing capabilities, just to name a few. "Creative tension" can inspire incredible innovations. However, circumstances such as this require strong leadership and clearly defined objectives so that brainstorming between departments can be properly channeled. This can lead to the creation of new ideas and unexpected outcomes.

Most of us view daily stress and tension in a negative frame. But can stress actually be good for you? The answer is yes when it comes to *eustress*, which is a positive form of stress, supplying motivation that keeps us moving toward our goals. Imagine studying for a final exam in a class you're doing well in or preparing to be interviewed for a job promotion perfectly suiting your talents. Eustress pushes you to study and prepare, and that little bit of nervousness you feel helps prove that the outcome is important to you. It is the optimal amount of stress for the average person. In a sense, eustress is the opposite of distress, and its presence in our lives is vital to our overall mental health and well-being.

Hold the club as if you had a baby bird in your hand.
—Sam Snead, Hall of Fame golfer

Imagine teaching someone to drive who has never been behind the wheel of a car before. They're terrified of having an accident, so they grip the steering wheel super tight, becoming a "white-knuckled driver." One of the ideas you should explain to them is that gripping the wheel in that fashion will slow down all of their other reactions and defense mechanisms.

This includes the time it would take to release that tension-filled grip in order to take one hand off the wheel to hit the horn in an emergency.

In the sport of golf, driving is also an acquired skill. However, gripping a golf club too tightly can provide some rather negative results when driving a golf ball from a tee. A tension-filled grip can cause weak shots off the head of the club that slice off to either the left or right of the fairway. That's because the hinging of the wrist, which can be severely compromised by tension, is a vital source of power in driving a golf ball.

Baseball pitchers can grip a ball too tightly, limiting the pitch's rotation and movement as the seams slice through the air on the way to home plate. Pitchers can also tip off the opposing team which pitch they're about to throw, be it a curveball, slider, sinker, fastball, or changeup, by the tension of their grip, despite the ball being hidden inside their glove.

Distance runners often experience tension in their neck and shoulders, usually as a result of how they hold their head and rib cage. One popular method of combating this type of tension is to drop or lower the neck, providing short-term relief.

Profile: Teenage Angst to Fulfillment

Born with serious, congenital kidney disease, Tish Das entered adolescence with a good-sized chip on his shoulder. He was a skinny high school kid whose friends didn't always understand the culture that his parents had brought with them to the States from India. In an effort to prove himself physically, Tish, a good student with varying interests, developed a strong passion for sports. But his father, a cardiologist who also doubled as his son's primary physician, flatly refused to let Tish play high school football. "I couldn't win the football battle with my parents, which was probably in my own best interest. But I put up enough of a fuss that they let me join the wrestling team," said Das. "I was still very young and going through physical changes, which probably contributed to a further decline in my kidney function. I barely finished half a season and a nephrologist said absolutely no more contact sports."

Undaunted by the diagnosis, Tish, who was still looking for something to fill a void in his life, turned to martial arts. "I initially studied kung fu under strict supervision. When I was in college, I took the risk and played rugby with minimal protective equipment. Although I was not that good at that sport, my kidney and I survived and the experience helped build my confidence, making me feel much more complete as a person," said Das, who eventually went on to study multiple martial arts, including Brazilian jiu-jitsu.

Then Das learned that he needed a kidney transplant. "I remember that it seemed like my father felt he had failed me. That he'd looked at me too much like his son, believing I'd get better, and not enough as a patient he could view objectively," said Das. Though Tish shares the same blood type as his several siblings, his father, who was sixty-five at the time (the age limit for donating a kidney), decided that he would be the one to give his son the new kidney he so desperately needed.

"His idea was that if I ever needed another kidney in the future, then my siblings could step up. That this was his one chance to do this for me," said Das. "No one knew it at the time, but I made a point of telling my surgeon to put the kidney on my left side, so I could continue training in martial arts (believing I could protect that area better)." Today, Das's kidney function is within manageable limits. He went on to finish graduate school, pursue a successful career, and currently leads a healthy and productive life.

He and his wife, Amisha, have presented his parents with two more grandchildren to spoil. "I know that martial arts really helped me in approaching my mortality by giving me a set of tools to live a better and more complete life," said Das, who applies a protective pad to the left side of his abdomen whenever he's on the jiu-jitsu mat. "Instead of believing I have bad luck or was cursed with this condition, I have the confidence to see it as an opportunity to learn something about myself and continually find ways to address all of the challenges that have been presented to me. I believe that it's all about having a great group of people who can help support you to reach your goals, and then, in turn, it's about continuing to pass that energy on to help others succeed as well."[13]

13 Tish Das interview with Paul Volponi (March 12, 2022).

Reflect on the Tension Principle when . . .

- **Motivating the Team:** Your company employs several dedicated sales reps so you create a strong incentive program to reward top performers, and the tension created by the internal competition ensures the highest output from each team member.
- **Exploring Options:** You're unsure of the right course of action at a significant crossroad in your life, so you decide to play devil's advocate in a healthy debate with a friend to ensure all essential truths are considered before a decision is made.
- **Creating Accountability:** You've failed in your independent weight-loss efforts for years, so you decide to publish your goals on social media in hopes that the tension created through increased accountability will help you stay on track with your goals.
- **Diversifying Teams:** You purposely construct your team with people of varied backgrounds and problem-solving styles to create the healthy tension that ensures challenges are addressed from all angles.

Tension as a Catalyst for Change

In "Letter from a Birmingham Jail," Martin Luther King Jr. speaks of a "constructive nonviolent tension" as an opportunity for social growth and change. Tension can often be the catalyst for those in conflict to open new avenues of communication, to analyze and address their concerns. In his 1963 letter, King states, "I must confess that I am not afraid of the word 'tension.' I have earnestly opposed violent tension, but there is a type of constructive, non-violent tension which is necessary for growth. Just as Socrates felt that it was necessary to create a tension in the mind so that individuals could rise from the bondage of myths and half-truths to the unfettered realm of creative analysis and objective appraisal, we must see the need for nonviolent gadflies to create the kind of tension in society that will help men rise from the dark depths of prejudice and racism to the majestic heights of understanding and brotherhood."

Scan here to learn the combat application of

The Fork Principle

Chapter Fifteen

The Fork Principle

Optimizing outcomes by pursuing win-win equations.

The trap had a ghastly perfection to it.
—Stephen King, author, *The Gunslinger*

In jiu-jitsu, our ultimate goal is to create a dilemma in which our opponent has no positive options remaining and can only choose to submit. We call this the Fork Principle. Why? A fork has multiple prongs or tines. Yet each one delivers the same result. Perhaps you're familiar with the phrase: *Stick a fork in me because I'm done*. That's how we want our opponent to feel on the mat, as if there is almost no sense in continuing the struggle against us. We want to be the architects of their dilemmas. Imagine your opponent, who is trapped beneath you, with only two choices to find an escape. Unfortunately, both of those temporary lifelines lead directly into a pair of equally potent submission techniques with the trap waiting to be sprung.

The hardest part of obtaining a submission is usually applying the very final stages of a particular technique. That's when the opponent senses the end is near and fights with their last ounce of strength to avoid it. But when the opponent chooses one prong over another, their momentum in that direction actually helps to seal the deal. Remember, jiu-jitsu is the art of efficiency, and the Fork Principle is a supremely efficient path to victory.

Consider the River Principle: It's very *reactive* in flowing past potential obstacles. Conversely, the Fork Principle is very *proactive*, limiting the opponent's options in the specific directions of our choice. How can we achieve the efficiency of the Fork Principle on the jiu-jitsu mat? Don't think in limited terms of establishing just a single technique. Instead, become a creator of dilemmas. That requires a certain amount of preparedness and patience to wait and then capitalize on the situations you've created. Experience is also a huge factor. You may set up what you conceive to be a dual-prong dilemma for your opponent. However, someone with more experience, and therefore more vision, may see a three- or four-prong dilemma from the exact same starting point.

A New Way of Thinking

To me, the Fork Principle represents the absolute highest level of jiu-jitsu on the mat. In life, the principle teaches us to pursue optimal outcomes for multiple stakeholders in a given situation. That way everyone involved benefits and can claim a victory, which in turn increases the likelihood of sustainable long-term success for any personal relationship or business initiative. It's not only your classic win-win scenario; it also has the capability to stretch beyond that to a win-win-win or even further, depending on the number of stakeholders and prongs to the fork. Of course, growing up in the Gracie family, the very notion of a win-win situation was completely foreign to us.

During the early days of the Gracie challenge matches, we were solely focused on defeating other disciplines. Our philosophy was that somebody had to win and somebody had to lose, so make sure the loser is *them*. It was a necessary belief for that time period if Brazilian jiu-jitsu was ever going to rattle, disrupt, and gain the foothold it deserved in the martial arts world. That intense rivalry, though, created a very unique relationship for me with these other traditional martial arts. I basically came to dislike and distrust them, as if I were personally involved with karate, kickboxing, or kung fu in a never-ending grapple for superiority. But as I began to mature, develop opinions of my own, and move forward in my thinking, this false feud faded into my personal rearview mirror.

When Ryron and I took over Gracie University, we realized that the overwhelming number of martial arts schools taught traditional arts. And if the hunger for Brazilian jiu-jitsu, spurred on by the triumphs of Royce and our family at the Ultimate Fighting Championships, was ever going to be sated, we would need to somehow find a way to partner with these traditional schools. We couldn't teach classes everywhere at once, so my brother and I decided to start an Instructor Certification Program (ICP) to train other martial artists on how to properly teach our proprietary programs.

We certainly needed to cross a bridge of trust on our part to make this a reality. After all, we had been schooled to believe that these other artists were our heated rivals. Could we really partner with them? Refer to them as our extended family? Ultimately, we set aside our past prejudices and fully embraced the thinking of a new era. The response was incredible and provided us with a deep pool of qualified martial artists with an interest in teaching our courses.

Now, martial arts schools of any discipline can supplement their offerings with Gracie Combatives, Gracie Bullyproof, Women Empowered, and other trademarked programs. Our message to them has always been simple and consistent: Your school is amazing. Just add jiu-jitsu to whatever it is you teach, and you'll undoubtedly attract more students. Three decades ago, it would have been nearly impossible to fathom the idea that traditional martial arts schools would be our biggest allies in both spreading and cultivating the seeds of Brazilian jiu-jitsu. In this era, some of my closest friends run traditional schools. We interact and support each other via the Fork Principle, and as is true with most authentic win-win relationships, each time we partner with a traditional martial artist there is a third beneficiary: the students.

The Squared Board

Jiu-jitsu practitioners aren't the only ones who employ the Fork Principle. Chess players are also masters of reaping its rewards. It is one of the basic tactics in the game and brought into play whenever one "forking piece" simultaneously attacks two or more of the opposition's forces. Lowly but useful pawns can fork bishops and knights, creating an unequal trade of pieces for the opposition. Though all chess pieces are capable of being used in such a tactic, the knight, because of its unique ability to jump over pieces, often cannot be captured by the forces it threatens.

Obviously, forked attacks on the opposing king are the most severe threats and can box the opponent into an inescapable position. When a chess player has no positive options but must move anyway because you cannot pass your turn at chess, it is referred to as a *zugzwang*, a German word meaning "all of the options are bad." The same way a jiu-jitsu practitioner must learn an abundance of techniques to successfully employ the Fork Principle, chess players must have a total understanding of the board and each piece's abilities and value to capitalize on the tactic. If you're not at that level yet, it's certainly something to which you may aspire. After all, every jiu-jitsu and chess master was a beginner at one time or another.

Contracts with Kids

In our everyday lives, we probably don't want to box our family, friends, and coworkers into "no-win" situations. So let's flip the Fork Principle around and see how we can use its nuances to create "win-win" situations for those in our immediate orbit.

Suppose your kids are suddenly having a tough time at school. They normally achieve grades in the range of A–. This semester, however, their report card average is a B–, a full grade lower. They're busy on the weekends with sports and other activities you believe will be helpful in making them well-rounded individuals, so you don't want to disrupt that pattern. Instead, you concentrate on creating study blocks during the weekdays, limiting their TV and non-educational computer time. Your children are not exactly pleased with the new restrictions. That's when you decide to use the Fork Principle in reverse, setting up a contract with your kids so the study expectations and possible rewards are clearly spelled out.

If your kids hold up their end of the bargain, increasing their study hours on weekdays and weeknights, as well as raising their grades, something extra they'd like to have will be in the offing. Perhaps a trip to an amusement park or a party they'd like to host for their friends—something that they want, which is acceptable to you. How is it a "win-win"? No matter what, your kids will benefit from extra study hours. They'll also be assuming more responsibility in their scholastic growth. Both wins.

If their grades go up, the win-win becomes even sweeter. If not, that bargain can be extended to the next grading cycle, another win.

Consider the Fork Principle when . . .

- **Managing Dilemmas:** Your kids are arguing over the last piece of cake, so you give one child the authority to cut it in half and the other child the authority to choose which slice they want.
- **Leveraging Relationships:** You invent a product but you have trouble bringing it to market so you decide to license the underlying technology to a competitor with a stronger distribution network.
- **Fostering Independence:** Your teenage son wants you to buy him a car outright so he can have more independence, but instead you agree to match him, dollar for dollar, if he gets a job and starts working to help pay for his car.
- **Donating:** Your closet is overflowing with clothing you haven't used in years, so you donate more than half to a local shelter, allowing you to help the less fortunate while clearing space at home (plus, you get the tax deduction!).

Scan here to learn the combat application of

The Posture Principle

Chapter Sixteen

The Posture Principle

Identifying the source of the problem, and then targeting your resources accordingly.

Posture for combat is so vital.
—Conor McGregor, former MMA champion

Few things are more important than the posture we assume in life. Are you fully engaged with yourself, those closest to you, and society as a whole? How do you treat the people in your daily sphere? And how do you expect to be treated in return? On the jiu-jitsu mat, we are keenly aware of our own posture. It's something we need to perfect to properly execute techniques, many of which have a preferred posture of effectiveness. But as our jiu-jitsu consciousness expands, we begin to see past ourselves and view our opponent's posture with a more discerning eye. That ability opens the door to putting the Posture Principle into play. Because if *we* need the correct posture to apply a technique, so does our opponent. And instead of being overly concerned about stopping a technique from being applied against us, we can combat that technique at its roots by denying our opponent the needed posture to properly perform it. *Don't defend the submission. Defend the position.*

Oftentimes, successful deployment of the Posture Principle will lean on other core principles, but none more than the Distance Principle and the Clock Principle. Disrupting an opponent's distance and timing will severely hinder their ability to maintain a preferred posture, as well as crippling their efficiency. When an opponent's posture is compromised, they will often try to immediately regain that posture. That's something you can anticipate and seize upon (Creation Principle) to initiate a technique of your own or simply gain a more advantageous position, including an escape. The ultimate goal should be to apply our strongest postures against our opponent's weakest ones.

One Way to an "A"

I attended West High School in Torrance, California, the home of the Warriors. During my senior year, I really buckled down in my classes and was headed toward a 4.0 grade point average for my final semester. It felt like a huge accomplishment since my family hadn't been one to stress academics to their kids, considering that so many of my relatives had made their mark in life through jiu-jitsu. My brother Ryron had urged me to take a keyboarding class as one of my senior electives. He'd tell me: "The world's already all about computers, bro. It's either catch up now or fall way behind." I knew that he was right.

My family was also one of the last in our neighborhood to have a computer in our home. Even as a high school senior, I was writing my essays out in longhand, after which my mom, who once had a job entering police reports for the LA County Sheriff's Department, would type them up for me. So keyboarding was a class that I was super motivated to take and one in which I really wanted to do well. It was being taught by a no-nonsense, straightforward instructor we knew as Ms. D. On the very first day, she informed her students that our grade in the course would come from an average of three sources: classwork, homework, and weekly speed tests that clocked how many words we could type per minute against any errors.

I was diligent and put a lot of effort into improving my skills. Of course, most of the other students, many of whom had spent a good portion of their lives keyboarding, were way ahead of me. Still, I was doing exceptionally well for a beginner. The weekly speed tests were the most frustrating aspect of the class for me. No matter how many times I registered a personal best on those tests, there were always a few students in the class who attained a higher score. Other kids just had more experience at a keyboard than I did, and I had to accept that.

With approximately two weeks remaining in the course, Ms. D sent us each a note telling us the final grade we could expect in the class. Mine read that I should expect a B. I totally disagreed. Both my classwork and homework grades were As. My speed test grade was a B. In my mind they averaged out to an A–. I immediately went to Ms. D, who pulled out her grading book to check my scores. She looked at my pair of As and a B, and without hesitation said, "This grades out to a B, Rener." I responded, "If you do the math, Ms. D, it should be an A–." She just shook her head at me and said, "Over the years, I've probably had close to a thousand students with this same set of grades. I always give a B under these circumstances. That's just the way it is." I could have been snippy about it or stormed off. But I didn't. I stayed focused on my goal, and even though my brother and I wouldn't pen the 32 principles of jiu-jitsu for another two decades, I put the Posture Principle to work by attacking the linchpin of her argument.

Yes, she may have always given that grade for those marks, but mathematically it was wrong. "Let's do the math together, Ms. D," I said, without making it personal. "If an A is a 4 on a GPA scale, and a B is a 3, then my grades add up to 11. When you do the division, the average comes out to 3.66. When you further divide 3.66 by the total possible score of 4.0, you end up with .915, which translates to 91.5 percent score in the class. According to the universal 0 to 100 grading scale in academics, anything from 90 to 100 percent is an A, which is why I believe that 91.5 percent is, at the very least, an A–. Now, I understand that you've been doing it like this for a long time, and I feel bad for everybody else who may have been shortchanged over the years. But giving the correct grade should start today."

The conversation ended there without a committed response from Ms. D. In my mind, I could see myself in student court presenting this same argument to the principal. Only it never came to that. Two weeks later, I had a string of As on my report card, preserving the 4.0 average I had worked so hard for. Today, as I sit here writing this book, my keyboarding skills are excellent, and I know that I have Ms. D to thank for starting me down that path.

Historic Arguments

In a debate context, as with the keyboarding example above, utilizing the Posture Principle often means focusing on isolating the linchpin of the opponent's point of view. This occurs constantly in court cases with trial lawyers attempting to destroy the foundation of the opposing side's argument. Sometimes those cases are about traffic-circle fender benders, property-line disputes, or slips and falls. Other times, they can be much more significant. In Brown v. Board of Education of Topeka, lawyer Thurgood Marshall, who was representing the right of Oliver Brown's daughter to attend a nonsegregated elementary school, argued that the notion of "separate but equal" was inherently unequal, thus violating the Equal Protection Clause, Fourteenth Amendment, and the US Constitution. Marshall continually hammered away at the foundation of the opposition's flawed premise, exposing every crack, fracture, and fissure. On May 17, 1954, the US Supreme Court, a body on which Marshall would eventually serve as a judge from 1967 to 1991, resoundingly agreed with Marshall's argument, voting 9–0 to end racial segregation in public schools.

Profile: Posture at the Piano

Jazz musician Howard Rees has a pair of passions in his life: music and martial arts. Many people, though, wonder about Howard's seemingly conflicting pursuits, considering that a professional pianist's hands are his livelihood. "Sometimes I'm one of the best nine-fingered piano players around," noted Rees, who has either broken or dislocated fingers on several occasions while participating in the world of martial arts.

When did he begin to understand that his dual pursuits had a shared synergy? "I started to recognize the concepts of my music teacher coming from the mouth of my martial arts instructor, and vice versa." Rees, a native of Toronto, Canada, studied piano with jazz great Barry Harris, who played with legends such as Charlie Parker, Dizzy Gillespie, and Thelonious Monk. "Barry used to preach that a jazz musician needed to study a martial art and a second language," said Rees. "I believe that was because those activities use different parts of the brain, and each can help you problem solve in those other areas. In both music and martial arts you need timing, rhythm, balance, and posture, which is especially important for your technique . . . Improvising with other musicians is almost like sparring. You can't approach it as if you know what your partner is going to do. You need an awareness and a self-assuredness to be tuned in and have a [spontaneous] blending."[14] As for Rees's second language? He fully admits his Spanish is "*un poquito*" at best.

Fortunately, good posture, like poor posture, is habit forming.
—Denise Austin, fitness expert

Static vs. Dynamic

There are two types of posture: static and dynamic. Most athletic endeavors demand superior dynamic posture for peak and efficient performance. But if someone doesn't have good static posture (chin parallel to the floor, chest out, shoulders even and back, weight evenly distributed on both feet) when standing at rest, it is certainly more difficult to compensate for that while in motion. Activities such as Tai Chi, yoga, and Pilates promote good posture by strengthening muscles, especially the core. Better posture equates to better overall balance. Reduced lower back pain, an increase in joint flexibility, improved circulation and digestion, and a boost in self-confidence can be the long-term health cache of improved posture. Your seated posture, another type of static posture, is also important. Chin back, shoulders not rolled forward, back fully supported, and feet touching the floor will help ease the

14 Howard Rees interview with Paul Volponi (February 10, 2022).

strain of hours at the wheel of a car or in front of a computer keyboard. Brief walks and switching positions at regular intervals can also lighten the burden on your body.

Dynamic posture is vitally important in both basketball and track (running events). The NBA's all-time leading three-point shooter, Steph Curry, is a prime example of mastering dynamic posture to deliver optimal performance. For a sharpshooter, elbow posture may be among the most important factors in their success. Defenders might take away your space on the court and even have you falling away from the basket on a shot attempt. But as long as a shooter can square his or her elbow (straight up and down) to the target, the ball can be delivered with a light and feathery touch. Upon the shooter's release of the basketball, you'll recognize the result of elbow posture when their wrist falls into a perfect gooseneck.

Suppose you're a runner, and every morning you go out with your next-door neighbor for a three-mile run. You can outsprint your neighbor hands down. You're clearly the faster runner over a shorter distance of ground. However, at the end of every three-mile foray, you finish a good forty yards behind. What might be holding you back is your running posture. Perhaps your stride is slightly pointing east/west instead of north/south. Maybe you're holding your arms too high or too low and failing to properly use them to deliver a rhythmic momentum. Meanwhile, the running posture of your neighbor is nearly perfect. Despite being the faster runner, every little flaw in your posture delivers a less efficient stride than that of your neighbor. And over the course of three miles, it all adds up to you being well behind. Will you ever improve your overall speed to make up the difference? Probably not. But if you improve your posture, you may find that forty-yard deficit being reduced thanks to a more efficient stride.

I want to get old gracefully. I want to have good posture, I want to be healthy and be an example to my children.

—Sting

Recall the Posture Principle when . . .

- **Negotiating:** Your partner is trying to impose a domestic role on you that reflects the way they were brought up, then you point out that their parents divorced after ten years of marriage, so they soften their stance.
- **Eliminating Distractions:** You realize that you have a bad habit of getting distracted by work-related emails during family time, so you turn off push notifications, which eliminates the source of your distractions until you're ready to allocate specific time for work.
- **Repositioning Employees:** A high-achieving employee is losing motivation due to the fact that she is surrounded by colleagues who don't carry their own weight, so you transition her to a role with greater autonomy and performance-based incentives to keep her fire burning.
- **Managing Emotions:** Your child is experiencing behavioral challenges and you suspect it's rooted in their jealousy of the time you're spending with their younger sibling, so you set aside one-on-one time with the older child to balance things out.

Scan here to learn the combat application of

The False Surrender Principle

Chapter Seventeen

The False Surrender Principle

Feigning compliance in the face of adversity, and then seizing the opportunity when it presents itself.

If you surrender to the wind you can ride it.
—Toni Morrison, author

Whether it's on the jiu-jitsu mat or in life, there's nothing better than facing an opponent who is overconfident. Why? Because your opponent may become dismissive of your ability to be victorious. Correspondingly, the False Surrender Principle encourages that type of overconfidence in your opponent, ultimately playing to your advantage. For you to effectively apply this principle, you must have a certain level of confidence in your own abilities, believing that nothing negative will happen through its application, that you are not really abandoning control of the situation but rather subtly taking a less aggressive type of control, one that blends the mental aspects of an encounter with the physical.

Unfortunately, there's a belief held by many jiu-jitsu practitioners that if they're not constantly advancing their position, either moving toward a submission or escaping one, they're falling behind in the encounter and not being efficient. But a false surrender, one in which you choose the appropriate time to send a signal to the opponent that you are defeated, can open a possible window of opportunity (consider the Creation Principle) to propel you forward in the grapple. I often teach this technique to the ladies in our Women Empowered program. If you are tackled or pinned down by a larger male opponent, don't be afraid to speak the words: "I'll do what it is you want, just don't hurt me." This often evokes a response in which the attacker feels he has complete control of the target, so much so that he may even loosen his grip to reposition himself. And that momentary lapse by the attacker can create a much-needed space for the target's succeeding action.

Remember, there is a communication of energy in every position between two combatants. You can dictate your own message, whether it's truthful or not. The False Surrender Principle is extremely synergistic to jiu-jitsu's other core principles. Timing is everything in its proper use (Clock Principle). You must yield while you still have a reserve of energy. Most people only surrender when they're completely out of gas. Your opponent has seen that to be true in past encounters (Reconnaissance Principle). That's why the False Surrender Principle can be so powerfully surprising and effective.

Profile: Standing Up for Myself

My wife, Eve Torres Gracie, is a three-time WWE Divas Champion and master instructor of Gracie University's Women Empowered self-defense program.

"I had just become an official member of World Wrestling Entertainment (WWE) after winning their Diva Search contest (a WWE contract award based on fan voting). At some point in the near future, I knew that I'd actually be inside the ring, wrestling professionals. But first, I needed to learn the ropes. The WWE asked me to go along on their tour of European countries as a reporter and commentator in order to build a relationship with the fans and the athletes with whom I'd be working. It was crazy to think about, but just three months prior, I had experienced my first jiu-jitsu lesson and started dating Rener. I'd been a successful academic and professional dancer. Now, I was on the brink of entering the world of professional wrestling.

"After one of the European shows, most of the wrestlers were relaxing in the lobby and bar of the hotel where we were staying. I didn't know it at the time, but I was about to both receive an education and give one back on how to build relationships with your coworkers. One of the male wrestlers approached me in the lobby and began to playfully harass me about my learning of jiu-jitsu. He had obviously been drinking too much and I was trying to politely end the conversation. His verbal jabs eventually led to some physical poking at my person, trying to get me to display some jiu-jitsu techniques. In the next moment, we were suddenly grappling on the lobby floor.

"This immense wrestler was on top of me, though I had him well secured inside my guard. It was something of which I wanted no part. I was there to get professional experience, not become part of an alcohol-fueled spectacle. Unbelievably, there wasn't any urgency in the crowd to break us apart. The grapple had probably gone on for close to thirty seconds before I used the False Surrender Principle, hoping to end this battle by not fighting back. It was successful. When I stopped fighting, people stepped in and finally pulled us apart (reflecting the mindset of that warrior-culture crowd). As I got up to my feet, I felt my eye beginning to swell. This fool had elbowed me in the face.

"Both the pain and the anger in me were really starting to build. He was being led away by someone and had his back toward me. That's when I rushed him, and the fight was on again. Only this time, it was completely on my terms. I latched onto him from behind, with my legs hooked onto his body. I put him into a rear naked choke and squeezed. The technique cut off his blood supply and I choked him unconscious. As soon as he fell to his knees, I released my hold, and he was snoring on the floor. Within a matter of moments, he was conscious again, trying to figure out what had happened. He didn't have to wonder for too long, because everyone there was rather pleased to inform him exactly how I'd dealt with his obnoxious stupidity. 'You got choked out by a girl!!' I left the lobby for my room that night with the early shadings of a black eye and a newfound respect among my coworkers for both me and the art of jiu-jitsu.

"Note to readers: I strongly advise against putting your jiu-jitsu to the test against an opponent who outweighs you by nearly 100 pounds after only three months of training."

If my mind can conceive it and my heart can believe it, then I can achieve it.
—Muhammad Ali

Playing Possum/The Greatest

The opossum is the only marsupial native to North America. This peaceful animal takes the False Surrender Principle, one of its natural defenses, to the next level by "playing dead" during tense and threatening situations. To lie there totally still while a predator considers you as its next meal means that the opossum, which can also bite and growl as a means of defense, has extraordinary confidence in its ability to deceive a foe. While in this state of playing dead, the opossum even emits a smell of decay from its glands, mimicking the odor of a rotting corpse. Now, that's how to really sell a technique!

Perhaps the best-known example of the False Surrender Principle was performed not on a jiu-jitsu mat but inside a boxing ring. It was superbly executed by one of the most recognizable people to ever set foot on the planet, heavyweight boxing champion Muhammad Ali. In October of 1974, in a fight nicknamed "The Rumble in the Jungle" because it was staged in Zaire, Africa, Ali fought then heavyweight champion George Foreman. During several stages of the fight, Ali, in a protected stance, allowed the six-foot-three, 220-pound Foreman to throw large numbers of punches at him without returning fire. The tactic was later dubbed "rope-a-dope." Most of the blows by Foreman during that sequence were deflected by Ali's gloves. That caused Foreman to expend massive amounts of energy on an extremely hot night, before Ali successfully counterattacked in the later rounds against an exhausted opponent.

The rope-a-dope and succeeding counterattack helped Ali post an eighth-round knockout over his opponent. Immediately after the fight, Ali told commentator David Frost, "Staying on the ropes is a beautiful thing with a heavyweight when you make him shoot his best shot and you know he's not [hurting] you. I gave George two rounds of steady punching, because after that, he was mine."[15] Years later, Foreman would concede of the energy-burning rope-a-dope tactic, "I'm the dope, right here."

You need to trust; to surrender.
—Karen Hackle, author

Profile: Breaking Free with Ed O'Neill

Actor Ed O'Neill, who among his many memorable roles played Al Bundy on Married with Children *and Jay Pritchett on* Modern Family, *is a proud holder of a black belt in Brazilian jiu-jitsu. The noted thespian and comedian also went to training camp with the Pittsburgh Steelers in 1969 as an undrafted free agent after playing college football at Youngstown State.*

When it comes to the False Surrender Principle, there's a moment shared alongside his father upon the family couch that stands out to Ed O'Neill. "We were watching a football game on TV together. It was the Cleveland Browns versus the New York Giants," recalled the Youngstown, Ohio, native. "The great Jim Brown was carrying the football and multiple Giants were desperately trying to tackle him. At one point, Brown was dragging a trio of Giants with him. Then just as Brown fell forward a bit and looked like he was going down to the ground, he surged again, breaking free of the defenders' grasps. My dad told me that was actually a technique in football and other sports: to relax your whole body, and when your opponent senses that, they'll relax too and you can put on another burst."[16]

15 "The Greatest: Remembering the Rumble in the Jungle," The42, the42.ie, October 29, 2014 (accessed on January 31, 2022).

16 Ed O'Neill interview with Paul Volponi (September 14, 2022).

Even famous actors can remain enamored by their childhood heroes. Later on in life, O'Neill gleefully got to meet and strike up a friendship with Jim Brown, the legendary NFL Hall of Famer who also made his mark in Hollywood films and, interestingly, was hired as a color commentator for the UFC, a role he occupied for the first six pay-per-view events.

Establishing New Baselines

Everyone in a committed relationship is probably familiar with mouthing the phrase, "Yes, dear," concerning something we have no intention of ever doing. That may well be the everyday equivalent of a false surrender. But let's take a more practical look at how the concept of a false surrender can actually propel us forward.

By challenging the idea of what it means to be depleted of energy, where the thought of surrender may first enter the competitive mind, we can use the basics of the False Surrender Principle to improve both performance and mindset.

Suppose you're training a group of kids to play soccer and you want to build up their endurance. You might bring them to the beach to train in the deep sand. Why? As you push off, the soft sand gives way, causing some of your potential energy (sometimes called "elastic energy") toward the next step to be lost. Correspondingly, the muscles in the lower extremities will work several times harder, while also engaging the core to maintain stability. Such shared-training methods can give a team of athletes a new baseline, which may far exceed that of the opposition, in what it means to be exhausted. This outcome has also been viewed in athletes who train at altitudes far above sea level (more than 4,000 feet) where they get less oxygen per breath, in places such as Denver, Albuquerque, and Mexico City in order to "trick" their bodies into producing more red blood cells, which will enhance performance when they return to sea level.

Do you know a student who looks at a 250-page book and automatically surrenders to the notion that it's too big to read? Beginning or less-than-confident readers are just like fledgling athletes. You can build up their mental and physical abilities through interval training. You'd never ask a novice to give you 250 push-ups in a single day—or maybe even in a week. Readers need to advance upon their goals slowly, gaining confidence, skills, and redefining what it means to become exhausted by a book (when you read but none of the words stick). Whether it's starting out with ten, twenty, or twenty-five pages in a sitting, a reader's endurance can ultimately grow by leaps and bounds.

Employ the False Surrender Principle when . . .

- **Surviving an Attack:** A man puts a knife at your neck and tells you to get in his car, so you cooperate temporarily just to get the knife away from your throat and then quickly exit the other side of the car when he looks away.
- **Leading Others:** Your team gets blamed for a mistake at work, and you quickly take full responsibility for the error (even though it wasn't your fault), which allows the team to save face while you build your reputation as a leader.
- **Negotiating:** Your spouse asks you to miss your favorite jiu-jitsu class to watch the kids while she gets a massage, and you comply because you plan on asking her to watch the kids all weekend while you surf with your friends.
- **Parenting Strategically:** Your teenage daughter asks for money to go out with friends, and you comply knowing that you're going to use chores around the house as a way for her to earn extra cash in the future.

Scan here to learn the combat application of

The Depletion Principle

Chapter Eighteen

The Depletion Principle

Overcoming resistance through patience, persistence, and pressure.

The world is too much with us, late and soon. Getting and spending, we lay waste our powers.
—William Wordsworth, poet

It doesn't matter if the fight is on a jiu-jitsu mat, athletic field, in a boardroom, classroom, courtroom, or the city bus during your morning commute; the combatants on each side of the equation are burning both physical and mental energy. But are they burning through these resources at equal rates? Perhaps not, and that's where the Depletion Principle comes into play.

Since jiu-jitsu is the art of efficiency, as practitioners, we are wholly committed to having our opponents burn their valuable energies at a higher rate than we do. This was always the main objective of my grandfather Helio, who helped invent Brazilian jiu-jitsu. As part of his superior technical wisdom, he realized that his opponents were going to be bigger, stronger, and more athletic than a smaller, slighter-built practitioner such as himself. So over the course of an encounter, he constantly made it his goal to turn those tables in his favor by lowering his own burn rate and increasing the burn rate of his rivals. That meant he would ultimately be focused on defeating a depleted and mentally frustrated opponent.

How do you implement the Depletion Principle? Slow down the opponent and make every movement for them more difficult. Whether you're on the top or bottom of a grapple, gravity can be your greatest ally in attempting to deplete your opponent. Be heavy with your body weight and holds, frustrating an opponent who'll most likely be focused on moving their own position forward. If the opponent hugs your neck, hug their neck in return and don't let go. Falsifying your conviction to slip out of such a hold, especially if you can properly sell it, will inspire the opponent to invest vital energy in keeping you there. For every ounce of energy that you spend on a technique, a hold, or falsifying a conviction, make sure your opponent spends several times more. You'll be budgeting energy, operating in total control at a discounted value, while you force the opposition to pay full fare. Correctly implementing such a plan will not only drain a rival combatant's energy, but their spirit as well.

Playing the Right Role

In 2004, a father walked his thirteen-year-old son through the doors of Gracie University. The son was an incredibly introverted young man of Mexican descent with penetrating blue eyes named Brian Ortega. His father did all the talking, explaining how his son had been in a few fights and needed to learn how to defend himself better. From the lightly framed boy's first moments on the mats with me during his intro lesson, I was incredibly impressed with his natural ability and believed that he could be a very special jiu-jitsu practitioner. During his first year of study, I had Brian shadow me around the school, giving him responsibilities and a deeper exposure to the art. Though he was still verbally reticent, Brian could beautifully express himself on the mats without hesitation.

At the end of Brian's first year of training, his father came to me and said, "Rener, I'm sorry. But our family can't afford to continue paying Brian's tuition." I wasn't about to lose a student of Brian's potential—a young Luke Skywalker training to become a Jedi knight and discover his true connection to jiu-jitsu's version of the Force. "Don't worry about the tuition," I replied. "Brian's a special student to us, and he'll always have a place here."

At the school, Brian became my literal sidekick, helping me with everything from mopping the mats to assisting me in teaching kids' classes. Then, after two dedicated years of practice, Brian disappeared for the first time. He was gone for several weeks without a word.

On the day that he returned, I ushered him into my office, where he told me about his cousin who'd been killed in a shooting. Brian conceded to me that he was in a gang himself, and not just as a passive member. He was truly immersed in the life. I could imagine what his parents were going through, trying to free him from the strangling grip of the streets. But what I understood about Brian was that he was intensely loyal to his friends and possessed a severe streak of stubbornness. The more we tried to pull him in one direction, the more he would be determined to go the opposite way. Instead of giving Brian a lecture, I offered him my support. And every day after that, I was determined to prove to Brian that there was a better life waiting for him in the future. With his parents' permission, I had Brian begin to accompany my team on teaching trips and seminars. He took his first plane ride with us and slowly started to experience a world outside of his neighborhood.

In approaching Brian's dilemma, I turned to the Depletion Principle. Being a gang member isn't easy. The pressures are immense. They can grind upon you night and day with a suffocating burden. In my heart, I knew that Brian couldn't tote that massive weight forever, that at some point, he would deplete himself. Did I also understand that during this waiting period Brian could die on the streets or be sent to prison? Yes. But being his support and a means of expanding his horizons was by far the best role for me to play, and perhaps the only viable one.

The Depletion Principle took some time in Brian's case. There were several more conversations in my office about his friends who had died on the streets. Eventually, though, Brian's loyalty to his crew started to run out of steam. With encouragement from me and others, Brian became fixated on competing as an MMA fighter. His talent as a martial artist was obvious, and his dedicated rise through the ranks of aspiring featherweights created a new life for him. In 2014, Brian signed with the UFC and won his televised debut. Seven years later, Brian Ortega fought for the UFC Featherweight Championship.

And though he wasn't victorious in the octagon on that night, in my eyes he'd become a champion—by overcoming a lifestyle that had so desperately tried to bury his bright future. I'm grateful to be part of Brian's journey forward, and I'm grateful for the Depletion Principle, which allowed me to remain in his life—not as an opposing force but as a steady means of support.

Brian's POV

Brian "T-city" Ortega is a top-ranked professional MMA fighter for the UFC and a Brazilian jiu-jitsu black belt under Gracie University.

"There's only one time I can remember when Rener took a stance with me. My mom told him that I wasn't going to school anymore. He didn't know that. My mom said to Rener, 'If you really love Brian, find a way to get him back into school.' So Rener sat me down and said, 'No school. No jiu-jitsu.' I was pissed about him taking my mom's side. He'd never done anything like that before. I really rebelled. I didn't go back to GU for maybe a month. I was even thinking that I might never go back. But I missed jiu-jitsu so much. I missed the whole environment there, and doing something I was good at," said Brian, who should have been in his senior year at the time, but only had enough credits to be a freshman. "I was able to get into a continuation school that focused on individual learning. It was a rough road, but I graduated.

"Even when I resisted it at times, Rener always seemed to know exactly the type of support I needed in my life. And he taught me so much more than jiu-jitsu. From finances to friendship and everything in between, so much of who I am today as a man and as a father was shaped by the years I spent with Rener."[17]

Purposeful giving is not apt to deplete one's resources.
—Anne Morrow Lindbergh, author and aviator

17 Brian Ortega interview with Paul Volponi (May 27, 2022).

Profile: Pushing the Limits

As a member of the 25th Infantry Division stationed in Hawaii, Aubrey Aldy, a former high school wrestler, excelled in his two weeks of hand-to-hand combat training. But it wasn't until the squad's first sergeant offered a day off to anyone who could complete the Honolulu Marathon that Aubrey developed a passion for competing and training others to compete in endurance events, including triathlons.

How does the Depletion Principle affect triathletes, who in the case of Hawaii's famed Iron Man (and Woman) competition are required to perform a 2.4-mile ocean swim, followed by a 112-mile bike ride, concluding with a full 26.2-mile marathon? "Depletion can come in many forms such as dehydration, nutrition, and mental fatigue. The brain of someone competing in their first Iron Man competition will probably set up limits, not knowing if this is something they can survive or not. But if you can take that same level of fitness into a second competition, you can almost guarantee a gain in performance with the brain recognizing that you can push harder," said Aldy, who views even those struggling to finish such competitions as part of the top 5 percent of the population in their display of inner resolve. "Pacing is everything. You only have a finite amount of fuel stored, and there's a very specific amount that you can take in and process during the competition. Your level of intensity will dictate how fast you burn fuel. Monitoring that is key so you don't run out of energy."

What sets a great triathlete apart from the rest of a field of competitors? "I've been able to work with some world-class athletes. It's not just their talent [that makes them successful]. It's the perfect storm of talent, tenacity, work ethic, and the ability to dig to the depths that most people might not understand. Not just doing it once or twice, but repeatedly . . . That's where the true mental strength is."[18]

18 Aubrey Aldy interview with Paul Volponi (March 8, 2022).

Waiting It Out/Load Management

How can the Depletion Principle be used in a nonphysical altercation? Suppose you're in a minor disagreement with your neighbor over who should pay for mending a fence that runs exactly down the middle of the property line between your homes. Your neighbor is usually a mild-mannered individual. But all of a sudden, they let loose with a profanity-filled tirade against you, laced with some intermittent physical threats. You have no idea what this is really about, but it's certainly not that fence, which was most likely just a flashpoint for some bigger problem in life. The neighbor's spouse, who's now on the scene, wrangles their significant other back. Other neighbors are coming outside to witness the disturbance. Your next-door neighbor's face is now beet red as the tirade continues. Smartly, you keep your distance. You remain totally silent, saying absolutely nothing that could further ignite the situation. After all, this is no longer a rational debate.

As the time slips past, your enraged neighbor is continually burning energy. It can't go on much longer at this fever pitch. So you remain cool and allow the verbal assault to slide off your back. Less than a minute later, your next-door neighbor, finally depleted of emotional and physical energy, takes a deep breath and stops yelling. Still at a safe distance, you say to your exhausted neighbor, "We'll discuss this fence business another time. I'm sorry it made you so upset." Then you go directly back inside your home with the satisfaction of knowing there was no physical altercation and that no one was hurt.

Baltimore Orioles shortstop Cal Ripken Jr. played in 2,632 consecutive baseball games during a span of 16 years, from 1982 to 1998. Over the last decade, however, pro athletes and sports ownership groups have become highly attuned to the Depletion Principle. That recognition began in Major League Baseball, where most teams used to have a rotation of four starting pitchers who took to the mound once every four days. That was replaced by a five-pitcher rotation. Then came the advent of the pitch count, both in a singular game and an entire season, meant to protect valuable pitching arms from becoming depleted before the playoffs and World Series, and to preserve the length of a pitcher's career.

The NBA soon followed a similar path. Many players and coaches began to embrace the theory of "load management" during their travel-laden 82-game season. That was to prevent players from becoming physically and mentally depleted prior to the NBA's nearly two-month-long playoff structure, in which players could conceivably add another 30 games to their season. The practice became so widespread that the NBA needed to institute guidelines for teams not dressing healthy players after several of the sport's biggest stars decided to sit out nationally televised regular-season games, hurting the ratings.

Distance yourself from negativity or it will deplete your well of optimism.
—Jeff Sheehan, author, marketing consultant

Consider the Depletion Principle when . . .

- **Pursuing Change:** You recognize that morale is low at the office, so you begin hosting monthly team-building events, and although buy-in is low at first, eventually the culture shift occurs and the positivity is palpable.
- **Overcoming Resistance:** You really want your spouse to try jiu-jitsu, but they're anxious about potential injuries, so you scour the internet for several instructional videos that show how safely it can be practiced, and eventually you win them over.
- **Rebuilding Relationships:** Your sibling has ignored you for years because of an argument, so you get in the habit or sending them messages of love and gratitude without expecting anything in return, and eventually they reply and the relationship is rebuilt.
- **Developing Habits:** You and your spouse are determined to adjust your infant child's sleep patterns, so you let the child cry in bed without providing any external soothing, which results in them learning to self-soothe and fall asleep on their own.

Scan here to learn the combat application of
The Isolation Principle

Chapter Nineteen

The Isolation Principle

Leveraging the influence of a crowd and the power of isolation.

No man is an island, entire of itself; every man is a piece of the continent, a part of the main.
—John Donne, poet, scholar, soldier

One of the realities of being in isolation, whether you're hiking solo through a dense forest or you've cut yourself off from the world for several hours to cram for an important exam, is that you're alone, dependent upon yourself without the help of others. On the jiu-jitsu mat, one of our main goals is to isolate an opponent's limb, to leave either that singular arm or leg minus the aid of its accompanying trio of appendages. We want a resource advantage over the opposition, and that's what the Isolation Principle can provide.

In chess, we might trade a pawn for a knight, or a knight for a bishop and a pawn. In the game of human chess occurring on the mat, just like on the squared board, creating a lack of resources (forcing a limb into isolation) will, at the very least, restrict your opponent's mobility, and, at the very best, create the opportunity for a fight-ending submission.

Isolating the Bully

A lot of people probably believe that because I was born into a famous family of fighters, I never had to contend with bullies as an adolescent. They would be absolutely wrong. In middle school and high school, you're always going to get tested by bullies, no matter who you are or whatever cachet your surname might hold. A school's social structure and hierarchy almost demands that such incidents occur. During my junior year at West High School in Torrance, a student named Nick, who considered himself to be a badass and had tormented plenty of other students, seemingly wanted to use my name as a stepping stone to build up his reputation. Though I had never had any heated confrontations with Nick, other students began to approach me saying that Nick was busy running his mouth that he could kick my ass. I've always carried immense pride in my family legacy, but in all honesty, the extent to which I carried that pride in high school would be considered excessive by today's version of myself. I simply wasn't equipped to accept the fact that, after spending my entire lifetime honing a unique skill set, a phantom assault by Nick was going to call my abilities into question. His bragging left a dark cloud hanging over me, so I decided I had to get rid of it.

At school, Nick ran with a clique of kids who were just subservient enough to keep his ego inflated. But rather than approach Nick when he was surrounded by his friends, for whom he might have felt that he needed to play the role of a tough guy, I decided to talk to him when he was alone and isolated from their expectations. I wasn't interested in embarrassing Nick, just setting the matter straight and giving him an opportunity to walk away gracefully. I normally left the school via the back gate because our house was just one block away in that direction. As I headed for the rear staircase after my final class, providence delivered me a gift in the form of Nick standing there alone at the bottom of the steps, probably waiting for his crew. I walked straight up to him and said, "I've been hearing from a few people that you've been bragging that you can beat me up."

Nick had never been belligerent to my face before, and this spontaneous meeting was no exception. He stood there in silence as I continued. "If that's true then I would be glad to give you the opportunity to prove it. Otherwise, you should stop talking like that. It's a little misleading and can create a lot of misunderstandings." Nick eventually replied, "Rener, I never said anything like that. We're good." It was the perfect surrender, powered by the fact that it was just the two of us, isolated from the social pressure of an audience. And to the best of my knowledge, Nick never spoke a negative word or propped himself above me to anyone again.

When dealing with bullies, isolation is often an asset. In other cases, however, a crowd provides value that isolation can't. In actuality, it's the Isolation Principle in reverse. A few months after the incident with Nick, I was at volleyball practice and the coach was running late. Instead of just sitting there waiting, I asked one of my teammates and friends if he'd like to roll, meaning grapple with me on the gym floor. He accepted and I submitted him in about thirty seconds. Another one of my teammates found it hard to believe, so he asked to roll with me next. The result was exactly the same, and just as quick. It caused a little bit of a stir in the gym and more of my teammates wanted to try me. In less than ten minutes, I submitted the remainder of the thirteen volleyball players in that gym. I made sure not to hurt anyone and it was all in good fun, but the display served me well. Word quickly spread of my skill set, and no high school bully ever stepped up to me again. That semester, outside of the academic classroom, I learned the power of what would become the Isolation Principle, and its counterpart, in doing something very publicly.

> *I'm the only one in my family who is deaf, and there are still conversations that go around me that I miss out on. And I ask what's going on, and I have to ask to be included. But I'm not going to be sad about it. I don't live in sad isolation. It's just a situation I'm used to.*
>
> —Marlee Matlin, actress

The Power of Isolation

Isolating a problem is often the best way to attack it. Whether it's an underperforming business, a social process of which we're a part, or even our computer malfunctioning, a systematic approach, such as one taken on the jiu-jitsu mat, can prove powerful. The concept of divide and conquer (which we'll also examine later on in chapter thirty-one's Centerline Principle) can isolate root causes and simplify problem-solving. With a computer, for example, isolating one software and hardware component after another can shrink the bigger picture to a more focused view. That can help us to uncover simple solutions that might have initially been overlooked. Yes, reboot and make sure it's plugged in.

In the classroom, educators and parents often come together to better understand a student's lackluster grades. Through a systematic approach, they might quickly discover that the student suffers from a basic vision or hearing problem before any deeper cognitive evaluations are required.

Social and Workplace Isolation

Team leaders, like teachers and supervisors, can play an essential role in combating the negative effects of social and workplace isolation.

Sometimes a student can feel isolated, even amid a packed classroom full of their peers. Every class of students is a blend of personalities. Not all students have the confidence to raise their hands and share their opinions. It often falls on the teacher's wide shoulders to make sure that a handful of extroverted students don't dominate the classroom discussion, while the quieter students become isolated. To counteract this, teachers will often call on students who don't raise their hands, giving them praise for sharing their thoughts in hopes of building a feeling of connectedness.

Anyone who owns or supervises a business should be concerned about whether their employees are experiencing feelings of workplace isolation. Such a condition will not only cause the employee personal unhappiness but can result in a lack of productivity. Hence, lots of companies invest resources in team-building exercises and even weekend retreats. But what can be done to prevent workplace isolation on a day-to-day basis? Communication is often the key. Those in management positions should foster an environment where the feedback and daily concerns of employees have a suitable forum in which to be heard.

Some people are introverts by nature and simply don't come to work to socialize. So identifying workplace isolation isn't as easy as observing who talks to whom and who doesn't. Speaking face-to-face with employees and hearing their concerns is often viewed as the best way to be vigilant.

Profile: The Duchess of Doom

Allison Fisher has won 79 pocket billiards titles and is regarded as one of the greatest billiards players to ever break a rack of balls. Here, she discusses her sport in relation to several of jiu-jitsu's core principles, including the Isolation Principle, Depletion Principle, Creation Principle, Tension Principle, and Momentum Principle, which is forthcoming in chapter twenty-one.

Two-time Hall of Fame billiards player Allison Fisher not only thrives on competition, but on the fact that in a single-player sport such as billiards, the idea of either advancing in a tournament or going home rests solely upon her own shoulders. "I don't mind the feeling of isolation. As billiards players, we choose that. I grew up playing team sports in school and so much of the outcome rested with your teammates . . . Competing in billiards tournaments can sometimes be a long journey. Yes, you have camaraderie with other players. But most of the time it's about you sitting alone in that chair either pleased with how you're playing or feeling depleted by a shot you didn't make," said Fisher, who grew up in southeast England.

Several of jiu-jitsu's core principles are certainly reflected in pocket billiards, which requires intense focus, a keen sense of touch, and a staggering amount of hand-eye coordination. Obviously, creating shots is key in billiards. "I think some people either see the correct shot on the table or they don't. You have to visualize the shot in your mind first. If you can visually see yourself doing it, then you'll execute the shot well," noted Fisher, who has amassed eleven Player of the Year titles.

Do tension and momentum play a part in a sport where the participants walk around a table? "There's certainly momentum in billiards and that often creates tension . . . In other sports there's usually a ball flying back and forth between players. Our momentum builds one shot at a time through focus and a thoughtful mental process . . . But you know when you're playing well and have another player on the hook. You can sense it and see it in the way they carry their body . . . Even in a tournament that you win, there always seems to be that one close match filled with tension that you could have lost, a match in which you truly needed to grind it out."[19]

Few billiards players wouldn't feel tension and daunting isolation at the sight of Allison Fisher—nicknamed the "Duchess of Doom" in large part for her focused ability to prove victorious in tough matches—chalking up her cue stick on the opposite side of the table from them.

Use the Isolation Principle when . . .

- **Testing Variables:** You want to know what specific changes you can make on your website that will yield increased conversion rates, so you identify a series of variables to test independently to isolate those that will have the biggest impact.
- **Communicating:** You need to have a difficult conversation with a friend, and you believe that the presence of an audience might adversely affect the outcome, so you wait until you're alone with them to talk.
- **Facilitating Growth:** Your child has trouble learning jiu-jitsu in a group environment, so you inquire about getting them some personal training instead.
- **Prioritizing:** You get bombarded with minutia at work daily, so you get in the habit of choosing one important task to complete every day before you check your email.

19 Allison Fisher interview with Paul Volponi (March 22, 2022).

Making an Impression

The artist considers his isolation, his subjectivity,
his individualism almost holy.
—Ingmar Bergman, film director

A bodybuilder will often isolate a muscle group during their training regime to provide greater growth and more chiseled-like detail. A musician might choose to isolate a musical note in a composition so that it really resonates with the listener. This is also true of playwrights and screenwriters, who may script their characters in isolated scenes, hoping their actions and words will make a greater impact on the audience.

During one of the most important scenes of the tragedy *Hamlet*, Shakespeare puts Prince Hamlet on stage alone to share his innermost thoughts through a soliloquy (a monologue addressed to oneself) in a moment that truly binds the character and the audience as one. "To be, or not to be, that is the question: Whether 'tis nobler in the mind to suffer the slings and arrows of outrageous fortune, or to take arms against a sea of troubles," ponders Prince Hamlet, during the internal debate as to whether or not to take his own life.

A modern monologue that has captured the emotions of a wide audience appears in the film *Taken* (2008), in which a former Green Beret, played by actor Liam Neeson, is alone on screen speaking to the faceless voice of his daughter's kidnapper. "I don't know who you are, and I don't know what you want. If you're looking for ransom, I can tell you I don't have money. But what I do have are a very particular set of skills." There are very few forms of communication that are as mesmerizing as an isolated actor standing alone on stage, delivering a supremely powerful speech.

Scan here to learn the combat application of

The Sacrifice Principle

Chapter Twenty

The Sacrifice Principle

Giving up something of actual or perceived value
to gain a tactical advantage in another form.

Success is no accident. It is hard work, perseverance, learning, studying, sacrifice and most of all, love of what you are doing or learning to do.
—Pelé, Brazilian soccer icon

Most people willingly make daily sacrifices in their lives. Whether those sacrifices are made in support of themselves, their family, their country, or society at large, they're usually done out of a strong sense of commitment. You might sacrifice your time, something of monetary value, or possibly even your health for a cause you deem meaningful enough. On the jiu-jitsu mat, the Sacrifice Principle can help you accomplish many things: escapes, submissions, counters, and sweeps. It's normally put into action when all other methods of moving forward have been exhausted. The practitioner offers something of perceived value to the opponent in the hope of gaining a tactical advantage in another form. Sometimes, the proposed offering is something of real benefit to the opponent, especially when the practitioner is in a perilous position with little other choice, but under ideal circumstances, the offering is a decoy.

As the opponent grasps for your apparent sacrifice, you have a chance to create a slim window of opportunity to reverse your fortunes. Correspondingly, on a chessboard, you might relinquish your queen to the opponent, either in a real or a sham sacrifice. A "real sacrifice" doesn't provide immediate benefits. Instead, the player losing the powerful piece stays alive in the match and hopes to gain position afterward. A "sham sacrifice" is usually followed by an immediate checkmate by the player giving up the queen, or perhaps it clears the way for a pawn's promotion to replace it.

Hitting "Send"

I understand that I practice jiu-jitsu, the art of efficiency. But not too long ago, there was a span of four months during which I was virtually paralyzed with indecision. I just kept putting off approaching an assignment I was given, one that had turned into a rather personal quandary. The problem was that I would need to swallow my pride and put aside my ego, a huge sacrifice for a type A personality like me.

Kenny, the professional responsible for promoting our instructional video series *The 32 Principles of Jiu-Jitsu,* on which this book is based, said to me, "Rener, if you want this video series to be a success, for a wide scope of jiu-jitsu enthusiasts to give it a chance, you're going to need testimonials from other experts in the field." It didn't matter that I knew he was right. Hearing that request was like a punch to the solar plexus. My brother, Ryron, and I had worked incredibly hard on the series' development and execution, and we were enormously proud of it. We wanted to share it with the world, but the thought of asking other jiu-jitsu masters for the *favor* of their opinion on our creation was virtually inconceivable to me.

Kenny had no idea about the clannish behavior of the martial arts world, and jiu-jitsu especially. Within Brazilian jiu-jitsu, there are several different affiliations or groups, like different denominations of the same religion, each with its own head instructor, and very rarely do they interact in any significant way, so cross-promoting between these master instructors was virtually unheard of. Most of them had probably grown up in the same way that Ryron and I had—to believe that their brand of the art was correct and everyone else's was wrong, even if that belief was based on a difference of a single technique.

Though I knew a lot about these masters and their accolades, I had never met most of them personally. Would this be the right introduction, me asking for a favor? My ego really began to play tricks on me as I formulated several scenarios of interpretation. If I'm asking them, does this mean I'm below each in stature and searching for their approval? Or will they take it to mean that I see myself as superior, having co-created a jiu-jitsu series on which they should have a praiseful comment?

After four weeks of hearing all of this amplified inside my own mind, I finally decided to sacrifice my pride and approach the jiu-jitsu teaching elite. I wrote a personalized email to each master, acknowledging that I knew their time was valuable. I made sure to stress how a series like ours, focusing on principles and not techniques, for practitioners from novices to black belts, had never been attempted before. As for that part about me knowing their time was valuable, I suppose I included it as an easy out for someone to say they were just too busy. But it was also there to protect my ego in case I was turned down, so that my sacrifice didn't come back to sting me too hard.

Eventually, I swallowed hard and hit "Send." Two seemingly longer-than-usual days later, the first response came back in the affirmative. Then the next response and the next after that in what became a succession of world-class jiu-jitsu experts happy to review our series. I was simultaneously shocked and thrilled. Sometime after that, their enthusiastic video reviews of the series arrived. In my heart, I know that their endorsements helped open the door to a wider audience, and for that I'm eternally grateful.

Within the first 72 hours of commercial availability, *The 32 Principles of Jiu-Jitsu* generated over $1 million (USD) in sales, making it the most successful martial arts instructional video launch of all time. The experience of approaching these masters taught me a powerful life lesson. The mental anguish and time I had squandered during my internal debate was simply about my ego, nothing more. The Sacrifice Principle, though I refused to see it at first, served me perfectly. I sacrificed something of perceived value, my ego and pride, to gain something of equal or greater value, the respect and opinions of others.

As for the possibility of "having it all," career and family with no sacrifice to either, that is a myth we would do well to abandon . . .
—Sonia Sotomayor, US Supreme Court justice

Your Own Business

If you have a desire to become an entrepreneur and start your own business, then the Sacrifice Principle will undoubtedly be part of your future. A real entrepreneurial spirit will include making sacrifices in many areas of your life during the first several years of work, while you struggle to gain position in the marketplace. Unless you retain a previous job concurrent with beginning your business venture, you'll certainly be sacrificing security. Yes, you're the boss, and you obviously won't fire yourself, but that still doesn't guarantee you a paycheck. In fact, even when your business is scraping by economically, you'll probably be sacrificing wealth in terms of the benefits a more established company might provide. There's also no time clock for the boss. You'll always be on call to address any situation that arises. That will mean a sacrifice of your time, as well as a definite blurring of the line between your work and personal life. So your family will be making a sacrifice of time too, even if that's just time away from you. Entrepreneurs know all about the Sacrifice Principle, because they live it every day.

Profile: Conquering the Iditarod

Sled dog teams are handled by human mushers, who have a lot more in common with jiu-jitsu practitioners than most people would believe at first glance. The Sacrifice Principle, Depletion Principle, and Isolation Principle are referenced below. But there are also strong parallels to the Connection Principle (with their dog team), River Principle (traveling a course presenting natural obstacles), and Clock Principle and Velocity Principle (racing at the right speeds) for these mushers during a race.

The Iditarod Trail Sled Dog Race is Alaska's most prominent sporting event. It presents a grueling challenge for both mushers and their teams of Alaskan huskies, which must traverse over 900 miles of wilderness from Anchorage to Nome, often in the face of frigid temperatures and frozen tundra, on an excursion that normally lasts anywhere between eight and fifteen days. The concept of "sacrifice" is something of which the participants are fully aware. "It takes a lot of time to prepare for something like this and you have to accept that you can't become a competitive musher overnight. It's a lot of time away from your family and other pursuits. And you're also tied to your dogs, who'll be with you until they're fifteen or sixteen years old. So it's a huge sacrifice and commitment," said Anna Berington, a Wisconsin native; she and her twin sister, Kristy, have become mainstay mushers in the Iditarod over the last decade.

"Our training starts in late summer with two- to three-mile runs with our dog teams every day," said Kristy Berington, who like most mushers, possesses a high tolerance for the cold and being uncomfortable. "Eventually, the dogs need to run 100 to 120 miles a day during the Iditarod, so we build their stamina up to that through middle-distance races held in January. Then in February, there are due dates by which we have to pack up and ship all the supplies we'll need, including dog food and human food, for a nearly 1,000-mile race."

Anna and Kristy try to run their teams together during the Iditarod, supporting one another on the arduous and sometimes treacherous trek. Do mushers and dog teams ever deplete their energies? "There's certainly an ebb and flow of energy out there, for sure. That's why the rules state that you can start with a maximum of fourteen dogs and must finish with a minimum of five," said Anna. "Our main concern is always the dogs. If something doesn't look right with an individual, that dog is going home. As a musher, you're the weakest link on the team. We're always the most tired. But you eventually become trail hardened to the routine of running six to eight consecutive hours and then seven or so hours of rest in which the mushers might be lucky enough to get forty-five minutes of sleep after tending to the needs of the dogs."

For the front-running teams and mushers racing ahead of the large pack, the feeling of isolation on the frontier can be quite overwhelming. But there's also a positive to being in such a situation. "It can be a really cool feeling to be alone in the middle of nowhere with your dog team," said Kristy, who plays the role of coach, nutritionist, therapist, and parent to her competitive canines. "It's pitch-dark outside and you turn your headlamp off. Your path is lit by the moonlight, stars, and aurora above. You can't see any artificial light at all. It's really an amazing sight."[20]

It is not the mountaintop we conquer, but ourselves.
—Sir Edmund Hillary, among the first party to reach the summit of Mount Everest

Remember the Sacrifice Principle when . . .

- **Driving Sales:** Your company wants to attract new customers, so it offers one of its best-selling products at a massive discount with hopes that the new customers will continue to purchase other regular-priced products after the sale is over.
- **Parenting Teenagers:** You want to get a new car, but rather than sell your existing car, you decide to give it to your teenage son under the condition that he get a job to pay for the insurance and gas on his own.
- **Missing Out:** Your friends drink and party every night after work, but you decide to start doing jiu-jitsu instead, so even though it's less time with them, you're learning a new skill and getting in better shape with every class.
- **Providing:** You work two different jobs during the winter months, so that you can enjoy some time off with your family over the summer.

20 Anna and Kristy Berington interview with Paul Volponi (March 30, 2022).

The Decoy Touchdown

Here's an example of the sham or decoy sacrifice beautifully translated into the game of football:

While deep in opposition territory, with just twenty-five seconds remaining in a game in which the Miami Dolphins desperately needed a victory, Hall of Fame quarterback Dan Marino hurriedly brought his teammates to the line of scrimmage. Conventional wisdom called for Marino to spike the ball into the ground in order to stop the running clock, preserving precious seconds from ticking away. As Marino received the snap from center, he stood straight up, and for a brief instant, angled his shoulders toward the ground as if he were about to sacrifice the play via a spike. The opposing New York Jets defense took the bait and relaxed for a moment. In the next instant, Marino fired the football to one of his receivers for a game-winning touchdown, perfectly synergizing the Sacrifice Principle with the False Surrender Principle and the Clock Principle.

Scan here to learn the combat application of

The Momentum Principle

Chapter Twenty-One

The Momentum Principle

Recognizing where things are headed and knowing where things need to go.

When you're that successful, things have a momentum, and at a certain point you can't really tell whether you have created the momentum or it's creating you.
—Annie Lennox, singer

We are all familiar with the concept of momentum. Whether it's swinging our arms for added ease of motion when we're walking and jogging, or arching our shoulders forward then back as we rise up out of a chair, we understand how using momentum makes us more powerful and efficient. In jiu-jitsu, the Momentum Principle teaches us to capitalize on the momentum of a physical mass in motion. Remember, jiu-jitsu is the art of efficiency, so we always need to be attuned to free energy sources, especially when your opponent is the one generating the momentum. The momentum upon which you capitalize can also be generated by you, or you may be the source that provokes your opponent into providing that momentum. So right away, you'll notice the obvious synergy of the

Momentum Principle with both the Velocity Principle and the Creation Principle.

Catching a Meaningful Wave

In life, momentum can be an incredibly powerful force, a curious one too. You might hitch a ride on the momentum of some natural event unfolding in front of you, or you may be swept along by the momentum of an event that you put into motion yourself. Either way, the ultimate destination at which you arrive might be richer and more satisfying than you had imagined.

In 1995, my father sold his stake in the Ultimate Fighting Championship, right after UFC 5. Over the succeeding years, the UFC has experienced some highs and even drastic lows. It changed ownership twice more before taking the fight and entertainment world by storm, exploding into a $7 billion corporation that's currently traded on the stock exchange. When my brother, Ryron, and I came of age, we decided that becoming professional fighters wasn't how we were destined to make our marks on the world. Instead, we dedicated ourselves to teaching and cultivating the art of Brazilian jiu-jitsu, with an energy and desire to achieve that goal in multiple new formats.

Feeling a closeness to the UFC, we began creating YouTube videos called *Gracie Breakdowns*, in which we illustrated important aspects of the previous night's card of UFC fights, especially how they related to jiu-jitsu. Realizing there was just so much that the average viewer didn't understand about how each technique either came to fruition or perished on the vine of an ill-conceived setup, we were stoked to lend our knowledge to fans everywhere. Those videos eventually became our most powerful marketing vehicle, having amassed nearly half a billion views across all our social media channels.

Building upon the momentum of the *Gracie Breakdowns*, we started to include our insights on street fights, random attacks, and other viral videos, discussing how the innocent victims might have defended themselves better through simple techniques or perhaps even defused the conflict before it occurred. Then we saw the video of Austin McDaniel, a twelve-year-old boy from Indiana who was viciously attacked from behind at his middle school and knocked unconscious. That's when a lot of things changed for us. Yes, our Gracie Bullyproof program was being taught to children across the country. But witnessing what happened to Austin made us want to do even more. Ryron and I felt compelled to contact Austin's parents, though not just with a message of consolation. This would be an invitation for Austin and his entire family to come to California, all expenses paid, and train with us for a week. We wanted to make sure that this singular incident, in which Austin held zero fault, didn't define his future.

It wasn't easy to convince his parents. They were rightfully very protective and had been receiving an abundance of advice from family, friends, and strangers after the video of the attack went viral. So we felt both proud and privileged when they decided to trust us during this incredibly difficult period in their lives. Austin came to California and had an amazing week of training. He simply shined on the mats, returning home with a newfound confidence in himself.

With the family's permission, we video recorded *Austin's 1-Week Transformation* and shared it on YouTube. It has been viewed over three million times. More importantly, countless families who are suffering from bullying have been inspired to enroll their children in the Gracie Bullyproof program after seeing how profoundly the experience turned Austin's life around.

Since his time at Gracie University, Austin has graduated high school and decided to serve his country by joining the Marine Corps. There have been other young victims of violence and their families who've accepted a similar invitation and taken that weeklong journey with us, just a start on their road to recovery. How did these special young people come into our lives? For me, the answer is the Momentum Principle, a testament to how the motion of one event can lead you to the open door of another. And I'm thankful to jiu-jitsu for helping me to become part of the world's movement in that way.

Matthew McDaniel's POV

"When we first got the Gracies' message, I was skeptical," said Austin McDaniel's father, Matthew. "I'd grown up in a nonviolent household and that's what I wanted to teach Austin. We really researched the brothers and their work with kids. The last thing we wanted to do as parents was put our son in a bad situation after he'd been attacked, and possibly make things worse. But I learned that jiu-jitsu was nonviolent. They wanted to teach Austin the skills to restrict someone who was threatening him, to take that person to ground if necessary and say, 'Are you going to leave me alone now?' So we decided to go as a family.

"Austin really took to the jiu-jitsu. I could see that his self-confidence was returning. Before the trip, he was asking to be homeschooled. But after that week of training, Austin said, 'Dad, I want to go back to school. I'm not going to let anyone steal that experience from me.' I was so grateful for the turnaround that I've sponsored other kids, who have been in situations similar to Austin, to make that same trip to learn from Ryron and Rener at Gracie University."[21]

Austin McDaniel's POV

"Martial arts changed my life. Before the training, I just saw myself as a fat kid with a lot of hair. I weighed something like 240 pounds as a twelve-year-old. But that week in California with Rener and Ryron built momentum in my life. When I got back home, I wanted to do more things. It was the catalyst for me starting to work out, and wanting to go more places. It's what led me to become a marine, which is a big title to hold, and now I'm looking to join the army to work in aviation. The kid who jumped me? I never saw him again. But if I met him today, I'd shake his hand. Without him doing what he did to me, I don't know where I'd be. Before the assault I used to be sort of antisocial and just played video games. And I'm extremely happy with the place where I am right now. In a strange way, he caused the forward movement in my life."[22]

21 Matthew McDaniel interview with Paul Volponi (February 7, 2022).
22 Austin McDaniel interview with Paul Volponi (February 8, 2022).

Never surrender to the momentum of mediocrity.
—Marlon Brando, actor

Blending the Physical and Psychological

Momentum can have a powerful effect on many different facets of life. You can feel it in a courtroom when a talented trial lawyer begins making substantial point after point in front of a jury. One candidate running for office might clearly outdebate the other just days before an election, causing a surge in public momentum to be the deciding factor. Through the early stages of the COVID-19 pandemic, companies that specialized in home workout equipment gathered strong momentum and surged in the marketplace.

How can we make use of the Momentum Principle in our daily activities? Well, the relevant follow-up questions should be: Where does momentum that is not generated through physics come from? And what is the relationship between that ethereal type of momentum and Newton's mathematics-driven model? There's plenty of evidence to support the idea that momentum in the daily application to our lives is as much psychological as it is physical.

Consider a sports stadium packed with cheering people. It isn't difficult to isolate a point in an athletic contest when the momentum appears to change, suddenly favoring one team over the other. It's commonly called a "shift in old mo." That sweep of momentum, like the swell of an onrushing wave moving swiftly toward the shore, seems to lift up one team and its fans, carrying them to victory. Of course, something had to tangibly go well on the field to trigger that shift—perhaps an outstanding defensive play or scoring drive was the catalyst.

Suppose you're at work and you give an incredible answer at an important meeting. The boss praises you and then asks for more details. In rapid succession, you provide several more insightful points that leave everyone in attendance thinking, *There's someone who really understands this topic.* Did your initial answer help create a flow for you to continue on? Undoubtedly so. But you didn't pull any of those answers out of thin air. You were prepared to succeed by having a great grasp on the material in the first place.

Correspondingly, that team on the athletic field couldn't solely rely on the shift in momentum, both on the sidelines and in the stands, they still needed to execute on the field to win. It appears that recognizing opportunity, talent, and preparedness creates a blending that fosters the growth of momentum in our lives.

Consider the Momentum Principle when . . .

- **Fostering Growth:** Your child has reached an age where they love trying new things, so you go to great lengths to support as much exposure as possible in hopes that they find the activities they want to commit to in the long term.
- **Leveraging Success:** Your company has a product that is going viral on social media, so you optimize your website to capitalize on all the organic web traffic.
- **Chasing Goals:** You're achieving your weight-loss goals faster than you expected, so you invite several friends to join a fitness group to provide motivation for others while keeping the momentum going for yourself.
- **Supporting Others:** Your spouse got fired from their job and is lacking confidence, so you get online and begin looking at job posts they might like in hopes of helping them build momentum in a new direction.

To every action there is an equal and opposite, or contrary, reaction.
—Sir Isaac Newton

Grappling with Physics

Sir Isaac Newton, the eighteenth-century physicist and self-described "natural philosopher," would have certainly been an advocate of jiu-jitsu's Momentum Principle. In his principle of conservation of momentum, Newton states that in an isolated system (which could easily be a pair of jiu-jitsu practitioners mid-grapple), two objects that collide have the same combined momentum before and after the collision.

That means momentum is not destroyed in this type of collision but rather transferred between two objects, such as our pair of grappling practitioners. An example of this in baseball would be when a pitcher releases a 90-mile-per-hour fastball, the momentum of the ball is ultimately transferred to either the hitter's bat or the catcher's mitt. That's why a pitch with more momentum can fly farther off a baseball bat than one with less momentum. But if the batter swings and misses, it will also produce more of a sting in the palm of the catcher's gloved hand.

Scan here to learn the combat application of

The Pivot Principle

Chapter Twenty-Two

The Pivot Principle

Changing your perspective on a person, product, or process to increase your effectiveness.

Good art is art that allows you to enter it from a variety of angles and to emerge with a variety of views.
—Mary Schmich, Pulitzer Prize–winning journalist

Jiu-jitsu techniques are predicated on a trio of important factors: distance (Distance Principle), balance (Pyramid Principle and Kuzushi Principle), and angles. That leads us to the Pivot Principle, which focuses on using the mathematics of angles to increase the effectiveness of our techniques. Mastering the angles within an encounter will give you the mechanical advantage of having more leverage, equating to increased power. You can also pivot, or change the angle of attack, to put your opponent off-balance. Pivoting around a center point will increase pressure on the opposition in the same way a tourniquet placed around a damaged limb can restrict the flow of blood. Defensively, you can use the Pivot Principle to counteract an opponent trying to gain these same advantages over you. That's accomplished by never relinquishing the superior angle during a grapple. Most of us are familiar with the Pivot Principle as it applies to our daily world. We're constantly pivoting in our quest to attain the mental framework that will optimize our outcomes in our relationships, social lives, and business ventures.

From Dream to Reality

Sometimes changing your perspective, taking a new angle on what you've been studying for a while, can completely transform your reality and your results. When the idea for Quikflip, a hoodie that transforms into a backpack (see chapter nine), came to me, I had a vision in my mind that it would be perfect for theme parks like Disneyland. Think about it. You're standing in a long line for an attraction. One minute you're cold. The next minute you're in the sun and it's too hot. The choices are either hold your conventional hoodie or tie it around your waist, unless you want to sacrifice your spot in line and trek back to the lockers. That's where I envisioned Quikflip satisfying a real need and making people's lives more convenient.

Six months into its invention, we had already sold thousands. Fast-forward another six months and I'm standing on that entrepreneurial carpet pitching the product on *Shark Tank* to a national audience. Though the TV deal with Lori Greiner was never finalized, Quikflip received incredible exposure and we sold a ton of hoodies. Still, I knew we weren't quite there yet. In my mind, I could see the peak of the mountaintop ahead in the distance. That's where I wanted to take Quikflip.

But despite every ascending step I took over the next several years, I wasn't getting any closer to that goal. And at times, that lofty peak became so shrouded in clouds of doubt that I began to wonder if it was attainable at all. Then there came a call from Warner Bros. Studios. They wanted 3,500 Quikflips emblazoned with their iconic company logo. Over the next few months, there were similar requests from Google, Intel, and Equinox. Suddenly, it became amazingly clear to me. Quikflip didn't need to exist solely as an apparel brand. It was an apparel technology with a patented design that would allow companies twice the function and twice the branding opportunity when compared to the regular sweatshirts they were used to. I had been focusing on selling Quikflips direct to retail consumers one at a time. But the better business, by far, was wholesaling large volumes to companies who would then sell the custom-branded Quikflips to their own customers or distribute them as corporate gifts to their employees.

Almost immediately, my partner and chief operations officer, Jordan Talmor, and I pointed Quikflip in that new direction. We attended the largest promotional products trade show in the country and pitched the product to potential corporate buyers for three days straight. Every single person who walked by got an up-close introduction to the magic of Quikflip presented with the same "Renergy" that worked so well on *Shark Tank.* Every five minutes a new crowd of astonished onlookers gathered, and as soon as the pitch was over, they lined up to buy samples to take home and show their colleagues. Fun fact: During each eight-hour day on the bustling trade-show floor, not only did I not sit down once, but I never went to the bathroom. Even though I drank several bottles of water each day, I was sweating so much that I never actually had to pee.

The response from these trade shows exceeded our expectations and the orders started to come in fast. Among our new clients were Amazon, which asked for Quikflips made to represent each of their employment divisions, and Universal Studios, which wanted its *Ghostbusters* and *Jason Bourne* logos on our product. Then it happened. My initial vision, before Quikflip even had a name, came true. Disney opened the Avengers Campus at both their California Adventure Park and at Disney World in Orlando. To commemorate the grand openings, they produced the first-ever Avengers Quikflip and offered them for sale at the parks.

I opened my eyes and I was suddenly standing on that mountain peak admiring the once-in-a-lifetime view of the moment your dreams become a reality. My vision of how people at theme parks would make perfect use of my hoodie/backpack invention had come full circle, from my mind to *Shark Tank* to the years spent afterward trying to find the right approach. It had all hinged on a single pivot, giving me a new angle and a clearer perspective on the massive opportunity that had been there all along.

Profile: Poker Face

Pivoting at the poker table? You bet. Poker star Maria Ho is a master of the pivot with over $5 million in live tournament winnings to prove it. "The thing that elite poker players do best is they pivot. They're able to adjust and adapt to any type of dynamic or situation at the table on the fly. Lesser players have a problem deviating from their planned strategy but the best players can maneuver when things don't turn out the way they expected," said Ho, who studied hapkido as a teen, advancing to the rank of purple belt. "Both martial arts and cheerleading taught me respect for my teachers and coaches. To respect people with more knowledge than me. To surround myself with people like that and learn from them."

Part of Ho's discipline at the table consists of her ability to "play in position," utilizing jiu-jitsu's Distance Principle, Frame Principle, and Posture Principle. In simple terms, playing in position means betting last, giving you a more complete view of what's going on in a particular hand. "Poker isn't about the cards that you're dealt, it's about making the most out of the situation you're in, and taking advantage of your position at the table is one of them."

How might jiu-jitsu's Prevention Principle be witnessed around a poker table? "In tournament play, your strategy varies based on your chip stack. There can be stages of a tournament when you're just in survival mode. You're not trying to be the table captain or the most aggressive player. You're just trying to survive to the next stage," noted Ho, who participated in season three of *American Idol* and made it to Hollywood Week of the singing competition.

Is there a parallel between bluffing at poker and the False Surrender Principle? "Maybe someone gets caught bluffing. Well, they might want to be seen as this huge bluffer because they want to capitalize off that image later. You need to observe what your opponents have done and what they've seen you do. If you know how they perceive you, you may be able to manipulate that image to your benefit later on." Of course, Ho is always practicing the Reconnaissance Principle on the opposing players at her table. "I like feeling players out, studying their personality traits, as well as talking and interacting with them to determine how they may approach the game." Has that ability helped the perceptive Ho relate to people in both real life and during her stints as a TV commentator? "It has made me a better listener. I think I understand subtext better than most people. To hear and engage with people on a deeper level? I think it's definitely helped. But I'm also a little bit skeptical of people in real life, just a healthy amount, probably because poker has made me wary of them bluffing."[23]

The Workplace

Pivoting in the workplace is very common. Over an extended period of time, little stays the same in the free-flowing world of business. People pivot in midcareer for many reasons including economics, potential advancement, new opportunities, and personal fulfillment. Just like on the jiu-jitsu mat, understanding the synergy of your many talents will enable you to reflect them onto new tasks in a different work-related arena. And though you may technically be a novice in a particular field, your overall experience and the superior angles at which you choose to apply that knowledge will boost you far above the title of "newbie." Of course, sometimes it's not a person who's pivoting but rather an entire organization.

Consider Smith Corona, a company once recognized for manufacturing some of the world's best typewriters. What's that you say? You don't own a typewriter? Well, that's why today, Smith Corona is better known for manufacturing thermal ribbons used for barcodes. Smith Corona is a perfect example of a company that pivoted to survive. How do companies know when to pivot? Often the industry they're part of completely changes (like typewriters being replaced en masse by computers). But there are also more subtle indicators. Maybe their customers are currently more in support of the competition. It could be that their sales have plateaued or that only one of their many products is relevant in the marketplace.

23 Maria Ho interview with Paul Volponi (April 8, 2022).

There are many brands and companies with which we're extremely familiar that viewed the warning signs and pivoted to choose the best angle for success. For example, Twitter, which began as Odeo, was a network where people could find and subscribe to podcasts. But after iTunes seemingly cornered the podcast market, the outfit reinvented itself as a micro-blogging platform and became Twitter. Another example can be seen in Starbucks, which started off by selling coffee beans and espresso makers in the early 1970s. But by the 1980s, company CEO Howard Schultz, who'd taken an eye-opening trip to Italy, decided to pivot and have his stores emulate European-style coffeehouses, which naturally brewed their own coffee for sale. The rest is java history.

Perhaps you've heard of Nintendo, the Japanese multinational company that is responsible for developing iconic video games such as *Donkey Kong* and *Super Mario Brothers*. However, before making the pivot to video games in 1966, the company produced vacuum cleaners, playing cards, instant rice, and even started a small hotel chain. Could you imagine Mario and Luigi coming to fix the leaky faucet in your hotel room?

When I am performing live, I walk into a room, and I just try to get a feel for the vibe, and I am coming from different angles musically.

—Grandmaster Flash, DJ and rap artist

Kareem in the Pivot

In basketball, the player at the center position is referred to as being in "the pivot." That's because the center traditionally plays with their back toward the basket on offense, establishing a "pivot foot" off which the player can change angles, spinning either right or left. Upon his retirement, Kareem Abdul-Jabbar, perhaps the greatest player to ever occupy the pivot, had scored the most points in NBA history at 38,387. (LeBron James is currently closing in on that mark.) Despite his seven-foot, two-inch frame, Abdul-Jabbar moved like a gazelle in the pivot, faking left with his shoulders, then spinning right to shoot, or vice versa. He could release the ball off his fingertips with a feathery touch using both his right and left hand, executing a shot he called the "skyhook."

Abdul-Jabbar was a martial arts student as well, studying for several years with Bruce Lee, who preached the concepts of efficiency and explosiveness to him. "I took it to heart. I dedicated myself to preparation by maintaining complete focus during basketball practice and my training with Bruce. As a result, I became stronger, faster, and a much more intense player," said Abdul-Jabbar. "Bruce was an innovator and caused martial arts to move forward . . . The skyhook is the embodiment of an efficient shot that requires minimal movement but sudden speed."[24] The center even appeared in Lee's final film *Game of Death*, in which he serves as a larger-than-life-sized opponent for Lee during a five-minute fight scene.

Acknowledge the Pivot Principle when . . .

- **Marketing:** You've been marketing your product to a specific demographic and getting marginal results, so you decide to test your product with new audiences to determine the best path forward.
- **Influencing Decisions:** Your child is experimenting with illegal drugs, so you arrange for them to get a tour of the maximum-security prison, which causes them to pivot and reconsider the path they're on.
- **Saving Relationships:** Your relationship is suffering and you are desperate for a solution, so you agree to attend couples therapy in hopes a doctor can provide a neutral perspective that may help repair the relationship.
- **Adapting to Change:** A global health pandemic drastically affects how people interact in social settings, so your company is forced to completely reconsider the customer experience in your retail stores.

Cock your hat. Angles are attitudes.
—Frank Sinatra

24 Luke Norris, "How Kareem Abdul-Jabbar Used What He Learned Under Bruce Lee On and Off the Basketball Court," sportscasting.com, June 1, 2020 (accessed on February 7, 2022).

Pivotal View

Many different types of people search for a reason to feel good about themselves. For better or worse, in an ultra-competitive society, we often view ourselves in relation to others. That potential for having to cope with feelings of inferiority has led social psychologists to observe a remedy called the "status pivot." It comes about when someone readily admits, "It's true. My neighbor's house in much bigger than mine. But my garden puts theirs to shame." It's a mindful pivot, revealing the truth as *we* need to see it.

Scan here to learn the combat application of

The Tagalong Principle

Chapter Twenty-Three

The Tagalong Principle

Identifying trends, innovations, and opportunities that will help you reach your goal with greater efficiency.

You see, I don't know how to ride a motorcycle, actually.
—Henry Winkler, a.k.a. The Fonz

Within a grapple, there are usually plenty of "free ride" opportu-nities for practitioners who can successfully take advantage of our next principle, the Tagalong Principle. A free ride, or tagalong, occurs whenever your opponent moves in a particular direction, whether of their own choosing or because you provoked that movement, and you force them to carry your body weight as well, a concept that epitomizes efficiency. How does this synergize with the principles we've previously encountered? Consider the Depletion Principle and how your opponent will burn excess energy carrying your weight, while you conserve precious resources. To maximize the frequency and effectiveness of these rides, recall everything you learned from both the Connection and Detachment Principles, using the more than thirty body parts that can create a connection to your opponent. Make sure that the connectedness is more relaxed than rigidly sticking to your opponent like a wet blanket, weighty but not so heavy that your impending movements can be read in real time.

Role Models

The Tagalong Principle was an important part of my adolescence. It was something I absolutely leaned on in order to separate myself from the crowd, set my own course in life, and resist peer pressure. By the time I reached the eighth grade, a trio of my friends had started drinking and smoking weed. Of course, they wanted me to join them. That's the way it always seems to be when teens get involved with drugs and alcohol—they want company. The more the merrier, and the more people to share in the risks and potential blame.

I grew up in a household where my parents never drank alcohol or used recreational drugs. Instead, we achieved our physical and mental highs through the art of jiu-jitsu. It was a model that both my grandfather and father had displayed for all of their children. In essence, it was the Tagalong Principle. The parent sets the example, and quite naturally, young kids want to follow along, emulating what they see. I'm not naïve to the world. I know there are plenty of circumstances that can derail and sidetrack a promising journey, no matter the example set at home, and there are also those who lacked a positive role model growing up yet still found their way clear of obstacles and unhealthy addictions.

As for me, I never wanted to disappoint my family. That was a huge part of the reason I declined the offer to pursue the path my peers were on. I simply wouldn't have been able to face my parents and my grandfather. I held too much admiration for them. But there was something else that helped me with that choice. Training as a martial artist gave me the confidence and self-esteem to stand on my own two feet, apart from whoever was considered the "in crowd."

Before we got married, Eve and I had a serious conversation. I wanted to maintain a dry household with no alcohol allowed. But Eve had come from a family in which wine might be on the table during dinner, or champagne uncorked at a celebration. It was incredibly important to me to provide our future children with the same tagalong opportunity that I had as a youngster.

After a lot of serious discussion and debate, Eve finally agreed. Even though I prompted the discussion, in the end, she acknowledged that my need to create this reality for our children was stronger than her desire to maintain a relationship with alcohol. And while her choice may have initially been for the benefit of the family, over time Eve has come to understand all the ways in which the change improved her own health, strengthening her conviction in the correctness of the decision. Today, our two young sons, Raeven and Renson, are being raised under that example. It brings me directly to that adage: Leading by example isn't simply the *best* way to teach. It's the *only* way to teach. Obviously, we'll have no control over what they choose to do as adults. But we hope they'll continue to tag along with us, moving forward on the clear-minded path we've paved. And when the inevitable day comes that they are hit with peer pressure from friends who've strayed, we're thankful that they'll both have jiu-jitsu in their lives as another positive point of reference.

Common Occurrences

How can the Tagalong Principle fit into our everyday lives? Think about car pools (ride-sharing) and the high-occupancy vehicle (HOV) lane on a highway. Like jiu-jitsu, they are models of efficiency, saving time and resources, as well as being environmentally friendly by decreasing the amount of carbon monoxide and other greenhouse gases emitted into the atmosphere.

The Tagalong Principle in reverse? Recall all the times you offered to carry packages or groceries for someone who was either elderly or overburdened at the moment. How about the doors you held open for others? Perhaps you were on a bus and there was only one open seat available, but you allowed someone else to sit there because they seemed less able to stand over a prolonged period than you. Or maybe you're a firefighter whose unit is responding to a call in another county due to a lack of essential equipment. On a larger scale, devastating occurrences such as earthquakes, wildfires, and building collapses often see neighboring, out-of-state, and even multinational response teams helping to carry the weight of serving others in times of tragedy.

Suppose you're a high school student or possibly an adult taking a civil service exam. You're feeling good about your test answers. You've taken the time to study the material in advance and you're moving through the questions at a realistic pace. The instructor at the front of the room has looked up from her computer screen several times to glance in your direction, even clearing her throat to get your attention on the last occasion. That's when you notice that one of your good friends, sitting one seat to your left, has his eyes subtly shifted in the direction of your exam paper. In response, you slide the answer sheet over to the right-hand side of your desk and reposition your left shoulder, blocking his line of sight. Up until that point, you had been unaware that your friend was in the midst of a "tagalong" concerning your answers. At the end of the exam, the instructor collects your answer sheet without saying a word to you. As you exit the classroom and step into the hall, your subtle-eyed friend approaches you with an annoyed look on his face. Just as he opens his mouth, you decide that you need to take control of the situation and speak first. What do you say? Will your opening words be positioning your friend to deliver an explanation or an apology?

Lots of people want to ride with you in the limo, but what you want is someone who will take the bus with you when the limo breaks down.
—Oprah Winfrey

Profile: Sticky Hands

In several other martial arts, sticking to your opponent and forcing them to carry your weight or energy is also a central concept. Wing Chun kung fu has a training exercise called *chi sao*, or sticky hands, in which a pair of practitioners stick to one another wrist to wrist, using both hands simultaneously, in order to sense the opponent's next move and respond with the appropriate technique. Sifu William Moy has been playing "sticky hands" for approximately forty years and is widely recognized for his unique ability to exhaust an opponent who must support the blanketing weight of his energy.

"When you can stick to someone, you can sense their movements, start to feel if they're going to be more offensive or defensive. Then you can begin to affect their balance. Also, when they're carrying your weight, your energy, they start to get tired much faster . . . and there's less space between you. That makes it harder for them to start a movement and generate their own energy," said Moy, whose father, Moy Yat, studied with the legendary Yip Man (there have been several major films made about his life) in Hong Kong and was a younger classmate there to Bruce Lee. "Being a martial artist trains you to be calm and relaxed, physically and mentally, mind and body. It keeps your mind in focus and helps with the way you interact with other people, along with your understanding of others. It also saves time in your life, teaching you how to multitask, which ultimately makes you very efficient."[25]

Recognize the Tagalong Principle when . . .

- **Trying Something New:** You want to try jiu-jitsu, but you're scared to go alone, so you ask one of your friends to join you for the introductory class and both of you decide to sign up.
- **Leveraging Technology:** You're writing your first book about life, and you want to include an audio-visual component for the reader, so you capitalize on a modern technological trend by adding a scannable QR code at the beginning of each chapter.
- **Nurturing Relationships:** You get a job as a new salesman at a car dealership, so you nurture a relationship with one of the top sales reps in the company and ask her if she will mentor you.
- **Influencing Decisions:** Your teenage daughter says she wants to be a police officer when she grows up, so you arrange for her to get a ride-along with a local cop to help inform her decision.

Life has got a habit of not standing hitched. You got to ride it like you find it. You got to change with it.
—Woody Guthrie, American balladeer

25 William Moy interview with Paul Volponi (March 2, 2022).

Scan here to learn the combat application of

The Overload Principle

Chapter Twenty-Four

The Overload Principle

Identifying where you have a unique advantage, and then doubling down to maximize your success.

The ass bears the load, but not the overload.
—Miguel de Cervantes, author, *Don Quixote*

Allocating multiple resources to focus on an opponent's single body part is referred to as the Overload Principle. On the mat, its obvious strength is combining several potential power sources (arms, legs, knees, hips, and others) to increase our leverage in order to overwhelm a singular aspect of our rival's offense or defense. This is usually done with a specific objective in mind, such as executing a sweep, hold, or submission. The Overload Principle clearly can be observed whenever a lone individual attempts to fight off two or more attackers. In society, we can see its ramifications in areas such as business, sports, and the military.

Betting on Myself

The Overload Principle teaches us to play to our strengths, doubling down on our best attributes and abilities. Besides jiu-jitsu, that special ability for me has always been connecting to other people. After all, it's why I became a teacher. During the early stages of introducing Quikflip to the public, I decided to combine my connective ability with the uniqueness of my product to create a powerful social media video featuring one-on-one pitches to strangers at the Third Street Promenade in Santa Monica, a beautiful open space where people stroll, shop, and enjoy the Southern California sunshine. I brought along four cardboard boxes, containing eighty Quikflips in all, with the goal of demonstrating how quickly they transition from a hoodie to a backpack, and then seeing if I could get random people to trade the jackets off their backs in exchange for a Quikflip. Almost in unison, my support crew said, "No one's going to do that. People have memories attached to their clothing. Maybe it was a gift from someone they love. Nobody's going to trade with you, even for something brand new." My crew obviously had a valid point. But I believed that the tandem power of me and the product could pull it off (no pun intended).

The first person I stopped that afternoon listened to every word out of my mouth. Only, they were immediately intent on not trading. Then I demonstrated the transition and they began to waver a bit before walking away. That taught me something. My dual strengths—the charisma pitch and the Quikflip conversion—needed to occur simultaneously, so I moved the hoodie transition to the fore. Person number two, three, four, five, and six all traded the hoodies they were wearing for a Quikflip, and my support crew was suddenly both silent and impressed.

I next stopped a man and a woman walking together. She was wearing a denim jacket, and he was clad only in a T-shirt. After my pitch and demonstration, the woman was on the fence. Her jacket probably cost much more than a new Quikflip, so she ultimately decided to pass. Fifteen minutes later, though, they both returned. Only this time the man was wearing a hoodie (he admitted that he went into a nearby store and bought a hoodie *just* so he could trade it), the woman was still wearing her denim jacket, and *both* agreed to trade. I can't describe how satisfying it was to see how eager people were to trade. By the end of the afternoon, our boxes were empty of Quikflips and filled with used outerwear of every brand you can imagine, from Nike to Under Armour to Adidas and everything in between. What did I do with all these non-converting garments? Donated them to a homeless shelter, of course, before taking my crew to have sushi for lunch.

Where did I get this entrepreneurial drive? I can trace it back to an economics class I took at West High School. For our final project, the teacher divided us into groups of four and tasked us with creating a commerce-themed board game. I was freaking out because the project would be counted as half our grade for that semester, with everyone in the group receiving the same grade for the project. As a teen, I was totally into building and designing things, and I didn't really trust that my group mates were as committed as I was to getting an A. So I pitched them this idea: "I'll do all the work. The rest of you don't have to lift a finger, but you each have to pay me forty dollars."

"*Forty dollars?*" inquired my teammates.

"And if we get a B instead of an A, I'll give you each back ten dollars. If it's a C, I'll give you each back twenty dollars." All the way down to an F, where I would receive nothing.

I didn't know it at the time, but I was using the Overload Principle, betting on myself by doubling down on my building and designing skills. I was also applying a business strategy called "risk reversal" through my sliding-scale payment method to make the deal more enticing to my group mates. The trio agreed and I went to work. A few weeks later, I had created Oligopoly, a board game inspired by Monopoly. In a monopoly, a single entity controls the marketplace. An oligopoly, however, signifies a market that is controlled by a small number of key players. I used the breakfast cereal industry as the basis for my game because it is dominated by a quartet of large companies: Kellogg's, Post, General Mills, and Quaker. I even made tiny cereal boxes as game pieces (with rice inside for the sound effect) and put my own likeness on the faux money with the caption "In Rener We Trust."

The day of the presentation, I did all of the speaking. My group mates simply nodded their heads in the background and played along. The project received an A+ and I pocketed $120. For a high school student who wasn't getting paid from the family business at that time, it was quite a haul and kept me financially afloat through the forthcoming summer.

One of the effects of living with electric information is that we live habitually in a state of information overload. There's always more than you can cope with.
—Marshall McLuhan, philosopher, author

Workplace/Military/Sports Overload

Society's surge in technology has brought about an interesting question: How much information is too much information? The buoyant promise of the internet and social media is now continually balanced against a relative tsunami of useless, misleading, or incorrect data in which we sometimes find ourselves drowning. Though no singular outlet producing such information is attempting to overload us, each seemingly wants our attention for a span of three to five minutes. Their cumulative effect can easily put us in overload mode, resulting in a decrease in productivity. Smartphones and email have us connected to our careers and jobs 24/7. That type of access often results in work overload, with motivated and conscientious employees more susceptible to burnout and fatigue. What can administrators do to combat these negative outcomes? It isn't easy to block out extraneous data. But administrators can clearly prioritize the top several tasks upon which their workers should focus. Furthermore, many companies now require employees to take "mandated leave" in order to avoid burnout due to overload.

The human brain operates best when it focuses on no more than seven to nine pieces of information at one time (consider that phone numbers are seven digits long). Hypnotists actually attempt to use the Overload Principle when trying to give a subject a suggestion. In conversational hypnosis, the hypnotist will either use many numerous details in describing a scene or remove a piece of information from a statement. For example, *it was so cold finding my hat and gloves.* These techniques cause the brain to overload (searching internally for the missing words in the example above), making it much easier for a suggestion to slip into the subject's subconscious.

Military strategists have also realized the value of the Overload Principle. In their world, it's known as "combined arms tactics." That's where strategists use the strengths of different divisions to increase the overall power of an assault on enemy forces. It's been used since the beginning of recorded warfare. Forces with rudimentary clubs and spears were joined by others on hillsides throwing stones. The strength of the Roman infantry was magnified by chariots. Armored knights combined with columns of crossbows. Cannons enhanced the mounted cavalry, right up until modern times, when air and sea support augmented boots on the ground.

Football takes much of its terminology from the military, including the blitz (see "blitzkrieg" later in this chapter). On the gridiron, a blitz is a perfect reflection of the Overload Principle. It means to bring more defenders, usually with designs on sacking the quarterback, than the offense can conceivably block. It's a high risk–reward tactic, because bringing extra defenders toward the quarterback means that a receiver could be running free and unguarded. In turn, the offense can also use the Overload Principle by stacking all of its receivers on one side of the field, making it more difficult for the defense, which may lose contact by running into picks, to closely guard each.

Profile: Applying Pressure

Head Coach Ken Niumatalolo has spent more than a quarter of a century with the United States Naval Academy's football team helping to produce not only fine athletes but exceptional young leaders and a growing number of Academic All-Americans.

"At the Naval Academy, all of our players engage in combative arts training, some more than others, but everybody goes through the basics. I'm a huge fan of Brazilian jiu-jitsu and I believe that the combative arts are a positive for football players. In football, we have our own Overload Principle. It's called the blitz. It can be very disruptive to put our players on the opponent's side of the field. We accomplish the blitz by either overloading their pass protection, sending more men than their line can block, or through overloading their personnel. That's where we try to exploit their weakest players by not allowing them to have any help. We refer to that as *putting someone on an island*," said Coach Niumatalolo.

Does the Reconnaissance Principle come into play here as well? "We certainly do our share of reconnaissance as coaches go through hours of film study and keeping our eyes open during the game itself. We're always trying to test the opposing quarterback, both physically and mentally. We're also trying to test the other team's ability to communicate with one another when they see us lining up for a possible blitz. Sometimes just the threat of the blitz can overload a quarterback's thought process. Of course, it's more difficult to do in the pros. Great quarterbacks like Tom Brady and Peyton Manning were very hard to rattle. They were so intelligent and got rid of the football so fast. But you often see younger pro quarterbacks with great physical abilities who don't have the experience yet to mentally deal with overloading."[26]

We overload in our workouts so the game slows down in real life. It helps you become a smarter basketball player.
—Stephen Curry, two-time NBA MVP

Call on the Overload Principle when . . .

- **Choosing the Path:** You realize your child is more of an audio-visual learner than kinesthetic, so you enroll him in twice as many art and music classes as you do sportive activities.
- **Prioritizing Work:** Your mental capacity is at its highest in the morning hours, so you try to tackle all of your creative work before lunch each day.
- **Nurturing Relationships:** You discover that physical touch is one of your spouse's love languages, so you go out of your way to make contact a priority every time you enter a room together.
- **Overcoming Bullies:** Your child hasn't started learning jiu-jitsu and is struggling with a bully at school, so you instruct their older sibling to assist in confronting the bully.

26 Ken Niumatalolo interview with Paul Volponi (March 5, 2022).

Blitzkrieg

The German blitzkrieg of World War II was an extremely calculated and successful use of the Overload Principle. After losing the First World War, Germany was forced to sign the Treaty of Versailles (1919), which limited their army to a mere 100,000 soldiers. With fewer forces, German military strategists attacked only the weakest points of the allies' lines with spearhead precision, giving them an overload advantage in a very small area. But that pinpoint numbers advantage was enough to break through those lines, causing chaos and destruction on the other side. In just the span of a few weeks, Germany occupied all of France because of their lightning-fast blitzkrieg assaults (in the German language, *blitz* means lightning). How was this strategy eventually negated by the allies? The answer is production. The allies outproduced the Germans in terms of manufacturing. With more resources, they dragged out the time frame of the war, making it a battle of attrition. That eventually entrenched Germany on the wrong side of the Overload Principle.

Scan here to learn the combat application of

The Anchor Principle

Chapter Twenty-Five

The Anchor Principle

Committing wholeheartedly to the people, principles, and processes that optimize your effectiveness and impact.

The anchor holds on despite the storm.
—Unknown

Whenever you pin your opponent's body, resulting in a loss of their mobility in order to increase your own potential, you are putting into play the Anchor Principle. Often a pin technique—also referred to as a staple—need only be achieved for a brief instant to facilitate your goal. These pins can be either direct or indirect (using an intermediary connection) and can be used in both offensive and defensive scenarios. How wide-ranging and flexible are pins? They include pinning you to the mat, pinning you to yourself, or pinning you to the opponent. Conversely, a pin can also include pinning the opponent to the mat, pinning the opponent to themselves, or pinning the opponent to you. It equates to a moment of complete control both on the mat and, hopefully, in your life.

Curriculum and Culture

Jiu-jitsu exists in two distinct forms. The first is a complete system of self-defense designed to empower the weak against stronger, more athletic opponents in a violent physical altercation. That is how my grandfather originally intended the art to serve its students. But jiu-jitsu also exists today as a recreational sport. There are many schools whose main focus is sending their students to competitions where jiu-jitsu practitioners square off against one another to win a match, governed by weight classes, time limits, and a nuanced point system. While there are many benefits to be had in the pursuance of gold medals, it's not uncommon for students who were only exposed to the sportive aspects of jiu-jitsu to find themselves in unfamiliar territory during an actual self-defense situation, especially as beginners in the art. Since there are no punches or kicks permitted in traditional BJJ competition, the defenses against these common attacks are often neglected in the daily practice at sport BJJ schools, and this will often leave students feeling unprepared for the eventualities of a street fight.

In following our grandfather's approach to teaching jiu-jitsu, Ryron and I have always been intent on providing our students with a strong foundation in both curriculum and culture. Those dual pillars comprise the anchor of our teaching philosophy and business model. To that end, our beginning students follow a curriculum that is 100 percent geared toward self-defense, with an intense focus on the specific techniques that would give the average person the skills to defend against a violent physical assault on the street. Bullies exist in many places and phases of life. There is one place, though, where we refuse to allow our students to encounter such a bully. That place is within the walls of Gracie University headquarters or any of our certified training centers around the world.

Unfortunately, there are misguided mantras in many schools that *only the strong survive* and *jiu-jitsu isn't for everyone.* My grandfather despised that kind of thinking (especially since he *was* the weak person who needed jiu-jitsu to give him a chance against larger adversaries). Training under such conditions can create a culture of aggression and a "food chain" mentality where newer students are used as grappling dummies for more experienced students holding rank to pat themselves on the back. Jiu-jitsu was designed to empower the weak against the strong, and it's a shame that at so many schools around the world, the very people that BJJ was originally intended to serve are precluded from learning due to the corrosive culture that permeates the mats.

In all of our Gracie University–accredited schools, the lower a student's rank, the more that student is protected and cared for on the mats. From day one, we make it explicitly clear that newer students are to be guided and encouraged by more experienced students, rather than beaten and broken down. Like my grandfather always said: There is no such thing as a bad student, only bad teachers. If a person who is small, weak, or unathletic has the courage to give jiu-jitsu a try, it is our responsibility, as their teacher, to exceed all their expectations when it comes to fostering a fun, safe, and positive learning experience on the mat. If someone tries a class and doesn't come back, it's not because they're weak, it's because we didn't do our job. This was my grandfather's belief, this is my belief, and this is the belief of the thousands of instructors my brother and I have personally certified to teach our programs. It's why over 350,000 students worldwide trust us to lead them on their jiu-jitsu journeys, and it's undoubtedly our most important application of the Anchor Principle.

One for All

Jiu-jitsu instructor Jonny Vasquez runs a Certified Gracie Jiu-Jitsu Training Center in Apple Valley, California. Despite being within driving distance of several other martial arts academies, some even sporting the names of recognized black belt champions on their shingles, Vasquez's establishment is thriving. "When I opened my gym as a blue belt (three grades below a black belt), I don't think those other schools in the area took us very seriously. But I knew what I wanted to bring to my students' lives and how I wanted to see them treated. There's no tough-guy mentality here. Everyone who walks through our door, no matter what their personality type or athleticism, is respected," said Vasquez, who now possesses a purple belt.

Prior to training with Ryron and me in Torrance, Vasquez experienced bullying in martial arts schools himself. "I'm glad I went through that, so I know what to keep out of our culture. People don't wake up one day and decide they're going to be black belts. They want to learn self-defense, and they want to do it without being harassed or embarrassed . . . The diversity on our mats is incredible. It ranges from average people who are completely out of shape to law enforcement officers who need the skills to stay safe out on the streets. Everyone's goals are respected here. If someone new walks in off the street who is totally nonaggressive and maybe even fearful of contact, we don't reject or judge that student. Instead, we embrace and cherish them, because that's what the Gracie brothers taught us."[27]

We should not moor a ship with one anchor, or our life with one hope.
—Epictetus, philosopher

Profile: More Than Anchoring the Beat

Drummer Peter Erskine was infatuated with martial arts as a pre-adolescent, buying magazines about it and visualizing himself moving forward through its ranks. Though music overtook that passion, and the practice of martial arts eventually faded from his life, it's amazing how many of jiu-jitsu's core principles are present in Erskine's discussion of his musicianship. The Creation, Velocity, Clock, River, Reconnaissance, and Anchor Principles are all referenced by Erskine below:

Legendary jazz drummer Peter Erskine, a professor at the University of Southern California, has been a musician for over half a century. Drummers are often viewed as the anchor or backbone of a band, establishing the beat. "The drummer's primary job is to provide rhythmic information for the other musicians. We function not only as a metronome in that we're providing a basic pulse, but we also provide the overall phrasing in the way that we treat the individual notes. The spaces in between the beats determine the style, and those rhythmic subdivisions determine the feel. So a drummer establishes not only time and tempo but becomes a reference point for the feel of a particular piece," noted Erskine, who sees a strong

27 Jonny Vasquez interview with Paul Volponi (May 29, 2022).

parallel between drumming and the martial art of boxing. "I often tell my students to watch the boxing highlights on the news. The knockout usually happens so fast that if you blink, you'll miss it. That's because it's not telegraphed like in a *Popeye* cartoon where he winds up, reaches back, and you see the fist for a few seconds. Instead, it's very quick with a kind of snap that doesn't require a lot of motion but provides substantial power. It's based on efficiency and economy of movement. That's how I approach the physicality of drumming . . . I've played with groups in the past where I'd be drenched in sweat halfway through the performance. These days, I play with a lot more efficiency. After all, drumming is one of the few activities where all four limbs are usually doing something completely independent from the others in terms of motion."

For a much longer piece, perhaps while playing as a featured guest with a symphony orchestra, Erskine will do a good bit of reconnaissance prior to taking the stage. "I'll sit in a quiet space like a dressing room and mentally run the piece, much like a downhill skier might before a race. I imagine the constructed music as it is written, not through any improvisation I might use, so when I get on the stage there are no surprises. I know where it's icy and where the sharp turns are placed. This really helps me navigate through a performance." Erskine firmly believes that everyone can better themselves and their lives through a basic course in music. "Everyone who takes a music lesson will not become a professional musician. That's not the point. Being in a larger group, like a band or a team, teaches people about being part of something greater than themselves. How the majesty, power, and beauty of your small part becoming an important piece of the whole can be fulfilling."[28] It's simply another parallel between music and studying martial arts.

The Boyd Belt System

Years ago, I had a great friend and student; his name was John Boyd. Even though he was a relatively small man (155 lb.) who started learning jiu-jitsu

28 Peter Erskine interview with Paul Volponi (May 2, 2022).

later in life, he committed more than a decade to the study of the art before earning his coveted black belt. One day, after completing a class, John (65 years old) came into my office, sat down, and said, "Man, Rener, I sparred with a young blue belt who was a monster, and I couldn't tap him out. I don't think I deserve this black belt." He was visibly upset, and it was clear that he held an anchoring belief that, as a black belt, he easily should be able to submit any lower-rank student, regardless of any physical disparities that existed, but he was wrong.

"John, the fact that you are able to survive against someone so much younger and so much stronger is the entire reason you do jiu-jitsu," I explained while he remained looking down at the floor between his feet. "Think of it this way, every ten years of youth and every twenty pounds of weight equals one belt advantage. So when you're sparring with this kid who's twenty years younger than you and forty pounds heavier than you, that's a four-belt advantage you're giving up the moment you bump fists." At this point, John looked up at me while I continued, "So even though he's wearing a blue belt around his waist, when you factor in the youth and the size advantage he has over you, it's easy to see how quickly he turns into a black belt. Now, the truthfulness of this equation might make you sad at first, but I want you to consider this: at sixty-five years old and one hundred and fifty-five pounds, imagine what your chances of survival would be against that same opponent *without* jiu-jitsu in your arsenal?" At that point he stood up and smiled, nodded his head, walked out of my office, and never again complained about sparring partners half his age. What John needed wasn't a new skill set, but rather a new anchoring belief on the mat. I'm so glad I was able to provide that for him.

A few years later, John tragically passed away when struck with his third heart attack. In his memory, I named this understanding "the Boyd Belt System." I have since published social media videos outlining this mental framework for others to benefit from. The videos have been viewed over 750,000 times, and I have been contacted by countless jiu-jitsu students who have stated that if not for the clarity and encouragement afforded to them through the Boyd Belt System, they would have quit jiu-jitsu.

Weigh Anchor

Whenever the Anchor Principle is levied against us, often by circumstances in our daily lives, it can make us feel like we're buried beneath an immense mountain of responsibility. Family, work, school, chores, and social obligations pile up until we can't find a free moment for ourselves. In response, we need to find a way to prioritize these obligations, to create a schedule, so that there's a moment or two out of each day when we can just clear our minds and breathe.

Something as simple as a few minutes of exercise, meditation, a walk around the block, listening to music, or occupying a space filled with complete silence can recharge our energies and spirits. And if you've been skillful enough to successfully juggle everything that life can throw at you, then maybe you can help a family member or friend begin to do the same. How? By executing the Anchor Principle in reverse and freeing up someone else so they can take a moment for themselves. Perhaps your neighbor is struggling with the needs of a sick or elderly parent while also having to look after their own children. You might give them some free time by babysitting or inviting their children to eat dinner with yours before hosting a movie night. Suppose you live out of state and your sibling is struggling with the same types of overwhelming responsibilities. Supporting that sibling can be as easy as coming into their home for a half hour using a video-chat app like FaceTime, Skype, or Zoom, and structuring an activity such as a game, storytelling, or even watching a TV show together. Anything that you plan where you're the leader and the burden can be lifted from their shoulders for a while will be of enormous help.

Martial Arts and the Media

Make no mistake, martial arts is anchored in our society by the men, women, and adolescents who train in the various arts and put their principles into practice on a daily basis. But another anchor for martial arts in our society has been the media's portrayal of the different disciplines in TV, film, and print media.

For example, in the Academy Award–winning film *Blood on the Sun* (1945), legendary actor James Cagney participates in a judo technique–inspired brawl with actor John Halloran, who was Cagney's real-life judo instructor. The furniture-breaking, bare-knuckled brawl still stands up today as one of Hollywood's best martial arts fight scenes. On a 1963 episode of *The Lucy Show*, Lucille Ball and Vivian Vance learn judo from Ball's actual private instructor, Ed Parker, in order to defend themselves from a neighborhood prowler. Peter Sellers often showed a comic side to martial arts as the bungling Inspector Clouseau in the *Pink Panther* film series. But off screen, Sellers, who was at one time president of the London Judo Club, was a serious practitioner. And Rorion Gracie, while still teaching out of his garage, served as technical advisor for *Lethal Weapon* (1987), in which actors Mel Gibson and Gary Busey face off in a final fight scene featuring a variety of Brazilian jiu-jitsu holds and chokes.

The Stunt Double

A champion at fighting, forms, and weapons, Christine Bannon-Rodrigues began studying martial arts as a teen. "It's really become a way of life for me. I was a shy girl and it gave me a lot more confidence: socially, at school, and in other sports. It gave me an attitude that I could achieve any goal to which I set my mind." Eventually, Bannon-Rodrigues's talents caught the eye of stunt director Pat Johnson, who cast her as Hilary Swank's stunt double in *The Next Karate Kid* (1994). In a film predicated on martial arts, the fight scenes had to be spot-on, and that's where Bannon-Rodrigues absolutely shined. "It would be nice if more people knew it was me, but that's a stunt double's job, to make others look good."

She also played Batgirl's (Alicia Silverstone's) stunt double in *Batman & Robin* (1997), where Bannon-Rodrigues seemingly had the film's entire production schedule riding on a singular kick. "It was during a fight scene and Uma (Thurman, playing Poison Ivy) had a knife in her hand. She ad-libbed by pausing to look at her reflection in the knife blade. The director liked it so much that he wanted to keep it in the scene. That's when he asked me if I could kick the knife out of Uma's hand without hurting her," recalled Bannon-Rodrigues. Accidentally sending a star to the hospital could mean massive shooting delays. But Bannon-Rodrigues confidently responded, "Piece of cake." The succeeding kick was perfectly on target.

Fight scenes for films often mean that martial arts efficiency takes a back seat to what looks best on camera. "You have to do everything you were taught not to do," said Bannon-Rodrigues, who was the fight choreographer for *Champions of the Deep* (2012). "Big round punches. Wide haymakers. Nothing short and straight. It's very wide, circular kicks. We cater to the audience, to make it look like the actor really got hit. You just can't send a professional fighter out there [with no experience in front of the camera] and expect that he'll do those things."[29]

To reach a port, we must sail, sometimes with the wind and sometimes against it. But we must not drift or lie at anchor.
—Oliver Wendell Holmes Sr., poet, physician

Acknowledge the Anchor Principle when . . .

- **Making Commitments:** You choose to engage in a discussion with your significant other about core values early in the relationship to determine if there are any known anchors on either side that would prevent a potential marriage from being successful long term.
- **Retaining Talent:** You catch wind that a key employee is considering leaving your company, so you increase their compensation and change their title to reflect your commitment to keeping them on board.
- **Strengthening Bonds:** As your child gets older, you fear that they will grow apart from you, so you decide to join them in learning a new skill (jiu-jitsu), and the newfound passion you share for the art serves as a major anchor in your relationship.
- **Preserving Values:** Your mother passes away so you decide to wear a pendant with her name on it around your neck as a constant reminder to treat others with the same love and selflessness that she always did.

29 Christine Bannon-Rodrigues interview with Paul Volponi (February 12, 2022).

Scan here to learn the combat application of

The Ratchet Principle

Chapter Twenty-Six

The Ratchet Principle

Believing that small, persistent advancements will add up to significant gains over time.

Hold on with a bulldog grip, and chew and choke as much as possible.
—President Abraham Lincoln to General Ulysses S. Grant

Forward advancement. That's what we want from our jiu-jitsu, and that philosophy is perfectly represented by the Ratchet Principle. A ratchet is a mechanical device that allows incremental advances in one direction, be it linear or rotary, without ever slipping backward. On the mats, we're willing to gain ground one inch at a time if necessary, as long as we keep advancing. It's a very persistent mindset, and in that vein, it shares a synergy with the River Principle's foundation of constantly flowing forward. The Ratchet Principle produces both "macro ratchets," which involve the entire body, and "micro ratchets," pertaining to advancing upon a hand, arm, or leg. Sometimes we use the Frame Principle or Pivot Principle as a way to increase leverage and mechanically drive our ratchet. Assuming more and more control while never relinquishing any part of that superior position is the basis of the Ratchet Principle.

Collaborative Journey

The first years of my life were dominated by ego. It actually makes perfect sense when I think about it. Growing up in a family of fighters, one where every member considered themselves to be the best, it was practically the only way to develop a perspective about myself. In fact, that Gracie family trait, as displeasing as it might have been to many outsiders, was certainly one of the driving forces that helped Brazilian jiu-jitsu emerge into the consciousness of the martial arts world. But as a fledgling business leader of Gracie University, that massive ego didn't serve either me or the business well. I was living under the burden of believing that every good idea about the business's direction needed to come from me alone. It was a massive weight to carry, and there were times that I thought I might collapse from the never-ending strain.

It took eight years to partner with enough martial arts schools around the country to establish approximately 100 Gracie University Certified Training Centers. Many of those schools were run by people who possessed greater business acumen than I did. But whenever a good idea would surface from one of them, I would be quick to dismiss it, simply because I wasn't its originator. It was my Gracie DNA at its most disadvantageous. Something happened, though, in reaching that 100-school mark. My stressful desire for each one of those privately owned schools to succeed in concert with Gracie University became too overwhelming and virtually unsustainable. I needed to make a change. It wouldn't be easy, but I knew I had to shed my egotistical shackles for the good of everyone involved, including me.

I began to recruit the voices of others and work more cooperatively with the instructors at our training centers, harvesting solid ideas from them and collaborating as a team to make those ideas even better. That initial spark of change led to our first instructor development conference, a three-day event in which we invite our school owners to come together to discuss their challenges, concerns, solutions to common problems, and innovations. This event proved to be a remarkable success, producing focus groups and crowdsourced ideas that have spawned marketing strategies, software improvements, and a mentoring program for new school owners. It's been a wonderful reflection of the Ratchet Principle, in which Gracie University and its certified instructors have moved our businesses forward incrementally in a collaborative fashion with an open ear to each other's ideas. How successful has this collaboration been? In just under four years following the event, Gracie University has certified an additional 124 schools, which means we more than doubled the number of Gracie University schools in half the time it took us to certify our first 100. Among my favorite corporate duties now is to make sure that everyone in the organization has a chance to be heard and to make sure that the individuals or groups who bring forth terrific ideas receive the praise they absolutely deserve. The same way you can't climb a rope without letting go of the rope, I had to let go of my death grip on the business to allow it to climb to new heights—one good idea at a time.

I'm not tough. I'm tenacious.
—Padma Lakshmi, author, activist

Ratchet Resolutions

Every January it's the same: Commercial airwaves are bombarded with pitches for weight-loss programs and gym memberships. That's because people everywhere are making New Year's resolutions to either drop a few pounds or get back into shape. If you find yourself fitting into either one of those categories, consider putting the Ratchet Principle to work for you. It doesn't matter whether you spend just fifteen minutes working out, barely producing a sweat. Why? It's a start upon which you can improve incrementally. Maybe the next time you're at the gym, you'll work out for twenty minutes, or maybe add an extra machine, or bump up the resistance a little. Jumping into a full-fledged workout routine is fine. But there's also nothing wrong with the building-block approach. Take in a few less calories on every trip into the kitchen. Substitute an apple for a cookie twice a week, or a glass of water for a soft drink. Maybe even count the number of times you open the refrigerator on a Saturday and then open it one time less on Sunday. Eventually, it will all add up.

If you're a teacher or in charge of a business, you might make a resolution to use the Ratchet Principle in reverse by making sure not to suppress the creative ideas of students and employees. Possibly your students will suggest the best day for an exam, most likely when another teacher is not giving one as well. Or they may suggest the format for the questions or the point distribution. Employees often notice details that their supervisors miss, so their opinions should be valued and be given a forum in which to be heard on a regular basis. All of these voices should ideally be praised for their interest, fostering an atmosphere of collaborative advancement.

You can witness the Ratchet Principle's philosophy being applied by a myriad of apps that round up your credit card purchases to the nearest dollar and use the spare change to build toward a monetary goal. The money might go into a savings account, be invested in the stock market, buy cryptocurrency, or go to supporting a charity of your choice.

One Class at a Time

Some of the most tenacious people are students who don't take the traditional route to college and higher education. Instead of attending such institutions straight from high school, they enter the workforce and maybe even have a family first. But the thirst for education and the drive to improve their position in life is never quelled inside them. So they often attain their goals the hard way, attending school while holding down a full-time job and other family obligations. They amass college credits one class at a time, be it in person or online, moving forward incrementally toward their degree. These incredibly persistent people are perfect reflections of the Ratchet Principle at its very best off the jiu-jitsu mat.

Profile: Among Baltimore's Best

Shel Simon is the living embodiment of the Ratchet Principle. A football star for his hometown Morgan State University in Baltimore, Simon put his education on pause at the age of twenty-one to focus on raising and providing for his newborn son.

"At first, I worked at manufacturing jobs, doing anything I could to support my child. Then I got hired by a pharmaceutical company and spent a decade in that field," said Simon, who wanted to make more of an impact on the youth of Baltimore City, either by coaching football or as an educator improving their life skills. In order to make that transition, however, he needed a degree. So Simon went back to school at night while continuing to work days. "It was incredibly hard moving forward one class at a time. I'd work nearly ten hours a day and then sit through classes at night. My son was about eight years old at that time. If it wasn't for my mother and his maternal grandmother splitting the babysitting duties, I would have never been able to do it. I'd literally pick my son up from their care at ten o'clock at night, take him home to go to sleep, and then start that exhausting cycle over the next day."

Simon's determination to incrementally move forward eventually paid off with a degree in information and technology from the University of Maryland. "That journey helped to build my character. It was something really rewarding and sweet to accomplish. And it left me feeling like I could do anything." That's when Simon began chasing his dream of helping adolescents in earnest. Today, Shel Simon is the program director for Next One Up, a Baltimore-based nonprofit that transforms lives one student at a time by providing adolescents of color a pathway to their goals through education, counseling, and sports. "My own son, who's fifteen now, is interested in football and boxing. But no matter what he chooses to do in life, I'm determined to be there for him and other adolescents just like him."[30]

We are the seeds of that tenacious plant, and it is in our ripeness and our fullness of heart that we are given to the wind to be scattered.

—Kahlil Gibran, poet, visual artist

30 Shel Simon interview with Paul Volponi (March 13, 2022).

Rely on the Ratchet Principle when . . .

- **Implementing Change:** You want to make a significant operational change at work, but you're concerned that it will fall flat if you try to implement it all at once, so you create a plan to introduce smaller increments, until the final goal is reached.
- **Chasing Dreams:** You're busy with work and being a parent, but you really want to become a licensed family therapist, so you begin taking online classes on nights and weekends in order to fulfill your dream.
- **Teaching Children:** Your child has an important school project that must be completed over a three-month period, and you help them develop the habit of working on it for thirty minutes a day so they aren't stuck cramming it all in during the final week.
- **Quitting Bad Habits:** You're determined to quit smoking cigarettes, but you know cold turkey won't work for you. Instead, you commit to reduce your habit by one cigarette a day until you work your way down to zero.

The Man in Black

In 1976, country music superstar Johnny Cash, a.k.a. the Man in Black, had a No. 1 hit with a Ratchet Principle–embodied song entitled "One Piece at a Time." Penned by Nashville songwriter Wayne Kemp, the song details a fictitious Detroit autoworker's plan to steal a Cadillac one piece at a time over the course of more than two decades before he retired. How? By sneaking a different car part out of the factory each day in his lunchbox and using a buddy's mobile home for the bigger pieces.

On the day that the worker finally assembles his dream car, he realizes that the pieces are an odd fit because it's comprised of so many different model years. Kemp was inspired to write the song after hearing about a US airman who tried to sneak a helicopter off his air base piecemeal. "One Piece at a Time" was such a mega hit that Johnny Cash's record label scoured hundreds of salvage yards to build him a real-life Cadillac that fit the song, supposedly with pieces of models ranging from 1949 to 1973.

Scan here to learn the combat application of

The Buoyancy Principle

Chapter Twenty-Seven

The Buoyancy Principle

Leveraging the predictability of human behavior
to build your allies and break your enemies.

A beautiful day with the buoyancy of a bird.
—Truman Capote, novelist, playwright

Ever notice how submerged air bubbles always flow to the surface? In fact, divers are trained that if they should lose their way while underwater, they can always follow the bubbles' path upward to safety. People, in all aspects of life, have a natural tendency to rise up in order to assume a more dominant and safer position. In jiu-jitsu, that's often the case for the practitioner who's on the bottom of a grapple. Therein lies the basis of the Buoyancy Principle. From the bottom position, its successful application can result in either surfacing (shedding the bottom) or triggering an expected and exploitable response from your opponent, sharing a synergy in that way with the Creation Principle. From the top position, it's easier to set traps for your opponent when you know their buoyant nature will make the desire to rise a priority for them.

Stealing Trust

The Buoyancy Principle shows us that the behavior of people generally follows a pattern, and that individually, there's a strong tendency for people to eventually reveal themselves for who they actually are. Over a thousand students attend in-person classes at Gracie University on a weekly basis. It is a trusted environment where people train together and support one another on their personal quests in life, of which for everyone there, jiu-jitsu is a valuable part. I spend as much time at Gracie University with my students as I do at home with my family. And to me, the school has always felt like an extension of my home. So I was both shocked and greatly displeased when a student reported to me that their phone had been stolen from an open locker. The idea of it was so out of place that even the victim wanted to believe that they had left it either in their car or at home by mistake. But sadly, that proved untrue. I suppose I could have made a big public speech about my disappointment in what had transpired. But instead, I turned to the Buoyancy Principle, waiting for the sneaky thief to strike again.

Two weeks later, it happened. A second phone went missing. Along with my staff, we instantly cross-referenced the names of the students who had attended both classes during which phones had been stolen. Seven names occupied both lists. I decided to still sit tight. The very next week, after my final Saturday class of the morning, a third phone vanished. After checking the three class lists, I learned that only one student had attended each of those classes. That was a seventeen-year-old young man named Daniel, who'd always been polite and never any trouble. I jumped into my car and phoned his father on the drive over to his house. I didn't give any specifics, just that I wanted to meet with their family about something important.

Fifteen minutes later, I was sitting at their kitchen table with Daniel, his father, mother, and older brother. Daniel looked tense as I laid out the circumstantial case against him. His brother jumped up and said, "My brother's not a thief, Rener!" I responded, "I can appreciate your loyalty and trust in your brother, but the facts are telling us a different story." With the weight of everyone's expectations on Daniel's shoulders, he slowly began to crack, with those air bubbles rising to the surface. He stood up, went to his bedroom, and returned with a single phone. "How about the other two phones?"

I asked, mentioning their existence for the first time. To his family's dismay, after a long pause in the conversation, Daniel eventually nodded his head and produced a second phone. The remaining phone he had already sold. "So the choice is yours from here," I calmly told Daniel, "you can either never return to the school, or you can show up to the next class on Monday night, explain your actions to your classmates, and help me restore the trust on our mats." Then I left and let Daniel and his family begin to sort out what had occurred. I didn't get a call until Monday morning when Daniel's father told me that he would bring his son to class that night. As much as I credit the Buoyancy Principle for helping me put an end to the thievery, I credit Daniel for choosing to become a better person on the other side of it.

Daniel's POV

"You know, it honestly wasn't that hard to take the first phone, to cross that line and steal something from a classmate. Then once I took it, I said to myself, 'Oh, shit, I can get away with this.' That's how screwed up I was in my thinking at that time. That Saturday morning, after I stole the third phone, I was on the way home with my dad, sitting in the passenger seat of our car. Out of nowhere, Rener called him and said that he was going to meet us at our house. I understood right away that he knew what I'd done.

"The anxiety started really building, and I felt the phone hidden inside my bag. When Rener got there, he was real respectful. He just laid out the whole thing piece by piece, like he knew my every move. I felt super bad because Rener had always been like an older brother to me, and I'd let him down. We had some back-and-forth with me trying to deny it, but I just couldn't hide it anymore and finally admitted everything. Over the next two days, I agonized about facing up to all of those people.

"That Monday at class, it was insanely hard to tell everybody what I'd done. The response wasn't what I expected, though. I figured that everybody would want nothing to do with me. But it wasn't like that. Even the people I stole from pulled me aside and spoke to me one-on-one. All of those conversations and the advice they gave me were positive. In a way, I was really grateful for the experience. I had been hanging around bad kids who were in gangs. I was getting immersed into that lifestyle, thinking it was cool to do bad things. The whole experience changed me as a person and I never stole again."[31]

Author's note: Today, Daniel is in his midtwenties. He's a diesel mechanic following one of his passions in life, turning wrenches and solving mechanical problems. He attended Gracie University for more than a year after the incident, took an extended break from training, but is now back taking classes again. He currently holds a blue belt in jiu-jitsu.

When writers make us shake our heads with the exactness of their prose and their truths, and even make us laugh about ourselves or life, our buoyancy is restored.
—Anne Lamott, author

Staying Afloat

Buoyancy is the upward force exerted upon an object that is either submerged or partially submerged in fluid. It occurs when the pressure beneath the object is greater than the pressure above it. Otherwise, the object would sink like a stone (negative buoyancy). This concept was first articulated more than two millennia ago by Archimedes of Syracuse, a Greek mathematician and physicist, who supposedly conceived of this concept as he entered a bathtub and watched his body displace the water therein.

Over time, people have achieved ways to control their buoyancy. Many underwater divers employ a buoyancy bag, which inflates and deflates, in an effort to achieve a neutral buoyancy so they may remain swimming in midwater. On a larger scale, a submarine both takes on and releases seawater in its ballast tanks, usually to attain a slightly negative buoyancy, controlling the depth of a dive.

The work of Archimedes has entered the lives of many modern-day athletes who are intent on having a higher percentage of lean muscle mass

31 Daniel Andrade interview with Paul Volponi (March 12, 2022).

while reducing their body fat. One of the most accurate measures of body fat occurs in a hydrostatic tank. First, a subject is weighed on land. After blowing all of the air out of their lungs, the subject is then submerged into the tank where a second weight is recorded. There will definitely be a difference. Everything weighs less underwater (due to buoyancy), but how much less is the key to measuring body fat. Fat is lighter than muscle and will displace a lower volume of liquid. Over time, those training and dieting diligently to lower their body fat, if remaining at the same dryland weight, will want their underwater weight to slightly increase. That heavier number will translate as an increase in muscle mass.

Profile: Just Keep Swimming

Coach Bob Groseth of Notre Dame University has been helping NCAA swimmers for more than two decades to both become faster in the water and mature as individuals. His teams and individual swimmers have captured a tsunami of championships while featuring over seventy All-Americans. Take note of how many of jiu-jitsu's 32 core principles that Coach Groseth references during his discussion with us on improving swimmers: Buoyancy, Posture, Creation, Pyramid, Connection, Kuzushi, Frame, and Momentum.

"I think there are a lot of positives that martial arts can bring to a swimmer—or any athlete. Among them are body control, balance, and leverage. Not leverage against your opponent, but increasing your own leverage," said Coach Groseth, who interestingly enough did not swim in high school or at the University of Indiana, but instead served as the student manager for both of those teams. How important is the principle of buoyancy to a competitive swimmer? "That starts early with beginning swimmers. I have them stand chest deep in the water, take a deep breath, and then tuck up into a ball. I ask them to float to the surface and wait until they stabilize. Then I instruct them to stretch out their arms and legs. That position gives them balance. So they use buoyancy to find their balance in the water."

Why is balance so important to a swimmer? "For a swimmer, there's less resistance when you're balanced and you're using less energy because you're in a position that causes less drag. That's the fundamental thing you want to teach a swimmer . . . In performing the breaststroke for example, swimmers will briefly go underwater. There's more surface tension at the top of the pool, where the water is actually thicker than the water underneath. So they push against their buoyancy and instead of making surface waves, remain underneath where there is less resistance. That's really important because at the collegiate level, the difference between making the NCAA Championships or not can be just a tenth of a second."[32]

My name may have buoyancy enough to float upon the sea of time.
—Richard Watson Gilder, poet, Civil War soldier

Consider the Buoyancy Principle when . . .

- **Overcoming Bullies:** Your child is being targeted by an incessant bully at school, and you know that the bully will continue the harassing behavior until your child learns the skills and develops the confidence to take a stand and disrupt the behavioral pattern.
- **Managing Employees:** You have an overly talkative employee who works in the warehouse and is distracting other employees, so you move them to the front office where they can interact with customers and put their outgoing personality to great use.
- **Controlling Temptations:** You know that you can't control your temptation to eat junk food when it's in the pantry, so you ask your spouse to stop purchasing it in order to help reach your fitness goals.
- **Solving Problems:** You realize that members of the general public hate sleeping on airplanes due to bobblehead, so you decide to invent the king of travel pillows to solve the problem once and for all.

32 Bob Groseth interview with Paul Volponi (March 1, 2020).

Uncoiling a Solution

Jordan Talmor is an ardent BJJ practitioner and the COO of Quikflip Apparel. When his son's four-foot-long pet corn snake went missing in his apartment on its first day home from the pet store, Jordan turned to the Buoyancy Principle for a solution. "Everyone in the house was distraught when we realized our brand-new snake was not in its terrarium, especially my son. My mom was a science teacher, and I practically grew up reading *National Geographic*, so I knew that snakes' natural tendency was to try to get to a heat source to survive when cold. Thankfully it was a cold night, so I shut off the heat in the apartment, boiled a pot of water, covered it with a blanket, and set it out in the middle of the living room floor. When I woke up the next morning, there was the snake, coiled around the pot. It was a perfect use of the principle in real life: knowing where someone or something wants to go next,"[33] reflected Jordan, who doesn't recommend losing a snake in the summer.

33 Jordan Talmor interview with Paul Volponi (September 21, 2022).

Scan here to learn the combat application of

The Head Control Principle

Chapter Twenty-Eight

The Head Control Principle

Identifying the primary source of influence in an organization and targeting your efforts accordingly.

When you react, you let others control you.
When you respond, you are in control.
—Bohdi Sanders, martial artist, author

More than any other body part, the head has a tremendous amount of control over a person's posture, mobility, and balance. On the jiu-jitsu mat, it is a prize asset to capture control of the opponent's head, thus limiting their ability to use several of the core principles to either defend or mount an attack. Offensively, you can use the Head Control Principle to break your opponent's balance, contain and control their ability to escape your applied techniques, and to effectuate a wide array of submissions. Defensively, it will allow you to avoid strikes through distance management and to better recognize possible escapes and reversals. While the combat applications of the Head Control Principle are entirely physical in nature, the life applications of the same principle extend far beyond.

Restraint over Brute Force

Gracie Survival Tactics (GST), our self-defense program designed to help law enforcement personnel humanely prevail against larger and stronger opponents in the field, has been taught to officers in jurisdictions throughout the country for the past three decades. But despite the program's success, I've always felt a tremendous frustration in speaking to police chiefs about increasing its implementation.

On average, police officers receive just two to four hours a year of defensive tactics training. In my opinion, not only is that amount of training woefully inadequate, it's embarrassing. Whenever Gracie University sends out a certified team of master instructors to work with police departments, we normally provide a full week of training. During this period, we certify the attendees as trainers so they can return to their agencies and teach the material to the other officers. The problem is that the agencies rarely provide the instructors we've certified with more than a few hours per year to share this valuable material with their colleagues. For the past twenty years, I've actually been advocating for end-user officers to receive ongoing training of at least one to two hours per week. In my opinion, this amount represents the bare minimum that an officer would need to develop muscle memory in the skills that will allow them to control subjects with the lowest level of necessary force while keeping themselves and civilians safe during each interaction.

Nearly every police chief with whom I've spoken agrees. Yet when it comes time to approve such ongoing training, they inevitably decline, citing the expense and potential loss of work hours through possible training injuries (workers' compensation). Their *shortsighted practicality* refuses to publicly acknowledge what would undoubtedly enhance the safety of citizens, suspects, and officers alike in every use-of-force encounter inside their jurisdiction. In 2019, both citizens and law enforcement officials in Marietta, Georgia, were shaken by a use-of-force incident that was caught on video at a local IHOP, after a man who didn't receive bacon with his meal became excessively upset.

Officers with a lack of training are more apt to lose their cool and overreact in such situations. Their emotions get hijacked by the amygdala, a part of the brain that can trigger an internal fight-or-flight response aimed at self-preservation, rather than allowing the cognitive functions of their prefrontal cortex to remain in control. As a result of that incident, the Marietta Police Department (MPD) mandated that all new hires, during their five months of police academy training, attend weekly classes at a local civilian-owned BJJ gym. In 2020, all 145 active-duty officers of the MPD were offered department-sponsored BJJ training at the same gym. A total of 95 officers opted into the program, and the results were undeniable.

For years, I had been trying to apply the Head Control Principle by speaking to police chiefs about implementing such a program. Now, thanks to the willingness of the MPD to think proactively, I had significant data to back my long-held beliefs. The data revealed that the BJJ-trained officers were 59 percent less likely to engage in a use-of-force incident. Serious injury to a civilian was 53 percent less likely during a physical encounter with a BJJ officer, including a 23 percent reduction in Taser deployments. As for the financial implications, the city paid a total of $26,000 for the classes over an eighteen-month period but saved an estimated $66,752 in projected injuries to officers. And, of course, that doesn't include the possible loss of life and jury award that a single use-of-force incident gone wrong could result in.

Since the emergence of this data, I have spoken to scores of police chiefs and agencies nationwide wanting to replicate Marietta's program, with Gracie University working diligently to meet the demands of more certified training centers. Of all the opportunities I've been afforded as a member of the Gracie Family, none fills me with greater pride than being a part of the policing revolution that advocates for humane and compassionate control tactics over brute force. For as my grandfather Helio Gracie always said, "A real jiu-jitsu fighter does not go around beating people down. Our defense is made to neutralize aggression."

We still have a long way to go, but thanks to the progressive law enforcement agencies that are committed to doing better and their open-minded chiefs, the future of policing in America appears to be headed in a direction much brighter than its past.

If you're yelling, you're the one who's lost control of the conversation.
—Taylor Swift, writer, performer

Dogs/Dealings/Meditations

If you walked your dog around your neighborhood this morning, you more than likely practiced the Head Control Principle by using a collar and a leash. We also bring this core jiu-jitsu principle to many of our daily business dealings both big and small. Suppose you're on the phone with your cable TV provider. You had previously accepted a deal in which you received a package of their premium channels free for a period of two months. To ensure that you remembered to cancel the package at the end of the subscription trial, you made a notation in your daily calendar book. Then you followed through by going online and opting out. But the next month you see there's a charge on your new cable bill, an increase of $14 per month. After waiting on the cable company's phone carousel for more than ten minutes, you finally get the human voice of a sales rep. You tell your story succinctly from beginning to end. Then you discover that the sales rep simply doesn't have the power to change the amount on your bill. So from experience, you automatically demand to speak to a supervisor. Congratulations. You already have jiu-jitsu's Head Control Principle in your life's toolbox.

If you're not speaking to the correct person, someone with the power to address your problem, then your efforts will be in vain. Similar scenarios could easily play out in a myriad of other places. For example, you can't settle an issue with your child's teacher, so you ask to see their administrator. There's an unresolved disagreement with a server at a restaurant and you call for the manager. And so on. How might you consider yourself to be a Head Control Principle Master? When you begin bypassing lower-level employees immediately if your issue is too complex and going straight to management, saving yourself both time and energy.

How can you practice the Head Control Principle in reverse? By keeping your own head and mind free and clear of obstacles and distractions. Consider meditating. Meditation is a mindfulness exercise often practiced daily by its practitioners. It can help increase mental clarity and self-discipline, reduce stress and anxiety, and in some cases it can even ease depression and physical pain. The practice of meditation has also been connected to the central nervous system's fight-or-flight response, something that a jiu-jitsu practitioner wants well under control in order to react rationally in times of crisis, without fear dominating the thought process.

If you're a total novice at meditation, don't stress. It's easy to start. Simply close your eyes, sit still, and practice. Stay focused on your breathing, and your mind will do the rest. When you find yourself lost in thought, that's mental awareness. A ten-minute meditation can feel exceedingly long to a beginner. No problem. Start with a length of time that suits you and gradually build up to longer meditations, creating a perfect synergy with jiu-jitsu's Ratchet Principle. Need help? YouTube is filled with guided meditations for beginners to help you on your way.

Profile: The Greatest Female Jockey of All Time

Hall of Fame jockey Julie Krone is one of the most accomplished riders in the history of Thoroughbred racing. The 4-foot-10, 100-pound Krone practically grew up on horseback and has visited the winner's circle more than 3,700 times during a career highlighted by stirring victories in major races as well as devastating spills. Pound for pound, jockeys are some of the greatest athletes in the world. Their unique ability to guide 1,800-pound Thoroughbreds around a racetrack via a bridle and a mouth bit makes a jockey's job a fitting parallel to jiu-jitsu's Head Control Principle.

"Growing up, all I ever did was ride horses. So by the time I got to the racetrack (at age fifteen via a forged birth certificate), I had learned a lot about horse psychology and how to get along with all the different personalities that Thoroughbreds could present," said Julie Krone, who received her earliest lessons from her mom, an accomplished horsewoman. "You can't force a horse to do anything. There are various stages of give-and-take with a horse. People think of them as being these big, spirited animals, and they are, but they're also really sensitive. You ask a horse to do something either with pressure through the reins or your heels. When they comply, you reward them by releasing that pressure and praising them," said Krone, who possesses an incredible gift of bonding with a horse, which in turn often resulted in an equine's top performance.

How does Krone communicate with Thoroughbreds? "It's definitely a balance between your hands and body. You need to have quick hands to release pressure on a horse after it has done something right. Then the horse will want to repeat that action for you. If you lean your body down across their back and squeeze your legs a little bit, a good racehorse will take off beneath you like a Maserati. But if you pull back on the reins and drop your hands on their neck, you can convince them to slow down. Then you can make their strides bigger, get them to relax more and breathe better. If you can accomplish that, they'll save something for a really big finish," noted Krone, who won the 1993 Belmont Stakes in that exact fashion aboard a Thoroughbred named Colonial Affair. It was the first time a woman rider had ever won a Triple Crown race.

"I thought all the time about how easy it was for me to ride Thoroughbreds and how they responded for me, especially the most challenging ones. I would think to myself, *I must really be blessed to have this special gift to do this.*"[34]

The highest possible stage in moral culture is when we recognize that we ought to control our thoughts.
—Charles Darwin, naturalist

Contemplate the Head Control Principle when . . .

- **Escalating Concerns:** You have a bad experience at a restaurant and the server handles it poorly, so you ask to speak to the manager on duty.
- **Seeking Approval:** Before seeking approval on a project, you conduct research to identify who has the authority to approve

34 Julie Krone interview with Paul Volponi (March 29, 2022).

your project, then you seek out that authorized person's advisors to get a vector from them before making your ask.

- **Managing Hierarchy:** You're seeking increased compensation but you know your immediate supervisor won't support it (for the wrong reasons), so you meet with the general manager directly to explain the challenges you're having with the supervisor and why you believe you deserve a pay increase.
- **Getting What You Want:** You want to go to a jiu-jitsu seminar this weekend but you know that doing it without your spouse's consent would cause turmoil, so you ask permission and even agree to watch the kids the following weekend while they go to a concert in order to create the win-win.

Equinity

One of man's earliest uses of the Head Control Principle arose from the domestication of the horse, more than 5,000 years ago by the Botai culture in what is now Kazakhstan. Learning to control these spirited and free-running equines enhanced military, commercial, sporting, and leisure activities. Horses are almost exclusively controlled via their heads, through a bridle used for direction, and reins used to give subtle commands such as to turn, slow down, and speed up. This is the origin of the modern-day expressions "free rein," meaning unlimited freedom, and "rein in," meaning to curtail one's self-governance or expenditure of energies. The span of a ruler's control over their dominion is also termed a "reign." Both "rein" and "reign" are derived from the Old French, each making their initial appearance in the thirteenth century.

Scan here to learn the combat application of

The Redirection Principle

Chapter Twenty-Nine

The Redirection Principle

Using unfavorable circumstances to create favorable outcomes.

When you can't change the direction of the wind, adjust your sails.
—H. Jackson Brown, Jr., author

Jiu-jitsu has long been lauded as an art that uses the opponent's own force against them. This can be accomplished in many ways. So far, we've witnessed various aspects of this concept in the Creation, Acceptance, Clock, Kuzushi, Tension, False Surrender, Depletion, Momentum, and Tag-along Principles. Redirecting energy is another valuable technique in turning an opponent's force in your favor. The Redirection Principle primarily focuses on a pair of ways to achieve this goal. You can either change the angle of impact of your opponent's incoming power (for example, replacing a 90-degree angle with a 45-degree angle to reduce the brunt of a blow) or intercept that energy before it is fully formed. These techniques will stifle your opponent's techniques, open the door for you to counterattack, and contribute toward depleting their energy.

Growing the Circle of Trust

In late May 2021, it seemed as if everyone in America who cared deeply about children being bullied at school had sent me a photo of a thirteen-year-old from Illinois named Charlee Funes. That photo wasn't particularly easy to digest. Charlee's face had multiple scrapes and bruises, and her front tooth was badly chipped. She also had the vacuous expression of someone whose confidence in their safety had been stolen away. Gracie University's work with Austin McDaniel, an Indiana youngster who similarly had been attacked (described in chapter twenty-one), received noticeable attention on social media, and now people across the country were directing these extreme cases to us. In response, we put out a call on social media to help us locate Charlee. Within twenty-four hours, I was on a video call with Charlee, who hadn't been back to school since being brutalized. Charlee, an incredibly kindhearted girl, appeared ready and eager to learn jiu-jitsu. Unlike Austin and his family, however, Charlee's mom couldn't take time off from work to escort her daughter to Torrance to train with us. It appeared to be a sizable quandary until I reached into my jiu-jitsu toolbox to find a solution.

Up until this time, these extreme-case bullying victims had only been taught jiu-jitsu by me or my brother. This time, though, the circumstances and logistics dictated otherwise. If we were going to be part of Charlee's turnaround, we would need to employ the Redirection Principle and introduce the talents of an instructor at one of our certified training centers. I turned to Jeff Kim, a lifelong martial artist whose school was in Elgin, Illinois. Admittedly, Jeff was nervous about the idea of taking on a high-profile student with such pressing and sensitive needs. But I knew Jeff well. I had confidence that he could be instrumental in assisting Charlee over the physical and mental hurdles that had been so unfairly shoved in front of her. And I needed to reassure myself as well that other instructors in our organization could succeed at this task.

Charlee and Jeff would have three vitally important months to immerse her in Gracie Bullyproof training before the reopening of Charlee's school in August. The results? From their first moment on the mats, they really hit it off. With a lot of hard work, everything fell into place and the pair didn't miss a beat. All summer long, Jeff proved himself to be an amazing leader and mentor to Charlee, who eventually moved from private lessons to group classes with students her own age. I couldn't have been prouder of them. In August, the first day of the new school semester arrived. I spoke with Charlee's mom about the jitters she might have in sending her daughter back. She told me that Charlee said to her, "Don't worry about me, Mom. I'm bully-proof now."

The Redirection Principle had supplied a pathway to personal growth for both student and instructor. Charlee and her family agreed to do a before-and-after video detailing her journey. The video currently has over four million views on Facebook and YouTube combined. That's important because acts of school bullying should never be swept under the rug, either in embarrassment by the victim or by school administrators who don't want to deal with the potential fallout. Instead, light needs to be shined upon them. That's the only way these incidents are going to be taken seriously. To me, the massive support of Charlee's transformation from people around the world signifies that society is ready to give this issue the attention it so desperately needs.

Something New for Student and Teacher

Jeff Kim began his study of martial arts in the mid-1970s under the tutelage of his pioneering father, Ken Ok Hyung Kim, who opened a school in Illinois after immigrating to the US from South Korea. Jeff has studied many different forms of martial arts and has a long and successful career as an instructor. Over the years, a multitude of bullied students and their parents have sought out his help. Why then did Jeff feel nervous about taking on the challenge of teaching Charlee?

"The nervousness I felt was twofold," said Jeff. "Rener already had a rapport with Charlee and her family. They didn't know me from Adam and would be driving ninety minutes each way for a one-hour class. That was a tremendous commitment on their part. Normally, when I teach, there are friends and family members of the students watching. But since the journey was being documented, I knew there would be a lot of eyeballs tracking Charlee's progress. It was a huge weight at the start. Rener and Ryron are the ones who have always taught these high-profile students. I've seen the impact they can make on such a student's life. This was the first time someone outside of Gracie University had been called upon to do something like this. I felt like I'd been handed the torch. I was really honored but I also didn't want to disappoint anyone. In the end, I think that Charlee and I both gained something very special from the experience."[35]

Every problem has a solution; it may sometimes just need another perspective.
—Katherine Russell, author

Redirecting Surplus Food

There are plenty of individuals and organizations throughout the world interested in redirecting unwanted food to combat hunger. Whether left-overs from a restaurant or food that's fast approaching a spoilage date on a supermarket shelf, there are established redirection routes ready to feed people in need. Among them is New York City–based City Harvest, which was born more than four decades ago when the organization's first director, Helen verDuin Palit, ordered potato skins in a restaurant. After discovering that the rest of the potato was being discarded, she made the Redirection Principle her passion via a meaningful, social cause. With the help of nearly 200 staff members and thousands of volunteers, City Harvest currently delivers 75 million pounds of surplus food per year to people in need. Kudos to all involved and their efficient jiu-jitsu–like model.

35 Jeff Kim interview with Paul Volponi (May 4, 2022).

Dealing with Anger

One of the healthiest goals you can attain through the Redirection Principle is learning how to redirect your anger. Many people in today's world of choosing-up sides and shouting at whoever voices an opposing opinion have a tough time dealing with their own anger and redirecting the anger of others pointed at them. Buddha said, "Holding on to anger is like grasping a hot coal with the intent of throwing it at someone; you are the one who gets burned." With that observation in mind, there are many ways to defuse such personal anger. For example, you can redirect those feelings into a workout or competitive sport. Lifting weights, riding a bike, jogging around the block several times, or smacking around a tennis ball can ease your tensions and blow off some of that rapidly building steam. As in the case of the tennis ball, hitting an inanimate object can be a substantial emotional release for many people. It should go without saying: choose something soft like a pillow and not a brick wall.

Often, writing down your feelings in a journal, diary, or letter, even one you have no intention of ever mailing, can be quite cathartic. If you can be alone in a car, letting go of a primal scream can also be a release that helps you to refocus. A scenario may occur where you become the subject of unwarranted or inappropriate anger. This can happen when you set a new boundary (an example of the Centerline Principle, which we'll discuss in chapter thirty-one) with someone. How can you deal with this? Realize that it's *their* problem, not *yours*. Don't allow their response to make you angry in return. Use physical distance (Distance Principle) to remove yourself from the situation. But no matter which direction the anger is flowing (you to them or them to you), try not to express yourself with a split-second reaction. Instead, if possible, replace that with a well-thought-out response.

Profile: Shattering Norms

Dr. AnnMaria De Mars, who holds an MBA and a PhD in educational psychology, has embraced the Redirection Principle her entire life. A master at deflecting the gender biases hoisted upon her as a pioneer of women in judo, De Mars continually redirected the negativity into motivating energy that supported her on every rung of life's ladder. The first American to ever win a gold medal at the World Judo Tournament (1984), De Mars grew up in an era when females didn't always have the chance to either compete or be praised for their desire to succeed at activities outside of what societal norms had reserved for them.

"I probably missed the memo at school that week about how a girl should act, and what she should care about. I looked in the mirror to comb my hair and brush my teeth, not to stress over my appearance. I grew up with a very positive body image. I didn't concern myself with whether my nose was too big or my breasts too small to fit society's definitions of beauty," said De Mars, who is the mother of four incredibly successful daughters, including former MMA champion Ronda Rousey. "I would tell my daughters all the time, 'It's my education that puts a roof over our heads, not my gold medal.'"

As an adolescent, De Mars spent time in both juvenile hall and foster care. "I got into judo and it helped me turn things around. While some of my friends were out getting into more trouble, I had to be at judo practice." Does De Mars believe that every adolescent should study martial arts? "What kids need most is at least one positive adult in their lives. Sometimes that comes from the home and sometimes from outside activities. It really doesn't matter whether it's judo, choir, or band. Although with judo, you know that young person will be physically fit and develop self-confidence," she noted.

How did math and judo blend together for the champ? "I had a serious knee injury, so I couldn't do half of what my opponents could while standing on my feet." That caused De Mars to study the statistics of the ultra-competitive sport, concentrating more on mat work instead of throws, and mastering those specific techniques through intense repetition. "I have that type of problem-solving mind and judo reinforced it in me," said De Mars, who has a significant interest in helping Native American adolescents, particularly those living in tribal regions, gain a foothold in mathematics. "Kids decide too early on that they're not good at math, and that really sets them back."

To that end, De Mars is currently the CEO of 7 Generation Games, a company that creates math-themed computer games for students, aimed at fostering both skills and a feeling of success in math. Recently, nearly 150 schools added her software to their curriculum. Despite all of her impressive credentials in education and working with adolescents, even PhDs sometimes get schooled on the basics. "I used to jokingly tell Ronda before her judo matches, 'I'll love you, honey, even if you lose, just not as much.' Then one day, Ronda, who was probably thirteen or fourteen, came to me and said, 'You know that really hurts me to hear.' After that, I'd say about anything she was doing (not just judo): 'You know, Ronda, if you don't win, I *will* love you just as much.'"[36]

You cannot look in a new direction by looking harder in the same direction.
—Edward de Bono, physician, author

Call on the Redirection Principle when . . .

- **Tactically De-escalating:** You see a man violently arguing with another smaller man, so you intervene and tactically empathize with the aggressor, "Don't waste your time, look at how small he is, the cops are on their way . . ." and this both strokes his ego and redirects his focus sufficiently to help prevent further escalation.
- **Directing the Discussion:** Your spouse is frustrated by how much time you spend doing jiu-jitsu, so you respectfully remind them that, above everything else, it's your time on the mat that teaches you to be calm, loving, and patient when you're off the mat.
- **Deflecting Anger:** An irate customer is on the phone telling you how disappointed they are in one of your employees, so you apologize emphatically before you redirect the conversation by asking them what system they recommend you implement to

36 Dr. AnnaMaria de Mars interview with Paul Volponi (February 8, 2022).

prevent this from ever happening again, and they immediately change their tone.

- **Managing Expectations:** Your child is begging you to go to Disneyland, but you can't afford it, so you let them know you're saving up, but in the meantime you can take them to watch the new Disney movie that just came out.

Appetite vs. Hunger

Yes, many people in this world are plagued by hunger. But for people who are either trying to improve their diet or lose weight, it's important to recognize the difference between appetite and hunger. Appetite is the *desire* to eat, often brought on by the sight or smell of food, sometimes even by the time of day. Hunger is the *need* to eat, brought on by the body's quest to sustain itself. Mostly, it's our appetite that pushes us to eat, especially those things we crave such as sweets, carbs, and salty snacks.

How can you redirect your appetite? Resist the immediate impulse to make a fast-food stop. Set an alarm for fifteen minutes in the future. When the appointed time arrives, the urge to satisfy yourself with food may have well passed you by. Take a piece of fruit or a stalk of celery. If you're not hungry for either of those things, then it's probably your appetite trying to control you. In an effort to redirect, you might consider leaving the room, kitchen, or restaurant where the food is tempting you. Go for a walk. Take a shower. Grab a book and head for the park. An appetite can very much become a fleeting desire, one over which you can take control.

Scan here to learn the combat application of

The Mobility Principle

Chapter Thirty

The Mobility Principle

Accepting the things you cannot change, while having the courage to change the things you can.

If the mountain will not come to Muhammad, then Muhammad must go to the mountain.
—Francis Bacon, philosopher and statesman

Mobility is an important success-achieving trait in endeavors ranging from business to sports to our daily social interactions with people. And, of course, mobility is one of the core principles of jiu-jitsu. The Mobility Principle is simple and direct: If you can't move your opponent, move yourself. Though jiu-jitsu employs many leverage-based techniques (consider the Frame, Posture, Pivot, and Ratchet Principles), sometimes it is just easier to reposition ourselves than a heavier, strongly positioned opponent. It is an energy-saving concept in an art based on efficiency. Some of the most common mobility applications on the mat consist of us circling, sliding, separating, pulling, and spinning relative to our adversary. These are movements with which you're probably well acquainted from participating in any number of sports and activities.

Sliding My Feet . . . Eventually

Sometimes even jiu-jitsu masters can't see the core principle staring them in the face. That was especially true for me when my ego got in the way concerning the California certification of Gracie Survival Tactics (GST), which trains police officers nationwide to use jiu-jitsu techniques with the goal of incurring less aggressive responses during use-of-force encounters. Our GST program had been an outstanding success for three decades, even in our home state of California, despite not being registered as an official program by the California Commission on Peace Officer Standards and Training (POST). To be clear, Gracie University received dozens of in-state inquiries every week asking if our program had California POST's seal of approval. Understanding that our program was head and shoulders above the rest, I resented the idea of conforming to the state's standards. I didn't like the idea of state bureaucrats telling me how to teach jiu-jitsu, and I definitely didn't want to reduce our normal class sizes by one-third, from 150 students to 50 students, as per their policy.

For years, my thought was to get California POST to change their policy to fit our needs. But that result never occurred and likely had little chance of ever happening. Even though the commission and I didn't see eye to eye on their certification regulations, I was asked to join a video call sponsored by the state, debating prospective techniques that could be used by California officers to keep both citizens and officers safer during encounters. I was quick to make the point that officers in our state should be given more than four hours of training every two years. That's when the moderator asked if I would join him on a private call after the session. On that call, he made the statement, "Rener, if you want to change the system, the best way to do it is from the inside, by being part of the system." The words were barely out of his mouth when it hit me—my ego had clearly stopped me from recognizing the Mobility Principle as a solution to this problem.

The commission wasn't about to change for me so I needed to display a willingness to adapt. In essence, it was an opponent on the mat that was too big for me to move without expending a significant amount of energy. That conversation, and subsequent realization, inspired me to change my stance. I recruited my good friend and longtime GST advocate, Officer Justin Wade, to help me fill out the necessary paperwork, since he had experience jumping through the same hoops to get the LAPD's curriculum approved by POST. We worked for weeks documenting our curriculum into terms the state recognized, and several months later, Gracie University's GST program gained state approval. Although we were forced to cut our class sizes by two-thirds, the California POST stamp of approval increased the demand for GST courses in California by a staggering 1,000 percent, more than making up for the discrepancy.

Gracie University headquarters is located in the city of Torrance, California. I had always been perplexed as to why the Torrance Police Department never officially sent any officers to train with us when we had officers flying in from all corners of the globe to attend our courses. It was something that never felt right to me, and it always left me feeling disappointed. Well, not long after getting POST certified, as I was leaving our facility for home, a Torrance police cruiser pulled into our parking lot. I asked the officer if I could help him with anything. He responded, "The chief sent me over to register several of our officers for your next training session. You are POST approved, right?" I nodded my head in delight, walked him into the building, and personally introduced him to Jackie, our GST coordinator, who got him and his team registered for our upcoming five-day instructor course. I have to admit it was a special feeling, almost like a kid at a sporting event who'd been gifted an official jersey by the home team.

While the process of achieving POST certification demanded I alter my business practices and my state of mind, it was totally worth it. Seeing what a massive impact it had on GST's growth within California, I immediately set my sights on achieving the same designation in every state in the US. I assigned the ambitious task of nationwide certification to Charlie Fernandez, director of GST operations, and, shockingly, in a span of less than eighteen months, we had been granted POST certification (or its equivalent) in 41 states, making Gracie University the only civilian-owned defensive tactics organization to achieve this distinction. Thanks to the awesome team we have at Gracie University, and the Mobility Principle, it's only a matter of time before GST is POST-certified nationwide.

A Number of Months Later . . .

As I pulled into that same parking lot early one morning, I had jitters. I was about to make a video in our Gracie Breakdown series, as I had done hundreds of times before. Only this time it wouldn't be about detailing a specific technique in an MMA fight. Instead, it would be about a controversial use-of-force incident between a police officer in Grand Rapids, Michigan, and a 24-year-old man named Patrick Lyoya that went horribly wrong, resulting in the shooting death of Mr. Lyoya.

I sat more than 2,000 miles away from where the tragic incident occurred, with a set of initial facts and the nationally released footage from the officer's body-worn camera. I understood that no matter what I said in that video, I would undoubtedly take heat from several different corners. That didn't matter to me, though. I felt compelled to speak about it. My experience in working with law enforcement professionals has repeatedly led me back to the same conclusion time and time again—police officers nationwide are woefully undertrained in empty-hand control tactics. When an officer enters into such a situation and feels that they have lost control of the encounter, it can often be accompanied by panic and a loss of rational decision-making ability that results in the officer going into survival mode.

When officers are too panicked or too poorly trained to respond with their empty-hand control skills, they usually turn to the tools on their duty belt, meaning a Taser or firearm. Of course there are certainly situations for which higher levels of force, including lethal force, are necessary and justifiable, but the optimal outcome for police officers should be to neutralize the threat with the lowest level of necessary force. In my opinion, every officer needs to undergo a minimum of one hour of empty-hand control training per week to feel safer in use-of-force encounters and to avoid the unnecessary escalation that happens far too often.

Without increased training, officers won't recognize the positions, or "islands," of safety that exist in every physical encounter. Above everything else, learning these relative safe havens allows officers to maintain activation of their prefrontal cortex, a critical factor in avoiding panic. Why did I *need* to make that video? Open myself up for the criticism? Because better training for police officers is a discussion society needs to have now more than ever. If I ever willingly walk away from that discussion to make things easier on myself, then I don't deserve a seat at the table where these problems will one day be solved. So I slammed my car door behind me, headed inside Gracie University, and hit "record" to earn my seat at the table.

It is a narrow mind which cannot look at a subject from various points of view.
—Mary Ann Evans (pen name George Eliot), novelist

Beach Blanket Bother

Implementing the Mobility Principle is one of the easiest ways to avoid conflict in your daily life. Suppose you're camped out at the beach with your family on a beautiful, sunny afternoon. You come out of the surf to discover that a group of loud and fairly obnoxious people have put their blankets down not too far from yours. They are so loud that your own thoughts have annoyingly become entangled in their conversation. When their language starts to become inappropriate, you rapidly come to the point where you've had enough. Is it possible to approach these people and let them know that you consider them to be rude? Obviously, you can. But that's a difficult talk to initiate with a group of strangers who will probably be your beach neighbors for several more hours.

Instead of trying to teach them to be considerate of others, wouldn't it be easier and consume far less emotional energy to simply move your family fifty yards farther down the shore, beyond the reach of their collective voices? Don't allow your pride or ego to talk you into the notion: *We were here first. They should be the ones to move.* If you were on a bus and somebody who sat next to you began coughing and sneezing, you'd get up and move without it being an internal struggle. What's the connection between the beach and bus scenarios? Well, the same way you can't cure someone of being sick by snapping your fingers, you can't teach obnoxious people to instantly develop manners through an impromptu speech or lecture.

Enterprise Mobility

The COVID-19 pandemic drastically pushed the envelope on the evolution of business practices worldwide. One of the most significant changes to emerge is the option being offered to many employees to work from home, signaling a seismic shift from the traditional central office model. This growing vision of a new workplace has been termed "enterprise mobility." It's obviously been made possible through the combined use of personal laptops and access to the data-sharing cloud.

What are the benefits of enterprise mobility? Increased productivity and a decrease in corporate and personal expenses are among the biggest. Consider that without the tiresome burden of a daily commute to a central office, workers are routinely more focused and possess a greater energy reserve to bring to their projects. Enterprise mobility smartly synergizes jiu-jitsu's Mobility Principle with the Connection, Distance, Creation, Clock, Tension, Depletion, and Pivot Principles in order to boost morale and optimize productivity.

Profile: Fighting Blind

Martial arts instructor John Giordano is a problem solver. When faced with the task of teaching a visually impaired student, he found a solution in the premise of the Mobility Principle. Since the student's perspective couldn't be changed, Giordano finally changed his own. "At the very beginning, I was becoming frustrated as a teacher. It was almost as if my student didn't understand what I was telling him. So I came up with the idea of blindfolding myself. For a short time, it would let me experience exactly what he was feeling, and it supplied us with the same spatial reference point," said Giordano, whose student eventually rose up the ladder of black belt degrees.

How did Giordano get his start in martial arts? "I grew up in the South Bronx. At about fourteen years old, I was running with a street gang. We saw a martial arts school and I said, 'Why don't we go up there and kick the teacher's ass?' That didn't happen. But we did go up there and I liked what I saw. The next day was my first class. The teacher wanted to demonstrate how to block a punch and asked for a volunteer, so I raised my hand. While he was still addressing the class, I tried to sneak punch the teacher. The next thing I knew, I was on the floor with a foot on my chest and this face smiling down at me. Needless to say, martial arts really changed my life."[37]

The power of hanging pawns is based precisely in their mobility, in their ability to create acute situations instantly.
—Boris Spassky, chess grandmaster

Reflect on the Mobility Principle when . . .

- **Making Commitments:** Your long-distance relationship is suffering, and your significant other can't relocate due to the job they have, so you decide to make the move and start over in a new city to give the relationship a chance.
- **Dealing with Distractions:** The person in the cubicle next to yours at the office speaks so loudly on the phone with customers that you can't focus, so you seek approval from your supervisor to move to a different cubicle.
- **Encouraging Children:** Your young child is terrified of their first jiu-jitsu lesson and won't exit the car, so you carry them into the building and let them watch the class from your lap, after which they are eager to give it a try because they see that the kids are having so much fun.
- **Managing Health:** You've suffered from obesity for twenty years and have failed every diet you've tried, so you decide to get gastric bypass surgery to help get the weight off and increase your chances of enjoying a healthy life.

37 John Giordano interview with Paul Volponi (February 3, 2022).

M-Learning

It used to be that the Mobility Principle for students was simply: *If you can't see the teacher's notes on the board from where you sit, get up and change your seat.* Not anymore. Today, the Mobility Principle is the driving force behind "M-learning" or "Mobile Learning," which is the act of using personal mobile devices such as smartphones and tablets to access learning materials through mobile apps. What are the advantages of M-learning? It's incredibly flexible and allows students to access materials at any time of the day and from anywhere. Imagine someone working a full-time job and trying to get a college degree or engage in graduate studies. Setting your own hours and location can be vital to moving forward educationally.

As for elementary, middle, and high school students, M-learning can make better use of their time, turning leisure-time video games into learning-based vehicles. It also makes them more tech savvy, and promotes individual-focused learning where students can move ahead at their own speed. Because the materials have 24/7 connectivity, it is one of the first educational systems with the ability to reflect whether individual students are more naturally suited to being morning, afternoon, or evening learners.

Scan here to learn the combat application of

The Centerline Principle

Chapter Thirty-One

The Centerline Principle

Owning your life by setting boundaries wherever they're needed.

Honoring your own boundaries is the clearest message to others to honor them, too.
—Gina Greenlee, author

Controlling the center of your world is important in all phases of life. On the jiu-jitsu mat, establishing control of the centerline, a theoretical line occupying the middle of two combatants, is also vital. Because bodies are changing positions during a grapple and not always directly facing one another, there can be two centerlines, yours and your opponent's. Maintaining control over your own centerline will increase your potential options, while controlling the opponent's will severely limit their options. Ideally, we'd like to stop the opponent's limbs and appendages from being able to cross over from one side of their body to the other to lend support. That's referred to as "splitting," mirroring the combative theory of *divide and conquer* (more on this phrase later). A successful split can also lead to a "break," a powerful result of trapping a pair of appendages in one of the four quadrants of a grapple: upper right, lower right, upper left, or lower left.

Establishing Boundaries

During daily life, the Centerline Principle is largely about setting boundaries for yourself and others. It's also about having the hard conversations that go along with establishing these limitations. The challenge for most people is that they typically won't set boundaries that they are not capable of enforcing, and this is where jiu-jitsu will often make the difference.

As a junior at West High School in Torrance, there was a boy named Martin in a few of my classes. We weren't friends, but we knew of each other from existing in the same orbit. And if the junior class had a bully, it was Martin. I was sitting in the school cafeteria one day when I heard this crash of plates and then a loud profanity behind me. I turned around to see Martin angrily standing directly in front of a freshman less than half his size. By all appearances, Martin looked like he was about to pound the kid, who wasn't putting up any kind of guard or resistance, into the food-stained floor. I didn't know what started the fire that I was looking at, but I knew I had to put it out or it was going to spiral out of control very quickly.

I got between them, standing face-to-face with Martin, and said, "Leave him alone. Just walk away."

"Yeah, but you don't know what he did, Rener," said Martin.

"I don't care," I replied. "This isn't going to happen."

I never verbally threatened Martin. But I had clearly established a boundary, realizing that if Martin chose to violate it, he and I would most likely be fighting. Did I believe that I was right? Yes. Was I ready and willing to accept all of the possible consequences? Yes. An instant later, an infuriated Martin walked away.

Later in my life, as a jiu-jitsu instructor, I needed to have a "hard conversation" with Yasu, a dedicated student who garnered a reputation for caring more about being perceived as the "winner" than about the safety of his training partners. When his name had surfaced more than once in relation to this problem, I knew it was something I needed to address. I brought Yasu into my office for a one-on-one discussion. "People don't feel safe rolling with you," I explained to him. Taken aback by the complaint at first, Yasu eventually conceded, "Maybe I do care too much about coming out on top." I made it clear to Yasu that this was the first and only time we would ever have this conversation, that he would need to solve the issue, and that the next complaint of this nature would mark his last class at Gracie University. That conversation took place one full year ago. Yasu is still with us, and no students have raised any issues in relation to him since. I knew that setting that strict boundary could have offended Yasu and caused him to quit. But that was a risk I was willing to take since the safe and collaborative culture of the school is much more important than any individual student's ambitions on the mat.

Having a hard talk with a single student at our Torrance location is one thing, but enforcing boundaries with a jiu-jitsu instructor who owns a certified training center (CTC) bearing the Gracie name is an entirely different challenge. This became my reality when I learned that a married instructor at one CTC had begun a romantic relationship with one of the students. On one hand, that might be viewed as the personal business of two consenting adults, and possibly none of mine. But the situation had grown darker. Several other students both knew about the relationship and had regular contact at the school with the instructor's still-in-the-dark spouse. In essence, that made those students part of an ongoing lie and cover-up, something they hadn't signed up for on their journey to study Gracie jiu-jitsu. On that basis alone, I felt obliged to call the instructor and immediately terminate our relationship with that school.

In a fight, the Centerline Principle teaches us to set physical boundaries to neutralize an adversary, and in life these boundaries are verbal, psychological, and sometimes emotional. But make no mistake, it can be a difficult task to set and enforce boundaries. You need to have confidence in yourself and your judgment, because what's on the line is, in many cases, your personal integrity or your personal safety. Boundaries also need to be fair if they're to be respected, have meaning, and carry weight. As the creator of those boundaries, you'll need to be able to both celebrate the progress they inspire and accept the actionable results they may incur.

Divide and Conquer

The Latin phrase *divide et impera* translates to "divide and conquer" or "divide and rule." Over the centuries, it has been used as a political, sociological, and military strategy built on the concept of breaking down a power structure into smaller individual sources that lack the continuity, mobility, and overall strength of combined forces (comparable to the aim of the Centerline Principle in jiu-jitsu). This phrase is perhaps most associated with Roman ruler Julius Caesar (81–45 BC), who famously stated, "All Gaul is divided into three parts," concerning his defeat and subjugation of the Gallic tribes. But the strategy has either been used or propagated by Napoleon, Sir Francis Bacon, James Madison, Thomas Jefferson, and philosopher Immanuel Kant. Today, techies may be more familiar with the phrase as it refers to a computer algorithm aptly called "divide and conquer," which attempts to solve a high-level problem by breaking it down into smaller subproblems until they become solvable.

Success comes from finding your center and self.
—Bryant McGill, author

Profile: Central to His Life

Ron Van Clief, also known as "The Black Dragon," is a martial arts legend. The seemingly ageless Van Clief starred in martial arts–genre films of the 1970s and is still competing in tournaments today as a jiu-jitsu practitioner.

"In many ways martial arts saved my life. Not only in situations on the streets when it was life and death, but in the rest of life too, dealing with the obstacles and adversities that everyone encounters. It gives you an opportunity to get a good overview of life's purpose and one's own personal choices," said Ron Van Clief, who was a teen on the streets of Brooklyn in the late 1950s. "I didn't start martial arts until I was fifteen. Prior to that, I was a gymnast and a swimmer. I only wanted to do martial arts so I would be good enough to go into the Marine Corps."

Van Clief spent a half dozen years in the corps, predominantly stationed in the South Pacific where he was exposed to a myriad of martial arts disciplines. As his martial skills and reputation grew, Van Clief was recruited to star in a number of Asian-made kung fu films and do voice-over work in scores of others. Some critics of the era referred to them as "blaxploitation films," contending that the characters being portrayed were stereotypical and criminally driven. But Van Clief, who believes he helped pave the way for future generations of Black actors to have starring roles in films, doesn't see it that way at all. "I don't believe in that term. Just because a film has a person of color in a dominant role, any positive example of character and proficiency is welcome in the public domain. My work in those films opened the door for other Black artists to star in Hong Kong films, and down the line to where we are today in the industry."

The martial artist is also widely recognized for climbing into the octagon at age 51 to fight champion Royce Gracie. "I had watched UFC 1 and UFC 2 on pay-per-view. I told my students at the time, 'I have to do this.' Everyone thought I had lost my mind. But when you see something and it inspires you to want to do it, you have to do it. You have to follow your chi. It was inevitable that I would fight Royce Gracie. You picked your opponent through a lottery using little balls and I chose Royce's number." Gracie ultimately defeated Van Clief with a rear naked choke nearing the four-minute mark of the match. "It was a great experience. Not long after that, I was made UFC commissioner and I helped write lots of their rules."

In his late sixties, Ron Van Clief decided that he wanted to study Brazilian jiu-jitsu. "A little more than eleven years ago, I took off my black belt and put on a white belt. I'd had fifty years of building my upstairs game but I didn't have a ground game. Right now, I have a purple belt with four stripes. I'm going to keep training until I get my black belt in BJJ," said Van Clief, who studies in Hawaii under Relson Gracie.

How does Ron Van Clief view his legendary career? "Martial arts has shown me the world. I've lived in New York, Los Angeles, Hong Kong, the Virgin Islands, and now Hawaii. I've competed in over 900 tournaments. I stopped competing in karate at age seventy-four. But I'm still competing in jiu-jitsu today."[38] That's why so many people around the globe refer to Ron Van Clief as "The Black Dragon."

38 Ron Van Clief interview with Paul Volponi (March 8, 2022).

The center that I cannot find is known to my unconscious mind.
—W. H. Auden, poet

Consider the Centerline Principle when . . .

- **Prioritizing Family:** You realize you are too easily distracted by notifications to your phone at home, so you place it in a drawer every time you're engaging with your family.
- **Communicating Concerns:** Your spouse has a habit of communicating condescendingly toward you when other people are present, and it's affecting your relationship, so you sit down with them to explain your feelings and why their behavior is so hurtful.
- **Proposing Change:** Your business partner shares equal ownership of the business but you do 80 percent of the work, so you respectfully ask to renegotiate the partnership agreement to reflect the actual workloads.
- **Revealing Intentions:** A suspicious person approaches you without permission, and you tell them to stop, but they keep coming so you know they have bad intentions and begin to plan your defense accordingly.

Paul's POV

I remember my first week in a martial arts school. There was an older gentleman training there who routinely recounted stories to the younger students. And whenever he began to speak, I'd always find my ears acutely attuned to his words.

One of his tales was about an adolescent boy who had recently suffered a black eye at the hands of a bully, and who was studying martial arts for the first time. The boy could barely take care of himself in a fight, let alone anyone else. But he found himself walking from the corner bus stop to his school with an old man. The pair, strangers to one another, had just gotten off a city bus together. Stepping off that same bus were two older teens who for some reason had targeted the old man. Just as the teens approached the man, the boy turned to him and bowed. The old man returned the boy's gesture in kind, before entering a tea shop beside the school. Taken aback by the exchange of bows, the two teens stopped the boy. "What was that about?" asked one of the teens. "That's how it is when you study martial arts," replied the boy. "You always bow to someone with more knowledge than you. It's a sign of respect."

"Was that the master of this school?" asked the second teen. "Did you get that black eye training with him?"

"I'm sorry, it's not something I can talk about with outsiders. But if I were you, I'd leave him alone," the boy answered directly. The two would-be bullies looked at one another for a moment and then quickly walked away in the opposite direction.

Whenever I consider the synergy between the Mobility Principle and Centerline Principle, I think about that boy, who accepted that he couldn't physically defend the old man. Instead, he found another way to protect him by establishing a boundary propped up by the fear and doubt he was able to instill in the minds of those potential teen thugs.

When the older gentleman was finished telling his tale, one of the younger students at the school asked him, "Were you that boy in the story?" He answered, "That's not really important. The real question is: Will that be you one day?"

Scan here to learn the combat application of

The Grandmaster Principle

Chapter Thirty-Two

The Grandmaster Principle

Living with the confidence of a black belt while learning with the humility of a white belt.

The mind is everything. What you think you become.
—Buddha

The blending and synergy of all of the principles you've learned come together in the Grandmaster Principle. I'm often asked: "What makes a Grandmaster?" Growing up in this family of fighters, if I didn't do the technique exactly as it was taught, I would pay for it. So rather than learning to think for myself, I became really good at memorizing techniques. I want to make sure that you don't travel that same road on your jiu-jitsu journey. To become a Grandmaster, you need to learn to think for yourself. It doesn't come from being taught every single detail, what to do right or what to do wrong. Rather, it comes from exploring possibilities, asking the right questions, and being open to alternatives. When you encounter roadblocks in life, and you undoubtedly will, there won't always be a teacher hovering over your shoulder, whispering into your ear what you should do. No, you're going to think for yourself, and in some situations, improvise on the spot to create a specific technique or solution based on everything you've learned up until that point. A really good teacher will facilitate this process. I hope that I have for you.

I remember the day I received my black belt and realized, *Wow, no one is going to give me all the answers. I have to learn to teach myself if I'm going to continue to improve in jiu-jitsu.* Of my current jiu-jitsu knowledge, I only "learned" 50 percent of it. The other 50 percent I discovered through my own exploration based on my knowledge of the principles and by asking endless questions. My grandfather Helio Gracie developed much of what jiu-jitsu is today through the same process. He didn't have a teacher for much of his life, so he had to be his own teacher. And he was able to do this because he embodied all the core principles of the art, even though he hadn't named them—the same way gravity always existed, but it didn't have a name until Isaac Newton showed up.

Even though he helped to invent the art of Brazilian jiu-jitsu, Helio never stopped seeking knowledge. He never believed that he knew it all, or that he was bigger than the art itself. Those types of thoughts never crossed his mind. Instead, he was constantly trying to evolve the techniques to accommodate his frail physique in approaching larger, stronger opponents. My grandfather was driven by an unyielding pursuit of efficiency, the apex principle of the art and the staple of every core principle we've explored. My brother Ryron and I are immensely proud to have learned so many valuable lessons about jiu-jitsu and life from our grandfather.

In turn, I'm equally proud to be sharing this knowledge with you. I know you will pass it on to others as well. As you approach life, now armed with a jiu-jitsu toolbox, I hope that the 32 core principles will ease your burdens and enhance the journey. These principles are now yours to explore, experiment with, modify, and use to create solutions or techniques to overcome the obstacles and adversity that inevitably await you down the road. Please, give yourself the permission to be your own teacher, so that you may evolve into the Grandmaster of your own life. Always remember that every problem is a technique waiting to be discovered, and the 32 principles are your ally in that search.

One's destination is never a place but rather
a new way of looking at things.
—Henry Miller, novelist

You know you're a Grandmaster at life when . . .

- **Every time you run into an obstacle,** the first question that comes to mind is: Which principle will best serve me?
- **Every time you experience a setback,** your first thought is: What can I learn from this that will help me down the line?
- **Every time you are successful,** the first thing you want to know is: How can I make this process more efficient?
- **Every time you reach a goal,** you celebrate, but soon after, you ask: What's next?

One of the Seven Wonders

Helio Gracie shared his name with the sun god of Greek mythology—Helios. The Colossus of Rhodes, one of the original Seven Wonders of the World, was an immense statue built to honor Helios and stood approximately 108 feet tall. Completed in 280 BC, the statue remained a remarkable achievement of ancient architecture for more than half a century before it was reportedly toppled by an earthquake.

Consider this: If the Colossus of Rhodes could have trained with Helio Gracie, it would have been comfortable being taken to ground. And more than likely, the Colossus would have fiercely grappled with that earthquake, eventually forcing it to submit and tap out.

On January 29, 2009, Helio Gracie passed away of natural causes at the age of 95. He never stopped practicing jiu-jitsu, and he spent his final days in the Brazilian city of Petrópolis surround by his family and loved ones. His final words were, "I created a flag from the sport's dignity. I oversee the name of my family with affection, steady nerves, and blood."

Acknowledgments

Rener:

To all members of the Gracie Family who came before me, thank you for all you've done to pave the way. Through your intense passion and persistence, you positively changed the world in a way that can never be undone.

To my brother, Ryron, thank you for being everything I could have ever asked for in a brother. No task is too difficult and no dream is too big with you by my side.

To my wife, Eve, thank you for being the missing piece in all my life's puzzles. Every day that I'm with you feels like I won the lottery, and having the privilege to raise a family with you is the greatest joy of my life.

To my sons, Raeven and Renson, thank you for inspiring me in ways I didn't know were possible and for being so patient with me as I pursue my black belt in parenting. I know I still have a long way to go.

Paul:

Thank you to my family for always encouraging me to express myself: Paul Volponi Sr., Mary Volponi, April Volponi, and Sabrina Volponi.

And thank you to William Moy for a decade of patience and trust in teaching me to think and respond like a martial artist.

Both Rener and Paul would like to thank Rachel Phares, Herb Schaffner, Joe Perry, Kim Broderick, and Jordan Talmor for their insightful editorial contributions to this project.

About the Authors

Rener Gracie is a third-generation martial arts master from the family that created Brazilian jiu-jitsu and the UFC. He is the co-founder and CEO of Gracie University, a global jiu-jitsu organization with hundreds of thousands of dedicated students. Rener has coached everyone from UFC champions to bullied children to Navy SEALSs and everyone in between. He is one of the most prominent jiu-jitsu practitioners and teachers in the world today. With over 25 years of experience teaching jiu-jitsu, Rener is most passionate about introducing the life-enhancing benefits of Brazilian jiu-jitsu to new audiences, hence the authoring of this book. Leaning on the principles of jiu-jitsu, Rener has achieved success in other areas as well. He invented a sweatshirt that converts into a backpack, used it to launch a company called Quikflip Apparel, and then got invited to appear on ABC's *Shark Tank* . . . all in his spare time. Send Rener an email at RenerGracie@GracieUniversity.com or connect with him on social media @RenerGracie.

Paul Volponi is the multi-award-winning author and journalist of 18 books. His novel *Black and White* is a staple in many high school English classes. His novel *The Final Four* is the recipient of five-starred reviews. Paul, who has received a dozen American Library Association honors, crisscrosses the country visiting schools and conducting writing workshops. He lives in New York City where he was a public school teacher for 16 years, including teaching incarcerated teens on Rikers Island for six years. Paul holds an MA in American literature from the City University of New York, and also works as a turf writer covering the sport of Thoroughbred racing. You can visit him at paulvolponibooks.com.